Staff Supervision
in a Turbulent Environment

Staff Supervision
in a Turbulent Environment
Managing Process and Task
in Front-Line Services

Lynette Hughes and Paul Pengelly

Jessica Kingsley Publishers
London and Philadelphia

The right of Lynette Hughes and Paul Pengelly to be identified as authors of this work has been asserted by them in accordance with the Copyright, Designs and Patents Act 1988.

First published in the United Kingdom in 1997 by
Jessica Kingsley Publishers Ltd
116 Pentonville Road
London N1 9JB, England
and
325 Chestnut Street
Philadelphia, PA 19106, USA

Second impression 1998

Library of Congress Cataloging in Publication Data
A CIP catalogue record for this book is available from the Library of Congress

British Library Cataloguing in Publication Data
A CIP catalogue record for this book is available from the British Library

ISBN 1-85302-327-2

Printed and Bound in Great Britain by
Athenaeum Press, Gateshead, Tyne and Wear

Contents

List of Figures

List of Tables

Introduction

This book grew out of our experience, when on the staff of the Tavistock Marital Studies Institute, of running courses for staff supervisors in a range of disciplines and agency settings. These courses challenged us to think about which of the concepts and ideas that we valued remained constant in their relevance to supervision amid the massive contemporary changes in the structure and ethos of health and welfare services; which needed adapting to be applicable to current supervisory dilemmas; and which might have become obsolete. The supervisory examples that run through the book are drawn largely from our courses (and occasionally from our own work as supervisors and consultants); they are the testing ground for the relevance of the ideas we put forward.

Aims

We have had in mind mainly first-line managers who supervise individual practitioners in social work, probation and health settings, but most of the issues we explore are also relevant for more senior managers, for supervisors who are not managers, for group supervisors and for other disciplines besides those mentioned. We do not, however, cover supervision in specialist treatment modes such as family therapy or psychotherapy.

While we tend to address issues from the supervisor's perspective, we give central importance at every point to the interaction between supervisor and supervisee, and much of our thinking is equally relevant for supervisees. We do not advocate one model of supervision; our aim is rather to explore a number of complementary conceptual frameworks and to prompt readers to pursue their own explorations. Throughout, however, we focus on our belief that effective supervisory work, promoting safe service-delivery, depends fundamentally on attention being given to the interactive processes in supervision and practice.

Sources and influences

We have drawn on so many experiences and ideas that it is hard to identify them all. Formative among them, however, was the experience of being supervised ourselves, as trainees and staff members, which confirmed in us 'the passionate belief that supervision is the worker's most essential professional relationship' (Morrison 1993, p.1). We were fortunate in having excellent supervisory experiences at crucial points in our careers. In our own work as staff supervisors in statutory settings we learned both the excitement of co-operative development and the weightiness of the responsibility.

Conceptually, we have drawn on the long tradition at the Tavistock Marital Studies Institute of applying psychoanalytic ideas, through research and training, to work in many front-line services – for example, local authority social work, health visiting, court welfare, work with those who are out of work, telephone helpline work and inter-agency collaboration (Mattinson and Sinclair 1979; Clulow 1982; Clulow and Vincent 1987; Mattinson 1988; Colman 1989; Woodhouse and Pengelly 1991). In running supervision courses we shared in the even longer TMSI experience of training and conceptualising in the field of supervision (Mattinson 1975, 1981; Dearnley 1985). We have benefited greatly from the tradition of the Tavistock Institute of Human Relations in applying psychoanalytic and open systems thinking to the study of group and organisational dynamics. We have also drawn – in a highly selective way – on other theoretical frameworks.

As we prepared to write, our thinking about the place of supervision in the currently changing agency context was sharpened by the ideas shared with us in semi-structured interviews with thirteen supervisors, managers (first-line and senior), consultants and trainers in a range of professions and settings, whom we approached because we knew of their commitment to staff supervision. Other experienced staff have also, over several years, helped to focus our thinking in jointly setting up and running supervision courses in various contexts.

Confidentiality and conventions

The heart of the book lies in the examples of supervisory practice, which (with a few named exceptions) refer to real situations. We have always modified details so as to conceal identifying features; sometimes the complexity of a situation has not been fully spelt out, in order to highlight the main issue. The consent of the relevant professionals (whether course participant, supervisee or consultee) has been obtained to our publishing their material in the form in which it appears.

In the main text, supervisors are always female and supervisees male, while the generic term service-user is usually employed for the recipient of professional services, whatever the setting. In the examples, the original genders are often changed unless we are highlighting a particular issue that arose from gender. Similarly, we often make no reference at all to age, race or other personal characteristics, unless drawing attention to specific issues related to these factors. Readers are therefore invited to monitor what assumptions they make about these characteristics of the supervisors, supervisees, service-users and others who appear in the examples, and to consider how they might construe the situations if they allocated the characteristics differently. A reminder of this invitation will be given in Chapter 6.

Structure and themes

Acting on our belief that supervision is potentially a microcosm of how an agency responds to its environment, including its service-users, we focus first in Chapter 1 on the contemporary turbulent conditions in which services must survive and work, before beginning to look at the place of supervision in the team and agency context. In Chapter 2, we turn to expectations of supervision – changing as services change and differing between professions and individuals – and some of the pressures on supervisors in making supervisory contracts. After these two contextual chapters, we move on to looking at supervisory tasks and interactions. Chapter 3 introduces the concept of supervisory triangles to explore the interrelatedness of participants, and of functions, in supervision. Chapter 4 addresses issues concerning the respective stages of professional competence and development, and the respective working styles, of supervisor and supervisee. Chapters 5 and 6 employ the concepts of countertransference, mirroring and drama triangles to highlight the importance of attending to the emotional impact of work and the dynamic interactions of practitioner and supervisor, teams and agencies. In Chapter 7, we explore how organisations become structured to contain or avoid work-related anxiety, and the implications of this for supervision; Chapter 8 looks specifically at the effects of how loss and change are managed. The last two chapters draw together many of the previous themes. Chapter 9 explores the struggle (mainly for the supervisor) to call a halt and face supervisory difficulties. Chapter 10 considers the underpinning concepts of authority and containment in the current context and concludes that, however difficult, the way a supervisor is able to exercise authority is as crucial as ever in ensuring a supervision that promotes safe and effective service-delivery.

Acknowledgements

Among the many to whom we are indebted for the direct or indirect help they have given us in writing this book, we should like to single out the following:

- ○ the Tavistock Marital Studies Institute, under its Director, Christopher Clulow, for its professional and financial support for the project

- ○ many of our former colleagues at TMSI, notably Evelyn Cleavely, who developed the thinking about staff supervision courses; but especially Felicia Olney, who formed a threesome with us to deliver supervision training, and whose clarity and capacity to confront difficult issues make her an invaluable co-trainer

- ○ our own past supervisors, especially Gill Bridge, Lorna Guthrie, Eleanor Murphy, Tony Page and Judy Treseder; and our supervisees, who have ensured that we continue to learn

- ○ the participants on our supervision courses, who took risks in sharing their supervisory dilemmas with us

- ○ the course participants and others who generously allowed us to use their material as examples

- ○ those who amid busy schedules agreed to be interviewed on their views and experiences of supervision – Alastair Bearne, Philip Bradshaw, Elspeth Cooper, Eric de Mello, Jim Harding, Nick Hervey, Dave Hill, Sue Hollinrake, Heather Hurford, Will Jones, Beatrice Stevens, Lesley Vincent and Malcolm Ward

- ○ those who, through shared work about supervision, have influenced our thinking, especially Jane Hicks, Bob Jezzard, David Lawlor, Sue Swann and John Wheeler

- ○ Maelor Griffiths, Grace Newball, Matthew Norman and Catherine Pengelly, who in different ways contributed to the production of text and graphics

- ○ Margaret Walker and her colleagues at the Tavistock Library, especially for their detective zeal in tracking down references

- ○ last but not least, Jessica Kingsley, for providing the kick-start that made us write, and for the patience and thoughtfulness that she and her staff have extended to us over many months.

However, just as supervisors and supervisees are ultimately responsible for their own actions, so we take responsibility for what we have written. Those whom we have acknowledged, like other readers, may find much here with which to disagree as well as agree; our hope, however, is that the reading provokes thought relevant to good supervisory practice.

Lynette Hughes
Paul Pengelly

CHAPTER 1

The Turbulent Environment
Needs and Resources – an Inevitable Tension

The challenge of managing the inevitable tension between needs and resources lies at the heart of provision in health and welfare services. Changes in the organisation of services are essentially changes in how the balance is considered and how the uncomfortable tension is either addressed or avoided.

Staff supervision is a means of developing and controlling the quality of service, taking account of the needs and rights of users and the quality of staff performance. The needs and rights of staff must also be attended to, in order to get the best from them as the major resource of the organisation. The functioning of supervision is thus inextricably linked to the way the organisation manages the tension between needs, resources and rights.

In this chapter, we shall try to elucidate some of the key aspects of the turbulent context in which health and welfare agencies have operated in the past decade or more. Only when this context is appreciated can we begin to consider the place of staff supervision within it.

The context of change

The reorganisation...called for changes in orientation and commitment and required an extension of functions. Social workers had to re-think their *raison d'être*, come to terms with new responsibilities, extend their work into unfamiliar areas, deal with feelings of loss of identity and recreate for themselves a new sense of belonging. During the initial phase of reorganisation when too much change occurred in too short a period, lack of a clear purpose brought upheaval and disorientation to the department as a whole and separately to individual members of staff...

Before it had a chance to establish itself, however, new legislation added further responsibilities to the department's already heavy load. It could not but fall short of widely held expectations. The question of appropriate resources to implement new legislation does not appear to have troubled ambitious politicians... In general, economic and practical needs are given priority over emotional and psychological needs. Crises take precedence over preventative work.

These quotations, which sound so topical in the 1990s, come from a key publication on staff supervision in social work written twenty years earlier, soon after the setting up of local authority social services departments (Westheimer 1977, pp.1–2). The term 'turbulent environment' was coined earlier still, by Emery and Trist (1965). Both these reminders of the perennial impact of change raise questions about how we construe our current experience that service-delivery organisations are in a state of continuous rapid change. Are we idealising a 'golden age' of imagined stability in the past as we struggle with the impact of great changes in the present? Resistance to change of any kind is a natural reaction; the comfort of familiarity is usually welcomed. As a sixteenth century essayist observed, 'there is no system so bad (provided it be old and durable) as not to be better than change and innovation' (Montaigne, transl. Screech 1991). Today, expressions of concern about the impact of change 'often attract the criticism of "wingeing" and invitations to leave the heat of the kitchen' (Sawdon and Sawdon 1995).

However, the 'across the board' changes of recent years have been on an unprecedented scale. There has been simultaneous, radical restructuring in the National Health Service, with provider health-care trusts, commissioning health authorities and fund-holding general practitioners; in the education service, with local management of schools and provision for opting out; in social services departments, with a purchaser–provider split in community care and the return of specialism by user group; in the probation service, with greater centralised control and the intended removal of its social work professional base; and correspondingly in the voluntary sector, increasingly indistinguishable from the private sector as providers of services to the public sector. What is left is a landscape of services with few familiar edifices. New routes have constantly to be explored and mapped to link the different structures. Within these frameworks, new job titles abound (e.g. care manager, business unit manager), sometimes reflecting new tasks, sometimes a new ethos. Many professionals, regardless of whether or not they welcome the changes, find themselves 'lost in familiar places' (Shapiro and Carr 1991) as they try to navigate along unfamiliar routes to attend to the familiar human problems of service-users. There is no longer a uniform shape to services throughout the country. At the centre of these changes lies the introduction into the health and welfare services of the ethos of market forces and business management, with the dynamic of cash limits, competitive tendering and short-term contracts.

The needs–resources tension: managed or avoided?

The proposals of the Seebohm Report (Department of Health and Social Security 1968) on the reorganisation of local authority social services embodied 'a wider conception of social service, directed to the well-being of the whole of the community and not only of social casualties', and saw 'the community it serves as the basis of its authority, resources and effectiveness' (para. 474). This optimistic but omnipotent vision prompted the last major piece of legislation to express the idealistic belief that the state would provide for all needs and that social services should expand. Parker (1967) was then a relatively lone voice in raising the question of resources:

> The existence of 'universal provision' has seduced many into believing that the problem of rationing no longer arises. As a result its political and administrative implications tend to have been side-stepped, and the problem all too often allowed to resolve itself without conscious planning or public debate – often to the detriment of the weakest and the most needy. (p.14)

The 1980s witnessed a reaction against such expansion of public provision, and a swing to focusing on the dilemma of finding financial resources to support the network of services. In the new emphasis on cost-effectiveness and cash limitation, previous assumptions about inevitable expansion and development were suddenly challenged, and many agencies went to the wall or became preoccupied with survival. In the meantime, the needs that services were expected to cope with were increasing for a variety of reasons, including: more sophisticated knowledge and technology (especially in the health service), demographic changes (particularly the ageing population and the increase in divorce), widespread unemployment and poverty, withdrawal of many supportive and preventive services, and the revelation (by tragedies, pressure groups and improved professional monitoring) of the extent to which services were failing to meet need and prevent abuse, especially of children. Recent legislation has also considerably expanded the duties of agencies in relation to need, particularly the Mental Health Act 1983, the Education Act 1988, the Children Act 1989, the NHS and Community Care Act 1990 and the Criminal Justice Act 1991.

At best, with more open planning and publication of service aims, the current climate allows for a realistic struggle to attend to the tension between needs and resources. The very concept of dividing agencies that assess need and commission and finance services from those that provide the services enforces consideration of the relationship between need and funding. The *Care Management and Assessment: Managers' Guide* (Department of Health 1991d) expresses this clearly:

> This separation does not solve the conflicts between needs and resources, but it does ensure that the respective interests of user and provider are separately represented. This enables any conflicts of interest to be recognised and managed, through a process of negotiation, in a more explicit and accountable way. (para. 30)

The *Guide* also anticipates (paras. 64 and 5.42) the potential alternative problem – that these two sections of community care provision might become split off from each other, ignoring each other's realities – and makes specific suggestions to limit this danger. In many settings, however, the actual experience so far appears to be of a gulf between purchasers and providers. In social services departments there can be confusion about the boundary between the two functions, with a consequent danger of gaps or duplications in service provision; this confusion may sometimes be accentuated by competitiveness over resources and status. In the NHS, meanwhile, there have been complaints of purchasers being ignorant of what is needed and therefore unable to commission effectively. Wells (1995), for example, provides evidence of this in the field of work with disturbed adolescents.

Even though it seems clear that purchasers' thinking would benefit from the knowledge and experience of providers, both sides may be wary that any co-operation might be seen as collusion. One may be sceptical, however, whether collusion can be avoided if the purchaser–provider 'split' is to achieve the government's aim of a 'seamless service' (Department of Health 1991d, para. 80); the contradiction was summed up for us by one senior manager's depiction of this as 'more like a stitched-up one'. While some of these difficulties might be seen as inevitable teething troubles in the early stages of major changes in service structure and ethos, the stress on needs-led assessment and user choice within at least the community care framework has, at best, underemphasised the reality of limited resources as the controlling factor and, at worst, totally denied it. Often quoted in this debate is the guidance letter issued to social services departments (Department of Health 1992b) which implied that, in order to protect themselves from legal challenge about not delivering the services assessed as needed, departments should not record unmet need.

Menzies (1979), in a paper on institutions for adolescents, recognised early that good professional practice requires decision-making authority over resources to be delegated as far as possible to staff in direct contact with users. Devolved budget-holding (e.g. to senior care managers in social services community care teams, or to head teachers under local management of schools) can be seen as such a step towards ensuring that decisions about spending priorities are made at a level flexibly responsive to local need. More negatively, however, such delegation may merely pass down the managerial hierarchy the painful experience of knowing about the gap between expensive needs and limited resources, allowing the more senior managers to know only about the financial aspect. The contradictory task now given to social workers when assessing elderly people for social care – to consider their interests and, at the same time, to assess them financially as part of a charging policy – epitomises the professional and ethical dilemmas that delegation can pose (Bradley and Manthorpe 1995).

Central government's attitude towards the struggles of health and local authorities to marry resources and needs can similarly attract either a positive or a sceptical interpretation. Marris (1991) points out that economic development amid uncertainty always requires that the least powerful be flexibly available to the decisions of the powerful; he argues that the temptation for the powerful is to make their own command over circumstances more secure by imposing a greater burden of uncertainty on others.

Clearly, the increasingly polarised party politics of the past two decades, ending the post-war political consensus, is highly relevant to the changes we are outlining. 'The welfare state formed the institutional embodiment of this consensus, receiving practical support from the social and economic policies of Socialist and Conservative governments alike, despite apparent differences in ideology' (Hewitt 1992, p.1). Governments since 1979, however, have been ideologically committed to limiting the public sector and extending the private. It is difficult today to remember that the expansionary Local Authority Social Services Act 1970, planned by a Labour government, was implemented by a Conservative government. As an illustration of the political change, Hewitt (p.45) contrasts the preamble to the first White Paper on the NHS (HMSO 1944), announcing the wartime (coalition) government's idealistic intention to bring 'the country's full resources to bear upon reducing ill-health and promoting good health in all citizens', with the statement in the White Paper *Working for Patients* (HMSO

1989) that today's health service is 'a complex multi-billion pound enter-prise'.

In this context, it becomes hard to tell how far a political decision is based on facing the inevitable, difficult tension between needs and resources, and how far on avoidance. There seems little doubt, moreover, that different political and social ideologies lend themselves to different modes of avoid-ance. Halton (1995) argues cogently that the current market culture of competition and self-reliance, embodying an attack on the dependency culture of the welfare state, is at least in part a defensive flight into unthinking manic triumph over neediness. On the other hand, the negative side of a culture concerned with the welfare of the vulnerable is professional pater-nalism and a passive expectation of an all-providing state, ignoring the reality of funding and the need for initiative. Halton sums this up:

> To treat passive dependency with a dose of survival-anxiety seems a reasonable proposition. It gets out of hand when a culture contaminated by the delusion of total social provision is transformed into one affected by the opposite delusion, that of alienated self-sufficiency. This transformation of values only replaces one delusion with another. (p.189)

In such a climate, words lose their meaning and credibility in euphemisms reminiscent at times of *Nineteen Eighty-Four* (Orwell 1949); terms such as 'downsizing' or 'streamlining' are used to deny cuts in provision, ignoring the impact of redundancy on those made unemployed and on those conse-quently over-employed as they struggle to 'do more with less'. Early left-wing criticisms of the welfare state's oppression of the powerless reappear, repackaged by the right, as calls for 'parental power' and 'citizen charters' (Hewitt 1992, p.37). The quality and quantity of unmet need becomes submerged under published figures emphasising 'throughput'. While any definition of need is always intrinsically a value judgement, there can be no more blatant attempt to blur the force and extent of neediness than the current use of the term 'consumers' for users of services; here, need comes to be synonymous with what can be bought, and the tension between needs and resources is ideologically obliterated.

Accountability: creative or destructive tensions?

Issues of accountability in the delivery of services have become sharper and more conflictual in the past two decades. The idealistic expansion of many services up to the 1970s was accompanied by growth in the numbers of professionals, and in optimism about the ability of professional intervention to prevent or alleviate human suffering. Despite left-wing criticism of the powerful social control function of professionals in public services, at the expense of citizens' rights (Hewitt 1992; Parton 1994), it took the right-wing preoccupation with spiralling costs to limit professional autonomy by introducing greater financial, organisational and public accountability. Meanwhile, public concern at evidence of incompetence or criminal abuse of position by professionals also highlighted the need for better systems of control and monitoring. Jones and Joss (1995) argue that 'what is emerging is a new and external definition of professions. It is based upon the idea of consumer-led definitions of the quality of service rather than professionally-led definitions' (p.19). This embodies a major conceptual shift, accentuated by increased state control of the content and assessment of professional training, especially in lower status professions such as nursing and social work (Yelloly 1995).

However, the backlash against professionals, whether in the media or in the speeches of politicians, has gone beyond the bounds of rational argument. Obholzer (1994b) offers one way of understanding this. He postulates that the 'irrational' function of public sector institutions is to contain on society's behalf the burden of human anxiety about life, death, madness, failure, sickness and violence; the decades of idealistic expansion, embodying society's omnipotent wish that all such anxiety could be removed, produced a backlash of disillusion at professionals when the latter's inevitable failure to do so became clear. A similar hypothesis suggests that professionals may become associated in the mind of society with anxieties arising from the troublesome problems of their user groups, and treated accordingly. In child protection work, for example, 'it is too painful for the community to face up to the horror of abuse, so the rage is often projected on to the messenger, the social worker...there is something deep and primitive in all of us that victimises those who work with victims' (Moore 1995, p.68). Valentine (1994) points out that it is only a short step from this 'to allocate blame, if the child is attacked, to the irresponsibility and failure of the social worker' (p.80). The government's recent decision that the probation service requires not social work qualifications but an injection of tough authority might embody a similar dynamic, seeing probation officers and their users in the same light of irresponsibility and subversiveness. Such dismissive attitudes towards professionals working with those in need are expressions of a predominant political climate that disparages dependency.

Whatever the motivations for attacks on publicly employed professionals, the need for them to be accountable remains. The classic potential tension between professional and bureaucratic accountability is well documented, though the experience varies between professions. Kakabadse (1982) describes how the amalgamating of local authority welfare agencies into large social services departments in the 1970s had the all too familiar effect of increasing hierarchical structures, establishing a 'role' as opposed to 'task' culture (Harrison 1972) with responsibility and authority attached to position in the hierarchy rather than to professional skill. In the NHS, the imposition of a managerial approach with clear lines of accountability is more recent and is closely linked to concern about 'value for money' in the delivery of services. Again, the actual experience of these changes leaves an ambiguity about how far they are addressing real problems and how far they are merely implementing a triumphalist approach of new 'managerialism' displacing old 'professionalism' – often importing into the public sector a rigid authoritarian attitude that is increasingly out of step with the development of more responsive, flexible management styles in many private businesses (Peters 1989). Too adversarial a view of professional versus manager, however, ignores the fact that managers are the new 'professionals'. It also tends to minimise the inevitable limits on autonomy and dynamism for managers in the public sector, compared to the private, because of the complex range of relationships of accountability they must keep in mind, particularly in their role on the interface between their organisations and the political process. The impact of politically-led initiatives is always to the forefront for managers as well as their staff. Many of the senior managers to whom we have spoken saw their work experience in terms of managing a three-way tension in relation to the users for whom their service exists. We have tried to depict this in Figure 1.1.

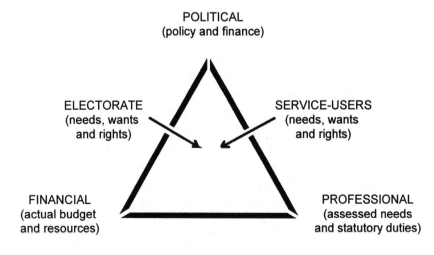

Figure 1.1 Triangle of tensions for senior managers

Within these structures, professionals are now required to evaluate the work they do in new and specific ways, through clinical audit, quality assurance, individual performance review and consumer feedback. Like any formal system, these measures may be relevant to achieving an evidence-led delivery of service and to providing constructive feedback that encourages the learning of the organisation, or they may be a merely mechanistic method of control, a superficial window-dressing which entails reducing complex interactions to the simplistic (Leiper 1994). For example, the increasing application of set procedures to practitioners' face-to-face work with serv-ice-users may be an enabling framework, or it may become a substitute for human contact and exploration, denying the necessity for professional judgement in assessing high-risk situations. Similarly, the idea we have heard mooted that social services departments should function like travel agencies, providing 'packages' of care for the choice of 'customers', ignores the quality of the human contact and interpersonal skills that are needed in the process (Nathan 1994). One child in a children's home regularly subjected to prescribed inspections by professionals and lay representatives summed this up when he complained that 'everyone visits but no one stops to listen'.

There is a danger that greater significance may be attributed to the words of mission statements, charter marks, policies, procedures and measurements than to the actions and meanings they are intended to articulate; or rather, that no distinction will be made, so that the words come to be treated as though they were the deeds. This overemphasis on the certainty of 'words' at the expense of acknowledging the uncertainties, confusions and anxieties that are part of human contact and inevitable human limitation, can be regarded as the social welfare equivalent of the fundamentalism that domi-nates much religious and political life today (Britton 1990).

Efforts to improve accountability to service-users have also been a significant feature in recent decades, often closely allied to anti-discrimina-tory strategies. Considerable work is usually needed in most localities to transform the idea of user participation, and consultation with special interest or pressure groups, from a 'fashionable dogma' to a 'professional necessity' (Devenney 1993). Again, mere 'words' are not sufficient. Political ideology and professional idealism, in hailing users as 'consumers' or 'partners' respectively, may too easily deny the potential tensions arising from severity of need, limits on resources, painful statutory duties and civil rights. Tunnard and Ryan's (1991) observation about partnership under the Children Act 1989 has a general applicability:

> Partnership is not about equal power, but about people working together towards a common goal. It is about empowerment, about

families having sufficient information to be able to understand and contribute to planning, and having some power to influence the outcome. (p.267)

Partnership also requires clear definitions of what is, and is not, negotiable and available. As Marsh and Fisher (1992) put it, 'partnership-oriented practitioners should be clear with clients where they have the freedom to reject intervention and where not' (p.21).

Contradictions

We have been discussing the recent major changes in services as though they had a uniform pattern and a coherent ethos. But the speed, pragmatism or political ideology of some major decisions, accompanied perhaps by failure to grasp the nettle of the needs–resources tension, have in many instances produced new contradictions or conflicts. These have exacerbated the task of professionals in adjusting to the changes and prompted cynicism about their value.

A few examples will illustrate the kinds of contradictions that have confronted staff, referrers and service-users as a result of recent changes (whatever their intrinsic merits):

1. The highly-promoted ideal of local accountability can be in conflict with extensions of central government control. The introduction of smaller, unitary local authorities may increase the imbalance between weakened local and strengthened central government.

2. A local education authority's plans to close a school may be overturned by the activity of parents who want to 'opt out'. The question of who most democratically represents local need becomes blurred by the political ideology of government commitment to opting out. As this highlights, the difficulty of proper long-term planning is a regular feature in all services, with so many conflicts of interest in a time of scarce resources.

3. In the 'mixed economy of care', the government's encouragement of private sector provision has at times been in conflict with its commitment to fiscal restraint, as Biggs (1994) points out in his discussion of the rising cost of payments for private residential care for the elderly.

4. Halton (1995) argues that the market structures introduced in the health and education services are 'aberrant' and self-contradictory, compared with 'pure' market values. In an 'internal' market, the

efficiency gains supposed to flow from the purchasing power of the user to demand cost-effective services are absent when user and purchaser are not one and the same, and the user in fact has no purchasing power. 'The purchaser is within the organisation, that is what "internal" means, and the market "force" operates within the organisation between its own members' (p.190). Further, in a 'managed' market, decisions about, for example, which units survive and which are closed, or which priorities are paramount, are as likely to be determined by politicians as by purchasers. Whatever the wisdom of such arrangements, the point is that their inherent inconsistency is seldom acknowledged.

5. Care management arrangements under the NHS and Community Care Act 1990, whereby a co-ordinating role was given to social services departments, can sit uneasily alongside the NHS-based 'care programme' approach for psychiatric patients in the community. It should be easier, one might imagine, in multidisciplinary community mental health teams, which are usually set up to respond to the needs of a particular geographical area in liaison with all local agencies, and define themselves as such in relation to local health commissioners. However, if GP fund-holders from other areas wish to buy the services of a good mental health team, the local focus may be distorted. This can raise issues within the team itself, especially if the GP comes from outside the local authority that employs the social workers in the team. A further complication is that social workers in such teams are frequently employed within the 'purchaser' section of their employing authorities, while the psychiatrists and community psychiatric nurses will be part of the 'providing' arm of the NHS.

6. The official requirement for agencies to 'work together' in partnership is inevitably hampered when every organisation is preoccupied with its own changes and its own survival. In the field of child protection, for example, established systems whereby a named person in the education department and in each school held responsibility for communication about child protection have often been destroyed by the introduction of local management in schools, and the struggle to cope with reductions in the number of teachers. The energy available for collaboration between services in area child protection committees has similarly been reduced. Competition for service contracts between agencies is as likely to

produce short-term planning or fragmentation as creative innovation. Even within services, the capacity to work together may suffer from increased rivalry between disciplines and specialisms, as each struggles to prove its cost-effectiveness and secure its jobs amid the ethos of the market-place.

7. Contradictions of a different order also arise from rapid change. Increasing discrepancies are likely between the perceptions of different staff, teams or levels of an organisation about their tasks – between what Lawrence (1977) called the *normative primary task* (the official task), the *existential primary task* (what staff believe they are doing) and the *phenomenal primary task* (what staff can actually be observed to be doing). It is in such situations that the new rhetoric of 'words' can be so dangerously misleading, as we noted above. Euphemistic terms may be used to deny harsh realities and sharply differing professional and ideological views amongst staff, many of whom may have difficulty in managing the contradictions within their own working experience.

BACKWARD STEP OR REDISCOVERING THE WHEEL?

Some recent changes appear to constitute a return to previous patterns, albeit in new guises. We would argue that this may sometimes be the reversal of earlier flights into mainly managerial or financial considerations which obscured the complexity of need. For example, the need for family support and preventive work has now been 'rediscovered' amid research findings on the weaknesses of over-reliance on procedures in child protection (Department of Health 1995). The need for psychological and emotional help has been 'rediscovered' in many health settings, with counsellors replacing social workers withdrawn by their local authorities.

The danger is that, as the past is contemptuously dismissed, learning from past experience will be lost or minimised (Cohen 1995) while old issues re-emerge in new settings (see Chapter 8). For example, will the new supervised discharge programmes for some psychiatric patients, which introduce key-worker responsibilities, draw on the cautionary experience (mentioned above) of procedurally-led services in child protection? Will the return of specialism by user-group to local authority services, and the division between adult and children's services, benefit from the experience of duplication and fragmentation of services to families that was a major reason for setting up comprehensive social services departments in the first place? It is certainly to be hoped that the current preoccupation with 'community care' will not ignore the experience of those who tried to implement the idealistic programme of the Seebohm Report (Department of Health and Social Security 1968), that is that 'communities' often fail to care for their most difficult, distressed (and distressing) members.

Personal and professional responses to turbulent conditions

In the rest of this book, we shall in effect be exploring the impact of this contemporary turbulence on professionals in front-line services, and the responses it produces, as we discuss aspects of staff supervision. A brief note here will therefore suffice.

Times of change are inevitably times of stress as well as excitement. Times of service reorganisation have been shown again and again to give rise to disruption and concern about the safe delivery of services (Department of Health and Social Security 1982; Department of Health 1991a). The uncertainty, contradictions and pressures we have described can readily engender overwork, demoralisation, disillusion and a defensive attitude of self-protection.

The experience of the changes and the meaning attributed to them will, however, be different for each practitioner, supervisor and manager, according to their personal and professional make-up. For example, the way professionals relate to the political and organisational handling of the needs–resources tension will be determined, at least in part, by their own experience of coping with this inevitable tension throughout their professional and personal lives. Menzies (1970) uses the concept of an 'internal society' to explore the connection between the individual and the social environment:

> An important element in the psyche is the internal society composed of images, concepts, memories and fantasies about people, in a great complexity of roles, functions and relationships. (p.61)

> The internal society never accurately reflects the external society. This implies that all our internal societies are different. However, since we all live in the same external society there tend to be significant areas of similarity in our internal societies arising from our being subjected to similar external influences. (p.62)

Throughout this book we shall attempt to keep in mind the subtle interconnection between the internal and the external societies inhabited by each supervisor and supervisee, and between the psychological and the social dimensions of their professional functioning.

Supervision in a turbulent environment

Amid incessant change, teams of practitioners in each organisation, with managers who are usually their supervisors, struggle to deliver a service. In this chapter it has taken a time to reach the point of focusing on supervisors and practitioners. We are sure this reflects the current preoccupation of members of organisations at all levels with the impact of contextual changes, reducing or postponing the availability of time and energy to focus in detail on the interactions involved in service-delivery.

We now turn our attention to locating the supervisor and supervisee, and the interaction between them, in their organisational context, using Figure 1.2 to depict key roles and boundary issues. While the diagram is based on large, hierarchical organisations with a number of operational teams, usually of one discipline, and with team or unit managers who are also supervisors, the issues for discussion are relevant to most supervisors working in an agency framework.

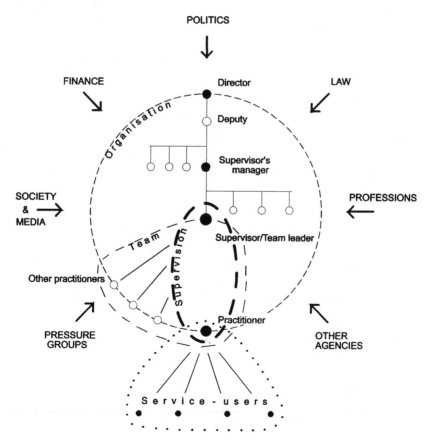

Figure 1.2 Organisational roles, boundaries and pressures

The open systems approach

An open systems formulation of organisational functioning (Miller and Rice 1967; De Board 1978; Zagier Roberts 1994a) stresses the interrelatedness of the individual, group, organisation and environment, with the management function being essentially one of managing issues at the boundaries between these. In Figure 1.2, the boundaries between the sub-groups and around the organisation are drawn in dotted lines to indicate that, though they need to be firm enough to demarcate and contain the unit they surround, they must not be rigid and impermeable. For the survival of the sub-group and the organisation, and for them to fulfil their tasks, information and resources need to cross the boundaries in both directions; managers of the boundaries need to be able to monitor conditions inside and outside, in order to regulate, anticipate and optimise the two-way flow.

Times of rapid change require 'relatively more open systems' to respond to 'more turbulent environments' (Bridger 1981); roles, structures and procedures need to be more fluid. The task of managers in maintaining a workable balance between firmness and flexibility of boundaries is thus even more vital. In reality, however, directors and senior managers are liable to become more and more preoccupied with outside issues; they must constantly respond to highly interventionist central and local politics and compete with other services for scarce resources, as part of the battle for the survival of their organisations. It is indeed hard for senior managers to maintain a firm enough outer boundary around the organisation to protect their middle and junior staff from being overwhelmed by external demands and change, let alone free themselves to focus internally on the organisation's tasks. The temptation for such harassed senior managers is to cease to look sufficiently in both directions, thus avoiding the painful internal issues that preoccupy their staff – about service-users' needs, staffing pressures and inadequate resources. The introduction of short-term contracts for many heads of organisations has exacerbated this, producing an individualised 'power culture' (Harrison 1972) focused on promoting change and future planning while neglecting the effect on (and views of) staff and other agencies. As Obholzer (1994b) points out, this tendency is encouraged in many public sector organisations by the politically acceptable new style of management, namely

> to give managers more power and to eliminate consultation [with staff] as 'inefficient'. It has become a top-down model, with dialogue and co-operation between the different sectors seen as old-fashioned, and

care staff increasingly excluded from policy- and decision-making. (p.173)

Practitioners and first-line managers often complain of senior managers' lack of interest in the 'grass roots' of the organisation and their preoccupation instead with 'macho' management. While there may often be truth in this view, it can also be espoused because staff find it more comfortable to see their managers as powerful and uncaring than to face that they may be highly anxious and uncertain whether they will be able to preserve the integrity of the organisation in a recognisable form. Senior managers may thus be confronted with staff who do not want to look realistically beyond their own positions in the organisation.

The organisation, the team and supervision

Kakabadse (1982) suggests that the key gate-keeping responsibility of looking both ways falls increasingly on middle and first-line managers, leaving directors and practitioners respectively freer to look outwards – the latter to service-users. In the past decade, however, increasing managerial demands at first-line level and the further removal of middle managers from involvement in practice issues have heightened the dilemma for first-line managers. Their struggle to maintain an appropriate boundary around the activities of their teams or operational units, ensuring that changes and requirements are known about without swamping their staff with them, may often feel like putting a finger in the dam to hold back the flood waters. It may seem to them increasingly hard to reconcile being members of manage-ment with meeting the concerns of practitioners, and some may take flight into identifying with one side or the other to avoid the tension.

However, a manager who looks only to the organisation outside the team will not provide a sufficiently strong boundary around the team or attend sufficiently to its members to allow them to co-operate and focus on their work with service-users. At the other extreme, a manager who shelters from organisational difficulties in the bosom of the team, identifying with prac-titioners and trying to ignore managerial accountability, enacts just as serious a failure. This may take the form of providing no clear boundary, no 'buffer' between practitioners and senior management, so that supervisor and team alike feel constantly harassed by the agenda of senior managers. Alternatively, it may involve trying to erect too rigid a barrier around the team, which then functions as though not accountable to or influenced by the main body of the agency – a defensive manoeuvre that leaves the team and its service-users in some danger. Team managers who are not sufficiently attentive to the way decisions are made in the organisation, and are unable or unwilling to communicate with senior managers, will be less able to argue the team's case effectively and may unwittingly mislead their staff about what is possible in their work (Downes and Smith 1991).

Teams whose work is already regarded as peripheral to the main work of the organisation, and who have had to struggle to survive within it, are particularly vulnerable, for example, court welfare teams in the probation service (Lane and Mackey 1995). This issue becomes acute in a climate where not only organisations but sub-groups within them may be competing with each other for scarce resources, and where redundancy or redeployment is common. The team manager's task of looking both ways can also be made more difficult if senior managers make it clear that they prefer junior managers not to raise concerns, and if team members exert a collusive pull on the manager to be 'at one' with them.

Clearly, the way the boundary around the team is managed (as well as boundaries within it, such as the purpose and structure of different team meetings) will also help or hinder the maintenance of a containing boundary around the supervisory relationship, be it in one-to-one or group supervision. In supervision, perhaps even more than in the team as a whole, the impact of the organisation meets head-on the impact of direct work with service-users and with other agencies. As Figure 1.2 indicates, practitioners are like senior managers in that they too are now exposed to increasing pressures as they operate across the boundary of the organisation. Meanwhile, as we have already noted, upheavals and wholesale restructuring across a range of services have complicated the work of co-ordinating intervention and communicating between agencies.

When considering the current heightened impact on service organisations of all the factors from outside, from the politicians to the service-users, we could easily imagine a different shape to Figure 1.2, with the circle flattened as the external boundary caves in under the pressures from outside, leaving the space inside collapsed, internal boundaries destroyed and no room for staff and sub-groups to think or consider their relation to each other and their environment. Within any service agency, the functioning of staff supervision – where the meeting of supervisor and supervisee brings face-to-face the concerns of manager and professional, policy and practice, politicians and service-users – will reflect in microcosm the state of the organisation, its relationship with its environment and how its boundaries are managed.

CHAPTER 2

Piggy in the Middle
The Place of Supervision

A weighty responsibility

It is a tribute to many supervisors and supervisees that, against the odds, work goes on in supervision. Though there is little formal research on the effectiveness of supervision, we would suggest that for most staff in the caring professions its impact for good or ill is palpable. On our courses for supervisors, we ask them to recall some of their own experiences of being supervised, and how these have influenced their own practice as supervisors. Experiences from up to twenty years ago are discussed with the vividness of yesterday. Both good and bad experiences turn out to have lasting sequelae, and the benefits and deprivations are precisely known. It is daunting for these supervisors, in touch with such feelings, to realise the power they now have to influence the professional lives of their current supervisees. A study of social services teams in the 1970s (Parsloe and Stevenson 1978) came to the conclusion that it was 'hard to exaggerate the influence of the supervisor'. It also revealed that the predominant emotion of a team leader in those days was not just anxiety but fear. How much more so now!

Ambivalence and tension in supervision

In the face of such high potential and intense emotion, both supervisor and supervisee can be paralysed by images of the 'ideal supervisor' with almost omnipotent attributes. The following emerged in a brainstorming exercise by a social work advisory group considering staff supervision in child protection work (Ash 1988):

> '– a warm wall – to give me support and firmness in bouncing off ideas;'

> '– a deep well from which I can draw strength and wisdom;'

'– a helicopter ready to winch me out of danger;'

'– a pilot to make sure I steer the right course through difficult waters;'

'– a harbour-master to ensure that I have safe haven in times of storm and stress.' (p.30)

This group thought supervisors

should be able to give advice, help with ongoing learning, know how to work the system, be supportive in relation to senior management, be able to pick up the frustrations of social workers with regard to resources, stress and emergencies and offer praise and encouragement. They should be available and aware of their supervisees as individuals as well as professionals, sensitive to feelings though not intervening inappropriately in personal lives. They should be able to help make the links between current work and previous experience, eliciting 'what you don't know you know'…(p.30)

Such idealised expectations can lead only to disillusion and, for supervisors, an inevitable sense of failure.

We shall now look at how the increasing statutory and organisational requirements and expectations of supervision over recent decades help or hinder the supervisor in managing the tension between professional and organisational accountability, without feeling merely 'piggy in the middle', buffeted from all sides and unable to maintain a consistent position.

Traditional patterns of supervision

'The supervisor–worker relationship is *the key* encounter where the influence of organizational authority and professional identity collide, collude or connect' (Middleman and Rhodes 1980, p.52). Statements such as this are scattered through the literature on supervision in social work and probation. While undeniably true, they tend to have a neatly balanced facility that belies the difficulty of the struggle (for both supervisor and supervisee) to make the supervisory experience an effective bridge between potentially competing or conflicting demands.

In social work in particular, supervision has traditionally occupied a significant, though potentially uncomfortable, 'piggy in the middle' position between management accountability and professional responsibility; between broad policy formulation and its application to individual situations; between the organisation and its users; between prescribed procedures and the emotional impact of high-risk work. 'This managerial–professional duality in supervision is often denied or at least obscured by participants, but it will always influence the transactions between them' (Brown 1984, p.4).

Different disciplines, however, have different professional and contractual traditions about the place and function of supervision, differences that may become salient in multidisciplinary interactions. Øvretveit (1993) spells out, for example, psychiatrists' and psychologists' traditional expectations of both 'case autonomy' over individual case decisions and 'practice autonomy' in organising and prioritising their work overall. Professional and, especially, organisational aspects of supervision have therefore often been peripheral in these 'independent practitioner' professions (Kraemer 1990). In other disciplines, such as hospital nursing, managerial accountability has traditionally been emphasised at the expense of the professional, often without a regular supervisory structure; other branches of nursing such as health visiting have tended to operate largely autonomously. Faugier and Butterworth (1992) describe how

> one of the major problems of nursing development has consistently been the tendency to view qualification as an end in itself, following which the prevailing culture deters qualified nurses from obtaining the professional supervision and support they need. Even the expression of such need has in the past been viewed very negatively as the indication of an inability to cope. (p.10)

Similar attitudes, of course, occur in disciplines such as social work and probation where supervision is built in and ostensibly valued; whatever may be idealised may also be depreciated. In these disciplines, however, the requirement for supervision, and for a supervision that brings together professional and organisational accountability, has not surprisingly been more pronounced and persistent, for a number of reasons – not least their lower professional status and their particular legal and societal accountability. In social services departments, accountability to local councillors has also been highly relevant. Probation officers were traditionally accountable to the courts; in practice this gave them a degree of autonomy which, however, was steadily reduced from the 1970s so that their supervision, once mainly professional, has increasingly incorporated managerial aspects. The powers exercised by approved social workers under the Mental Health Act 1983 provide a rare example of some social work autonomy in decision-making.

New factors have arisen with the expansion and professionalisation of counselling. National accreditation requirements have underlined the need for counsellors to seek regular supervision from an approved supervisor; for the growing numbers of counsellors employed in primary and secondary health care settings (as the social work role has contracted), such supervision is often unobtainable within the agency and outside supervisors are used. This, however, can leave line-management issues ill-defined or studiously avoided; Pengelly, Inglis and Cudmore (1995), for example, suggest that counsellors in infertility treatment settings 'may rely unduly on confidentiality for protection against the anxieties of being involved in decision making and, perhaps, accountability' (p.523).

The use of supervision has thus embodied, in microcosm, the way in which different agencies and professions have addressed or avoided issues of professional and organisational accountability and how they should be related.

Two pressures for change

The profile, expectation and even existence of supervision in different disciplines, settings and types of work have been substantially changed in the last two decades under pressure from two major developments, both part of the turbulence described in the previous chapter. They are, first, the impact of child abuse scandals and, second, the new business culture's emphasis on political and financial accountability for public services.

Beginning with the inquiry into the death of Jasmine Beckford (London Borough of Brent 1985), a fresh wave of reports on child deaths in the 1980s (like the previous series in the 1970s) has highlighted with depressing repetitiveness the failures of supervision in social work, and often health visiting, and re-emphasised the central importance of effective supervision in promoting safe practice (Waters 1992). While the Jasmine Beckford report stressed particularly the need for clearer procedures and structures to ensure statutory and organisational accountability, it linked that requirement with broader issues about the importance of a proactive supervisory stance in thorough decision-making, exploring family dynamics, relating to workers' feelings, and so on. This was expanded in later reports, and in summaries of research (Department of Health 1991a and 1995). The following much-quoted description of the purpose of supervision for child protection social workers is relevant to other disciplines and areas of work:

> The purpose of professional supervision must be to help...provide the most appropriate form of service to the client and to assist workers to maintain their objectivity. The managerial supervision must ensure that the work is being carried out according to the policies of the agency and that they have reasonable resources for the job... It is the role of

the supervisor to ask searching and pertinent questions which enable
the worker to assess the strengths and needs of each family and work
to a plan in accordance with these needs. (Social Services Inspectorate
1986 p.29)

It is striking that, although the marrying of managerial and professional
aspects of supervision has long been a core expectation in probation and
social work, the need for it has constantly had to be restated. These early
reports on child deaths in the 1980s, which prompted the introduction and
development of clearer procedures and systems for managing the supervision
of child protection work, aimed once again to facilitate this marriage.

Further scandals concerning the abuse of young people in residential care
drew attention to the need for supervision in settings where previously it
had received little official or public attention, and prompted more specific
recommendations on matters such as frequency of supervision than those
laid down for fieldwork settings (Department of Health 1991c and 1992a).

The second main pressure for change in supervision has come from the
new emphasis on financial accountability and political control, through the
introduction of clinical audit, quality assurance and resource management in
health and welfare services. Pressure to 'get more for less', and an ethos that
may see supervision only as a luxurious prop for dependent professionals,
have in some areas threatened the survival of any professional discussion in
supervision. Even where supervision *per se* has not been formalised, these
changes have had a powerful impact on professional functioning. One effect,
both in the NHS and in some care management arrangements in social
services departments, has been to create more situations where line managers
are of a different discipline from practitioners, or are sometimes administrators with no background in practice – thus highlighting in new ways the
relationship between professional and agency accountability. In the NHS in
particular, while clinical audit and tighter financial control have changed
perceptions of managerial accountability, these have not necessarily included
a supervisory function focused on practice. Indeed, the innovations have
often served to make senior medical, nursing and other staff more remote
from clinical practice and less available for clinical consultation with junior
staff. In other settings, the emphasis on consistent accountability and
appraisal for staff has given rise to centralised prescriptions of managerial
and supervisory functions.

The swing to proceduralism

The introduction of clearer procedures and systems resulting from all these influences offers at least the possibility of more professional, and organisationally accountable, services. The necessity for this was apparent in, for example, the research of Davies (1988) in the probation service, which demonstrated a serious need for greater consistency, purpose and understanding of the work of supervision. However, most studies of supervision in the last decade speak critically of a mechanistic, procedurally controlled, 'check-list' type of supervision, with little or no space for exploration of the work or of workers' feelings about it (e.g. Waters 1992; Department of Health 1995). While these studies refer mostly to child protection work, a procedural approach in other fields, for example care management, is no more likely to encourage a thoughtful style of supervision. Research into the response of services to the Hillsborough disaster highlighted that even within a creative, innovative and procedure-free initiative, 'the responsibility for supervising what was acknowledged to be potentially difficult and traumatic work was completely abdicated' (Newburn 1993, p.46). Kearney (1994) succinctly locates these developments in the context of defensive, procedure-led organisations. In social work there is the sense that lip service is constantly given to the central place of supervising practice, but with little organisational commitment of resources and thinking, while in many organisations supervision of staff with less professional history (for example, home carers) has never been established at all. In its study of nine local authorities the Social Services Inspectorate (1986) reported

> that in all authorities there was a general assumption that supervision is necessary but no social services department had a clear and explicit written statement about the nature of supervision, and no authority prescribed the method of supervision in detail. (p.30)

The situation has certainly improved since then and many agencies now have thoughtful and developing policies, but we remain sceptical about how many departments seriously evaluate the supervision they prescribe, or even monitor whether it is happening. With all the quality assurance mechanisms in place for other activities, this could be a glaring omission when supervision is necessarily a highly expensive and time-consuming practice. We also wonder how many agencies give adequate – or any – attention to training for the transition to first-line management, and especially for starting to supervise staff, despite the oft-confirmed view that 'in a social work career, the biggest step of all is from being a practitioner to being a first-line manager' (London Borough of Greenwich and Greenwich Health Authority 1987) – a perception that applies to other disciplines too.

Perennial ambivalence about supervision

In a cogent paper about ambiguity and ambivalence in social services departments towards supervision of practice, Clare (1988) warns against creating a myth of the golden age of social work supervision. He quotes Westheimer's (1977) comments on the then newly-established social services departments:

> There are two misconceptions in management: one is that 'mature' people can operate independently under any conditions at all times; the other arises from a lack of appreciation of the anxiety-producing nature of the work and the consequent feeling of depletion. (p.4)

Clare further quotes Younghusband's (1978) assertion, after researching the literature on pre-Seebohm services countrywide, that supervision and consultation were then almost unknown in local authority services – though we are aware that in clinical settings the situation was probably different.

Ambivalence about supervision in social work is thus long-standing. Not all the problems can be attributed to recent changes or the introduction of a business culture. We suggest at least two elements which would contribute to this ambivalence at any time.

First, organisations and individuals may have very mixed feelings about this key encounter, which embodies the often painful and unequal meeting of human need and limited financial, organisational and professional resources – an encounter that has the potential for querying the value of all organisational and professional effort, as well as the possibility of satisfaction and achievement. Supervision of practice highlights the needs–resources tension discussed in Chapter 1 in an intense way. Small wonder that at times supervisors wish to turn a blind eye to what is really going on, or that even supervisees who want supervision may at times fear it would be too persecuting to face the realities of their work (Kraemer 1990). Nowhere is ambivalence about the importance of supervision, as a place to examine and develop work, more clearly seen than in the fact that it is rarely discussed in the literature or in departmental policies except in terms of first-line managers' supervision of practitioners. Riley's (1995) chapter on the supervision of social services managers is a welcome exception. A prevalent, albeit usually unspoken, belief would seem to be that once you are senior and 'really grown up' your work should not need the benefit of professional help or need to be monitored. Dearnley's (1985) observation on the pressure experienced by first-line managers to act as though they can do everything applies even more strongly to senior managers.

Second, ambivalent attitudes to supervision may be specifically related to the experience of some kinds of direct work with service-users. Clulow (1994) points out that in high risk statutory work in child protection and probation, for example, the very word 'supervision' is used for practitioners' task of combining 'care' and 'control' when monitoring service-users' functioning – a struggle that may contaminate professional belief that it is possible to do this in staff supervision in any constructive and developmental way. Conversely, in community care, it is easy to imagine that the striking absence of reference to staff supervision in relevant literature and directives might reflect the new optimistic ethos that users may 'choose' and not need to be 'supervised', that professional freedom may replace 'restrictive' authority structures and that, for example, mental health teams of different disciplines may co-operate 'seamlessly' together. When the term supervision is mentioned in this context, it usually refers to patients who are considered potentially a risk to others. Perhaps as concern continues to grow about the failure to monitor and care for potentially dangerous psychiatric patients in the community, staff supervision with its emphasis on professional and organisational accountability will have a higher profile.

Increased pressures and contradictions

The long-standing ambivalence towards supervision is currently being exacerbated by new pressures. First-line managers have never been more overloaded: with new tasks (for example, budget management or negotiation with user groups); by the amalgamation of posts and responsibilities; by increases in team size; by taking on the management of other disciplines such as administrative workers; by a proliferation of procedures and paperwork; by the removal (literally or through busyness) of middle tiers of management previously attuned to practice issues. Cockburn (1990) is one of many authors who highlight the diminishing time and attention available for supervision amid the many tasks of such first-line managers. Under these pressures, moreover, supervisors may often be tempted to cancel or postpone even the supervision sessions they do arrange – as being, in one team leader's words, 'the most malleable area of work'. The current Management of Practice Expertise Project at the National Institute of Social Work, funded by the Department of Health, is a timely initiative in acknowledgement of this crisis (Kearney 1994). Some agencies and professions have responded to the unavailability or lack of practice involvement of first-line managers by providing alternative arrangements (for example, supervision by senior practitioners, or peer 'supervision' in nursing) which, though potentially valuable, raise issues of defining accountability and prompt a new form of the question: 'who is supervising the supervisor?' Aspects of these issues will be developed in the next chapter. It remains to be seen whether such arrangements, intended to fill a vacuum where practice supervision is overlooked, will serve also to demote supervision to a task for less senior staff while promoting other core management responsibilities.

Meanwhile, contradictions abound. As procedural 'check-list' supervision increases, Department of Health publications are more and more preoccupied with the impact upon safe decision-making of interpersonal processes in supervision (Department of Health 1991a and 1991b). As the quality of supervision in area teams in many social services departments has decreased, that in some residential settings is, for the first time, receiving serious attention. In some departments, where agency-wide supervision policies and management training used to exist, they have disappeared with the division between adult and children's services – or with the introduction of an internal market environment, where supervisors in provider units may be understandably reluctant to discuss their vulnerability with supervisors in purchasing teams. In others, on the contrary, increased specialism by user group and task has prompted the development of supervision policies for the first time. Some voluntary agencies have found that having a firm supervision structure has increased their success in obtaining contracts. There is little sense, however, that commissioning authorities consistently require guarantees of adequate supervision in the services they purchase, or are willing to pay the added cost that effective supervision would incur.

At best, the supervisory task is like undertaking a balancing act, managing the tension between the need for space to think and the need to act, between proliferating tasks and limited time, between checking through every case and detailed discussion of one or two, between exploring possibilities and making decisions, between ensuring agency policies are followed and attending to workers' emotional responses to the work. It can leave a good supervisor feeling pulled in all directions, struggling to manage the balance between feeling stimulated and feeling chronically frustrated and unsatisfied. This is the uncomfortable position of 'piggy in the middle'.

Two amid the turbulence

Let us return to the supervisory space inhabited typically by one supervisor and one supervisee (though the following comments may equally apply to group supervision). Paradoxically, though we have been discussing the intrusive organisational turbulence surrounding the supervisory interaction, once inside it the two people involved can sometimes feel too entrammelled in an intense personal interaction to be able to consider the welter of external issues banging on the door of the supervisory space. In order to work effectively they must find a way to mediate these internal, interpersonal issues too, remaining aware of them, attending to some of them and yet not getting overwhelmed by them. There will also be local issues related to the team's current situation and resources.

We now highlight six factors that may influence either or both of the two participants – leaving aside the major influences of organisational change and ambivalence towards supervision that we have discussed. Underlying all these factors will be the core influences of age, gender, personality, class, culture, race and sexual orientation.

First, *current or recent life events* may enhance or detract from the energy and concentration available for work at any given time. Falling in love, marital stress, bereavement, the birth of a grandchild: all these will effect an individual's work capacity in different ways. Supervisor and supervisee may of course not be aware of each other's current life situation.

Second, *certain types of work or specific cases* may reverberate with personal experiences past or present, either causing distress and difficulties or sharpening effectiveness (Sayers 1992). For example, however competent a professional may be in working with severely depressed or suicidal people, a certain piece of work may suddenly and unexpectedly stimulate fears of a personal nature. The age of one's own children, or a worry about ageing parents, may at certain points of professional life prompt difficulties about working with service-users of corresponding age groups, and these factors need to be acknowledged. Some areas of practice, for example disaster work in recent years (Newburn 1993), can cause particular stress not only because of the horrors involved but because of the ease of professional identification with the victim, as everybody feels 'it could have been me'. Less obvious and more deep-seated might be, for example, the difficulty of working with service-users whose way of dealing with anxiety is similar to (or markedly different from) one's own.

Third, *the professional backgrounds and histories* of supervisor and supervisee, even when from the same discipline, will be highly relevant. Assumptions about each other may be ill-founded, and open discussion of professional histories, values and ideologies may be essential for a more accurate appreciation (Brown and Bourne 1996). The influence of theoretical ideas in particular is, in our experience, rarely discussed. Checking out each other's understanding and experience of the purpose and methods of supervision is also a crucial foundation (we shall discuss this further in Chapter 4). On our courses, we have been struck by the frequency with which supervisors refer to experiences of managers or supervisors who have 'collapsed' or 'had nervous breakdowns', and the effect this has continued to have on their capacity to develop robust supervisory relationships.

Fourth, *recent events and history in the team or agency* may be so taken for granted as to be overlooked. Disciplinary hearings felt to have been badly managed; the reason why the previous supervisor left; the suicide of a service-user with whom all the team were involved; a child death in a neighbouring area; all these may affect the temperature of supervision at any point in time.

Fifth, *clarity of work policies and availability of good, relevant professional advice* can greatly reduce anxiety and facilitate a work focus; inconsistency in these areas causes stress. Especially in statutory work, amid a rapidly changing legislative context, to be able to call on thoughtful legal advice is vital for practitioners' – and supervisors' – confidence.

Sixth, *the interface between agencies* is a site where supervisors and first-line managers are often active; their clarity and facility of communication with other organisations, plus their knowledge of individuals in them, will greatly ease the task of planning for supervision and of gauging the meaning of what supervisees say about their contacts with other agencies. As we highlighted in Chapter 1, when organisations all around (as well as one's own) are changing, this interface requires constant attention and management of uncertainty.

By this stage, the supervision room that was supposed to enclose two people is very crowded! The task for supervisor and supervisee is to acknowledge all these influences, so that the pressure is not experienced solely as a struggle between two individuals, while at the same time facing that it is through the human and professional encounter between the two of them that these influences must be mediated to promote better service-delivery.

Defining the parameters of supervision

The supervisory space needs a boundary clear enough to afford a safe focus on the work, but at the same time open enough to allow realistic influence from the agency and from the user group. We would suggest that in approaching the question of establishing this boundary, especially in a new supervisory arrangement, the following issues need to be in the mind of the supervisor (and preferably the supervisee too), though the extent to which they will need active discussion initially will vary according to circumstances.

A. PARAMETERS AROUND SUPERVISION

1. *The purpose of supervision.* Nixon (1982) shows how supervisor and supervisee may have quite different priorities and expectations. We shall focus on the functions of supervision in Chapter 3; here we note the importance of discussing previous experience as well as relevant departmental documents such as supervision policies and anti-discriminatory codes of practice.

2. *Frequency and timing of sessions.* Forward planning and clear arrangements are essential to an efficient supervisory framework. In most settings, 'on-the-hoof' supervisory contact between sessions will also be needed, especially where there may be crises in statutory work or in group settings. Some definition of the criteria for such contact is important, however difficult, both to ensure adequate availability and to prevent the over-use of quick, casual discussion (Hawkins and Shohet 1989).

3. *Interruptions and cancellations.* The established expectation should be that supervision will be given high priority, but in busy statutory agencies some prior discussion of possibly acceptable grounds for interruption or cancellation may be more useful than 'ideal' arrangements that are bound to fail and lead to disillusion.

4. *The supervision room.* This should preferably be the same, adequately sound-proofed location each time, with an 'engaged' sign on the door and telephone arrangements that prevent any but the most urgent interruptions (see 3 above).

5. *Confidentiality.* Defining the extent and limits of confidentiality is of core importance. Without initial definition, supervisor and supervisee may act on vague assumptions about maintaining confidentiality until a crisis exposes the severe limits on many aspects of confidentiality in an accountable agency context. Moreover, a supervisor's need to be free to discuss her supervisory work with her own supervisor is often ignored. Some definitions of the exceptions to confidentiality, based on the need to know, and ensuring that wherever possible the supervisee knows what sensitive information is being shared, should be seriously discussed in the initial stages.

6. *Recording of supervision.* This is linked to the question of confidentiality. Supervisors usually take responsibility for writing notes about the sessions, but clarity is needed about their purpose

and status, whether both supervisor and supervisee have copies, how disagreements are noted, and who has a right of access to the notes. This is distinct from supervisory decisions written directly into case files. In our experience, it is easy for supervisory notes to focus on discussions about service-users and to leave out or minimise discussion of supervisees' practice. The need to maintain appropriate privacy and the reality of struggling to write notes amid a busy day suggest that simple expectations of recording are best. Richards and Payne (1990, p.26) and Stanners (1995, p.189), among other writers, give useful outlines for recording.

7. *Appraisals and individual performance reviews.* 'Whilst appraisal has the specific function of evaluating staff performance at set intervals, its broader range of functions overlap with, and rely upon, the supervisory process' (Kemshall 1995, p.147). The respective functions of appraisal, individual performance review and supervision need to be organisationally defined before any explicit statement can be made on the relationship between them. Some statement is necessary, however, for the integrity of the supervisory process, as these issues touch also on questions of confidentiality and right of access to information, and are particularly sensitive where performance-related pay has been introduced.

8. *The social-professional boundary.* Supervisors cannot ignore information gained in social contexts that is relevant to their supervisory responsibilities, although careful thought may need to be given to how they can use it sensitively. This can be a particularly delicate matter for supervisors who are promoted from within a team and who had previous peer relationships with those who are now their supervisees.

9. *The boundary between supervision and other meetings.* The work of supervision will be affected by how clearly the tasks of other related meetings (for example, team allocation or case discussion) are defined. This touches on the perennial dilemma of combining the supervisory and team leadership aspects of the manager's role. Clarity is particularly important in group care settings where the nature of the work makes some group, as well as individual, supervision not only valuable but essential (Kahan 1994). We would suggest caution, however, in using the word supervision for too wide a range of meetings, especially those where the emphasis is on mutual help by peers; however valuable these may be, to call

them supervision tends to blur the aspect of managerial accountability for practitioners' work (some texts on supervision in group settings seem to us to introduce this kind of blurring, e.g. Roscoe 1995).

10. *Dissatisfaction and disagreements.* A supervisee dissatisfied with a supervisor's performance, or a supervisor and supervisee unable to resolve a disagreement, will benefit from being clear in advance whom they would be expected to approach in such circumstances.

B. PARAMETERS WITHIN SUPERVISION

1. *Power differentials.* Acknowledgement of the realistic power difference arising from the supervisor's authority as manager is important at the outset; likewise with any potential perceived differences in power arising from, for example, race, gender or age, however tokenist it may appear to be and however impossible at that stage to understand fully the implications for the two participants. Acknowledgement provides a base line which can be referred back to if difficulties arise later, either in exploring differences or in mediating the boundary area between difference and prejudice.

2. *Agenda-setting.* In reality it is likely that agendas will be set at the start of each session rather than in advance as sometimes advocated. It should be expected that supervisor and supervisee come having given some thought to items for the agenda. A plan for shared agendas may be appropriate but should not ignore the supervisor's responsibility, if necessary, to make the final decision about priorities. It can sometimes be helpful to plan in advance to use some supervision sessions for specific purposes, for example to focus every fourth session on one case in depth. This may be one way of ensuring that not only crisis work is discussed. It may also help to ensure that space is given to work that is going well, and that praise of the worker is not overlooked.

3. *Working concepts and skills.* 'There is nothing so practical as a good theory' (attributed to Kurt Lewin by Woodhouse 1990). Allowing space for supervisee and supervisor to share ideas they find helpful in the work, or to identify a need to seek theoretical knowledge that neither possesses, may enrich the experience of both. This is one of the ways in which 'external' influences may become 'internal' resources. Some initial acknowledgement of the extent

and limits of the knowledge and skills each possesses also provides the basis for later exploration of competence in the work.

4.   *The personal–professional boundary.* Supervision is not counselling. However, supervisors should make it clear to supervisees that they will actively wish to know about the emotional impact of the work, and in this context would be interested and available to hear of any personal difficulties that might be affecting it (as discussed earlier). Further, a supervisor may at times need to take the initiative in exploring whether a specific work problem might bear some relation to the supervisee's own life and not just arise from the work itself. In doing so, the supervisor may facilitate the supervisee's integration of personal and professional development through identifying links between different areas of anxiety (Pietroni, Poupard and Wilford 1991).

Nevertheless, both should be clear that supervisors have no right to insist on exploring personal dilemmas that they may consider exist in supervisees' own personalities or lives; and, equally, that supervisees have no right to expect a therapeutic service from their supervisors. The supervisor's responsibility is summed up by Kahan (1994):

> Supervisors' engagement with staff should be confined to the staff's ability to do their job, and care should be taken not to intrude into the staff members' personal lives in a way that cannot be justified by the terms of employment. (p.298)

A supervisor who blurs this boundary is abusing the supervisee; at the same time, one who holds too far back for fear of such abuse runs the risk of neglecting the supervisee's needs. Ash (1995), speaking of 'the personal and the professional', highlights that there is no clear-cut divide between the two. Such a truth does not, however, remove the supervisor's responsibility for struggling with this boundary of her responsibility. We shall explore further aspects of this in later chapters.

5.   *Case records.* It should be clear that the supervisor will expect to have access to case records (whether or not there is a requirement for the supervisor to record decisions there) in order to monitor the supervisee's recording practice, and familiarise herself as necessary with case developments. Advance discussion of how this will take place can reduce a supervisee's feeling of persecution if files are

read at a point of later difficulty. The supervisor's reading of records also ensures that good practice is recognised and not taken for granted.

6. *Methods and tools.* For much of the time supervision relies on verbal exchanges only. Process records, visual material, flip charts, role-play, audio or video recording may seem luxuries that belong only to training settings, but limited use of them might achieve more than much talking.

Direct observation or shared interviewing are, of course, normal practice in group care settings. Where supervisors have no automatic access to direct observation of supervisees' practice, such strategies are often employed only at times of exceptional concern either about a supervisee's functioning or about some difficulty in a case. They could, however, be valuable sources of information and exchange for both supervisor and supervisee at other times if built in as an occasional feature. Professional training (including postgraduate training) nowadays often requires direct observation as a basis for assessment, which – at least in theory – should make it easier to incorporate it as an adjunct of staff supervision.

7. *Review and evaluation.* Whether or not appraisals are required, a planned review of supervision, perhaps twice a year, promotes a useful focus on the experience and effectiveness of supervision itself. Both supervisor and supervisee can benefit at other times, too, from discussing each other's observations about how they are working together.

The supervisory contract

The long list of issues above needing anticipation and definition could of course be extended. They are more fully described elsewhere in the literature on supervision (e.g. Kemshall 1995). As we have said, however, there is a danger amid busy professional life that when expectations become too ideal the baby may be thrown out with the bath water. Realistically, a contract covering the minimum requirements is a necessary starting point to any supervisory relationship (Brown and Bourne 1996). Without it, supervision cannot be fully purposeful, nor can it be evaluated. We are surprised, in today's contract culture, how rarely formal, written supervisory contracts seem to be used. We would suggest that a contract should include at least the purpose of supervision and the main responsibilities and obligations regarding frequency, timing and location; interruption and cancellation; confidentiality; review and evaluation; and recording of sessions.

Drawing up a realistic, shared contract can be time-consuming, and may be avoided for fear of its becoming the focus for work rather than the means. Making and keeping a contract will, moreover, be more burdensome when there is no agency policy on supervision that helps to remove many of the issues we have mentioned from the arena of individual debate. Morrison (1993) provides a succinct list of what needs to be covered in an agency supervision policy, and suggests that supervisory responsibilities should be defined in job descriptions. The existence of a policy also highlights that, however clear the advantages to the working relationship of a contract agreed between supervisor and supervisee, however essential it is for the views of each to be explored, and however well-defined the supervisee's responsibility for using supervision, many aspects of the contract are not fully open to negotiation and it is not a contract between two equal parties. Ultimately, maintaining the appropriate boundaries both around and within supervision is the responsibility of the supervisor not the supervisee.

CHAPTER 3

Three into Two Won't Go
Supervisory Triangles

> Professionals have been disturbed to find that they cannot account for processes they have come to see as central to professional competence...they cannot say what they know how to do. (Schön 1983, pp.19, 69)

We now begin to focus on what actually goes on between the participants in the supervisory session, and to relate the processes involved to the tasks and functions of supervision. Schön's words highlight, not that experienced professionals do not know what they are doing, but that they take for granted the skills and knowledge that they automatically pass on to the next generation. This is particularly true of the expertise of supervision itself. Moreover, there often seems to be a gap between the (frequently idealistic) exhortations of official or professional writings about supervision and the actual experience of supervisory work (good and bad) that occupies so much of practitioners' and managers' time. We need some maps of this essentially interactive process, in order to study the taken-for-granted skills that embody what Schön calls 'how professionals think in action'.

Functions and participants in supervision

The overall purpose of supervision is to optimise the service to users within the limits of agency task, professional knowledge and financial resources. Many texts on supervision in agency settings have drawn on the key work of Kadushin (1976), who identifies three major functions of supervision – *administrative*, *educational* and *supportive*. More recently, as the work has become more complex, the list of functions has lengthened (as reviewed by Faugier and Butterworth 1992 and Waters 1992). Some authors, for example, have added the function of *mediation*, recognising the supervisor's role in negotiating with other organisations and with senior managers (Richards and Payne 1990; Morrison 1993); or *communication*, referring to the supervisor's responsibility to channel feedback from practitioners to the organisation on policy and practice issues (Borland 1995). While the balance between these functions (and what is involved in each of them) might vary according to setting, profession and area of work, there is remarkable consistency in the literature on how they are defined. In practice, however, supervisors and supervisees alike may sometimes despair of keeping proper track of these functions, amid the sheer quantity of supervisory tasks that constantly accumulates.

Whilst we are not offering a definitive view, we have found it helpful to conceptualise the work of supervision in terms of two triangular interactions: between three participants (Figure 3.1) and between three functions (Figure 3.2) of supervision. The value of the triangular configuration is that it highlights how different aspects of the work are interrelated.

Supervisor

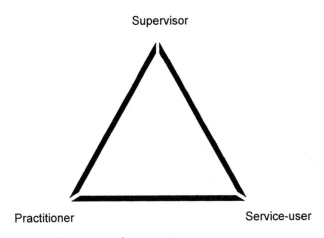

Practitioner   Service-user

Figure 3.1 Triangle of 'participants' in supervision

Figure 3.1 represents Mattinson's (1981) argument that when a case is being discussed in supervision there are, dynamically, not two but three 'participants' influencing the proceedings:

1. *Supervisor*, representing line-management authority and accountability;

2. *Practitioner*, bringing the experience of direct work with service-users and other agencies, and related professional needs;

3. *Service-user*, with needs, capacities, demands and rights.

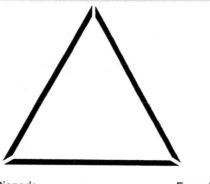

Managing service-delivery

Facilitating practitioner's   Focusing on
professional development   practitioner's work

Figure 3.2 Triangle of supervisory functions

The three functions in Figure 3.2 are linked in some ways with the 'participants' in the first triangle – never exactly corner to corner, though there is a particularly strong link between the 'supervisor' in triangle 3.1 and 'managing service-delivery' in triangle 3.2. The latter refers to ensuring implementation of statutory and agency policies and procedures; it includes monitoring the quality and quantity of work, prioritising and decision-making. The corner 'focusing on practitioner's work' refers to detailed exploration of individual pieces of work, as opposed to managerial issues covered in the 'service-delivery' corner.

While the supervisee is of course responsible for his own proper use of supervision, the functions described in Figure 3.2 are ultimately the responsibility of the supervisor. Though usually undertaken by one supervisor in relation to a supervisee, they essentially comprise the supervisory functions of the agency. Sometimes different functions may be undertaken by different people as part of the supervisory arrangements, especially in multidisciplinary or group-care settings. Although we shall mainly explore the application of the triangles to the more common one-to-one supervisory relationship (manager with practitioner), we will refer later to other arrangements, and also to the special pressures caused by some of the developments we have discussed in the previous two chapters.

'Two's company, three's a crowd'
Mattinson (1981) highlights the familiar feature in triangular relations of an excluding dynamic, whereby one participant or corner inevitably gets left

out from time to time; this point is also cogently addressed in the joint study of supervision undertaken by Wandsworth Social Services Department and the Tavistock Institute of Marital Studies (1989). Mattinson argues that the corner of a supervisory triangle most likely to be excluded is that which is causing most anxiety to the supervisor and/or supervisee. Conversely, we have increasingly noticed that supervisors or supervisees can become anxiously attached to their most worrying corner, unable to risk leaving it for another equally important, but less specifically anxiety-provoking, corner.

We shall give examples of both these interactions. Of course, certain corners of the supervisory triangles may at times be consciously put on one side in order to concentrate on one of the other corners, but we particularly wish to highlight the dynamic whereby one or other corner is avoided without any clear intention to do so. This process may be unconscious or barely acknowledged.

Three main points underpin our thinking about the application of the two triangles:

1. It is inevitably difficult, in any supervisory arrangement, to keep all three participants or all three functions in mind.

2. Nevertheless, the three corners are dynamically and functionally interrelated and cannot be regarded separately from each other.

3. Consequently, supervision and practice become unsafe if one corner is ignored or avoided for any length of time.

The following examples (imaginary but based on typical scenarios) will illustrate these three points.

EXCLUSIONS FROM 'PARTICIPANTS' TRIANGLE (FIGURE 3.1)
EXAMPLE 3.a

> A supervisor, sensitively concentrating on a practitioner's personal and professional distress in relation to a particular case, may find it hard to switch to getting the practitioner focused on the service-user's needs, and on ensuring that appropriate action is taken. *Service-user's corner excluded.*

EXAMPLE 3.b

> A new supervisor, more experienced as a practitioner than the supervisee (and more confident of her practice expertise than her ability to supervise), may be particularly prone to disregard the supervisee's position as the one who knows the service-user and is doing the direct work. She may jump quickly into telling the

supervisee what to do (meaning what she thinks she would do in his place), with no space given to exploring his actual experience, developing his ideas and valuing his judgement. The supervisee, either sensing the supervisor's vulnerability or perhaps anxious about expressing his own views, may go along with this. *Practitioner's corner excluded.*

EXAMPLE 3.c

A supervisor who feels unskilled compared with her supervisee in an area of practice which has developed greatly since she was a practitioner (e.g. investigation of sexual abuse allegations) may devalue the relevance of her own knowledge and experience in exploring the supervisee's work, and abdicate from doing so. *Supervisor's corner excluded.*

This last example illustrates how supervisees seen as good and experienced may sometimes be 'abandoned' by supervisors who underestimate the value of their own position one step away from the immediate impact of the work – a key position that affords greater professional objectivity than practitioners can sustain when closely involved in highly-charged cases. The importance of this aspect of supervision is particularly clear in the report on the death of Jasmine Beckford (London Borough of Brent 1985).

EXCLUSIONS FROM 'FUNCTIONS' TRIANGLE (FIGURE 3.2)
EXAMPLE 3.d

A supervisor may join a supervisee in not focusing in detail on the work being undertaken on a particular case (or group of cases). The degree of hostility, pain and conflict emanating from the case(s) may be so great that getting involved would raise fears for practitioner and supervisor of feeling helpless, becoming overwhelmed or being destructive themselves. These fears may be avoided by denial and by steering clear of exploring the practitioner's contact with service-users. *'Focusing on practitioner's work' corner excluded.*

In this kind of situation, a focus on procedure may be misused to provide a superficial clarity and certainty that avoids really thinking about what is going on in the case. Decisions based on the 'rule of optimism' (Dingwall, Eekelaar and Murray 1983) are the result of such avoidance of complexity.

EXAMPLE 3.e

A supervisor, furious with senior managers for their lack of interest in practice issues or their failure to provide adequate resources, may be tempted to deny her own identity as part of management and her proper concern with accountability. She may instead give excessive attention to what she enjoys doing, namely, consulting to practice issues in depth and exploring the worker's professional development. *'Managing service-delivery' corner excluded.*

EXAMPLE 3.f

The supervisor of a competent and experienced practitioner may give scant attention to his continuing professional and career development, especially when both may be feeling overwhelmed by the amount and intensity of the work. *'Facilitating practitioner's professional development' corner excluded.*

The interrelatedness of 'participants' and functions

The above examples, however familiar, present a somewhat false picture because of their static quality, pinpointing how one corner of one of the triangles is neglected at any one time. More dynamically, however, neglect of one corner will necessarily lead to neglect of another. In Example 3.a, for instance, if the supervisor – preoccupied with the practitioner's distress – does not in due course help him to think about the needs of the service-user, she has also abandoned her position as supervisor with management accountability for service-delivery; in effect, both supervisor and practitioner are left huddled together in the practitioner's corner. The supervisor in Example 3.e, over-focusing on a practitioner's work in a few cases, may be not only neglecting to ensure that agency tasks are attended to over the whole caseload, but also thereby giving the worker a skewed model for his professional development. In Example 3.d, on the other hand, the supervisor who avoids focusing in detail on a piece of work deprives herself of evidence on which to make case decisions, monitor whether agency policy is being implemented, or notice gaps in the worker's practice or knowledge that need attention. Moreover, it is only through close discussion of work that a supervisor can obtain information to feed back to senior managers about the need to adapt policy or procedures to ensure better service-delivery.

At the same time, this emphasis on interrelatedness does not remove the reality of frequent conflict between the demands of different corners at a given point in time. The conflict may sometimes lie in the pace of attention required (Dearnley 1985), for example when a practitioner's need to develop greater skills over time conflicts with the urgent need for work to be covered.

Moore (1995) underlines one aspect of interrelatedness in the context of child-protection work:

It is administrative supervision that ensures the rules and procedures of the department are carried out. But more than that, imaginative administrative supervision can discover quicker than the other types of supervision what is really going on between worker and user. Inflexibility in carrying out procedures shows that a worker has an acute fear about a case. Rules that are ignored may show the worker has got sucked in by a hostile client… Unwillingness to operate guidelines may reveal that the worker is afraid to confront the client. (p.65)

Thus the interrelatedness of the three corners in each triangle, and of the two triangles, becomes clearer. The dynamic processes of supervision are seen to be intertwined with its functions, tasks and outcome. It makes no sense to say, as we have frequently heard it said, that considering process is a luxury in this busy task-centred age. The dilemma lies in having the time, skill and experience to manage the difficult tensions, keeping in mind all three corners of the relevant triangle and the pulls and pushes that are influencing them. Supervisors and supervisees whose experience of working life has included little or no emphasis on continuing professional development may not easily appreciate the link between this and the requirements of service-delivery. Professionals whose training has afforded only limited in-depth consideration of process in their interaction with service-users may find it hard to see how this relates to service-delivery. On the other hand, those who have traditionally functioned in effect as independent practitioners may be slow to acknowledge Moore's claims for the value of good procedure in ensuring exploration of process. At best, as Kahan (1994, p.273) usefully points out, 'part of the importance of supervision is that it can assist staff to accept accountability without resentment because it demonstrates the link between verbal aspirations and practical reality'.

In agencies where the three main supervisory functions of Figure 3.2 are carried out by different people, it is important to be clear who holds overall responsibility for seeing that all three are being implemented, and that relevant information is fed back to this person so that s/he can hold in mind how the functions relate to one another. For example, in group care settings, information about a worker's functioning apparent in group case discussion led by one manager needs collating with what emerges in individual supervision with another manager, in a way that is clear to all concerned. Similarly, a duty senior responsible for managing the crisis work done by social work staff on a duty rota will need to draw to their regular supervisors' attention the strengths and weaknesses they show in that work – and not, as often happens, assume either that these are known or that such feedback is not her responsibility. Without such communication, an agency cannot make effective use of its most important resource – its staff.

The deadly equal triangle

The injunction to attend to all three corners of the supervisory triangles, however, comes with a major word of caution! Unless a supervisor allows herself to take the risk of ignoring one or two corners for a time, or from time to time, she may not get closely enough involved in the issues in any one corner to work effectively there. There is thus no easy solution to the management of these interconnected corners. The 'deadly equal triangle' depicted by Mattinson (1981) is one where rigidly equal attention to each corner turns the concept of the triangle into a procedure to be rigidly followed.

As in all triangular relationships, any 'third party' can be used as a distance-regulator to avoid close engagement between the other two (Byng-Hall 1980). Mattinson argues that not only is it inevitable that a supervisor will become caught up in a particular corner at times, but it is essential that she do so, allowing herself to be responsive to the pressures exerted by the supervisee or the work. Elsewhere (Mattinson 1975) she quotes Jung's (1931) maxim, 'you can exert no influence, if you are not susceptible to influence'. The supervisor therefore needs at times to become totally in-volved, for example, in discussing one big anxiety-provoking case and forgetting everything else; or to spend a number of sessions considering how to apply new procedures; or to put to one side for the moment any concern about professional development or decision-making in order to respond sufficiently to a worker's distress (and it may be only when the distress has been understood that its implications for those other tasks will become clear). We shall discuss further aspects of such 'influence' in Chapter 5.

It is not, therefore, a question of always being skilled enough to 'get it right'. The key issue for the supervisor is what capacity she has to stand back periodically and consider whether – in her supervisory work overall, or with certain supervisees or certain kinds of work – she is habitually neglecting one or other corner, and then to think diagnostically about what is giving rise to this. Similarly, a supervisor needs to check whether she takes refuge in neat but ineffective deadly equal attention. Both within a session and over time, the supervisor thus requires a 'helicopter ability' (Hawkins and Shohet 1989, p.37), being able to move in close but also pull back to a broader perspective, in order to fulfil the key supervisory task of initiating exploration in areas of difficulty hitherto neglected, avoided or overlooked. By consid-ering their own movements between the corners of the triangles, supervisors will of course also learn about the corners that they find difficult and the areas where they may themselves require further professional development.

Support: a means, not an end

Before moving on to consider the impact of recent developments on the supervisory triangles, we should explain why we have excluded *providing support* from our list of supervisory functions, when it is one so often mentioned in the literature (e.g. Kadushin 1976; Butler-Sloss 1988). By 'support' or 'personal support', texts on supervision usually mean attending to the emotional stress experienced by practitioners, sustaining their morale and valuing their hard work and achievements. The importance of this cannot be overstated, but we believe that to speak of support as in itself a function of supervision is to confuse means with ends. Certainly, a *supportive attitude* that considers the feelings of the worker and values what he offers is essential if a supervisor is to attend adequately to any of the three corners of the 'functions' triangle. If support is treated as an end of supervision, however, there is the danger of a collusive focus on the worker's needs for their own sake, rather than a focus on the worker in order to promote a better service. In work with service-users, an aim such as 'providing support to the family' has long since been recognised as lacking in purpose, ignoring the question of 'support to what end?' Too often it means little more than support of the status quo. We are highlighting the parallel in supervision.

We would argue that attending to the worker's emotional response to the work actually has a greater importance than merely 'support'. Particularly in a culture tending to a mechanistic focus on quantity of output, to define a worker as needing 'support' runs the risk of pathologising him, suggesting some personal or professional vulnerability that needs special attention. Instead, it is essential to recognise that strong feelings about highly emotive work may be inevitable, and a sign of health in a practitioner; and that they can also be a vital source of information about dynamic issues in the case that will need to be taken into account when making decisions about it. For example, debriefing after a violent incident not only allows feelings to be freed in a worker (rather than denied in a way that may inhibit future work), but may also provide learning for worker, supervisor and agency (Roscoe 1995). The rational and emotional aspects of supervisory work thus become linked rather than split (this will be a main focus in Chapters 5 and 6).

We would similarly argue that, however welcome the increasing provision by employers of counselling schemes for staff under stress, and however sensitively the confidentiality boundary is handled in such schemes, there is again a danger of confusing personal problems with quite appropriate emotional reactions to highly painful work or unsatisfactory work conditions. The term 'counselling' inevitably suggests emphasis on a personal crisis. While there may be no absolute division between what is a personal problem (even if exacerbated by work) and what is work-related stress, it seems to us that even detailed evaluations of the issues brought to counsellors in work settings (e.g. Fineman 1985; Sloboda *et al.* 1993) do not sufficiently address this question. The fact that counselling may help is not the relevant issue. We would argue that the provision, in the first place, of thorough consultation to individuals and teams about stress at work might not only produce greater learning about service-delivery (and suggest improvements), but also result in fewer staff seeking counselling and becoming the scape-goats of a pressured agency.

Current turbulence and the supervisory triangles

Some supervisors on our courses who, at the time, found the concept of the supervisory triangles a useful tool have more recently suggested to us that they look almost too clearly defined and sturdy to reflect the current reality of supervisory functions and interactions, beset by rapidly changing structures and increasing responsibilities. They wondered whether some more intricate, but precarious, image such as a spider's web might be more appropriate in these turbulent times. To us, this feedback has only confirmed the need for a clear conceptual structure such as the supervisory triangles, as a touchstone or reference point amid disorientating change; but it has also led us to think anew what factors in the current situation are putting what pressures on which corners of the triangles. In this section, therefore, we consider the implications for the triangles of recent developments.

Distortions in the 'participants' triangle

In drawing the 'participants' triangle (Figure 3.1), we paid no particular attention to which participant sat at the apex of the triangle, with no (conscious) intent to give greater importance to any of them. Many supervisors have commented on this, suggesting various alternative shapes of triangle and positioning of participants. The kind of experience we most often hear about is represented by the triangle in Figure 3.3, which depicts a strengthening of the corners of the supervisor and service-user, at the expense of the pivotal corner of the practitioner. The supervisor and service-user also frequently have a closer link than formerly. We do not intend this to be a definitive new diagram; clearly different settings and types of work will throw up differently-shaped triangles at different times. Supervisors might find it useful to draw the triangle that seems to represent their current experience most tellingly.

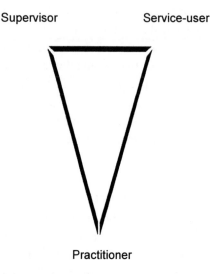

Supervisor   Service-user

Practitioner

Figure 3.3 Distorted 'participants' triangle

We summarise below, in note form, the ways in which the relative weighting of the supervisor's, practitioner's and service-user's corners may be experienced as increased or reduced by recent developments.

SUPERVISOR'S CORNER
Increased by:

- more procedures and administrative demands
- more involvement in policy development (especially where the management hierarchy is 'flattened')
- requirements of quality assurance units, and use of information obtained from such units about teams' or practitioners' functioning
- appraisal schemes
- budget-holding
- information technology, giving access to knowledge, for example about resources
- contracting and networking roles, giving broader contact with other agencies

- more direct contact with users/carers/community groups (e.g. over complaints, evaluation of services and local policy development)
- rapid decision-making demanded as crisis work predominates.

Reduced by:

- information obtained about team or practitioners by quality assurance units which bypasses supervision
- uncertainty about authority to supervise given by agency, and what sort of supervision is valued, especially in new areas and structures of work (e.g. care management)
- less communication about practice upwards to senior management
- supervisor's own supervision less available or providing less space for supervisory and practice issues.

SERVICE-USER'S CORNER

Increased by:

- agency publicity about services available
- statutory and procedural emphasis on partnership
- anti-discriminatory policies
- needs assessments
- complaints procedures
- outcome evaluation and quality assurance schemes
- influence of special interest and community groups
- advocacy schemes
- user participation in policy development.

Reduced by:

- busyness of agencies
- lack of resources
- evaluation based on quantity not quality.

PRACTITIONER'S CORNER

Increased by:

- practitioner's professional needs analysed through quality assurance schemes (occasionally revealing what is not being obtained in supervision, and highlighting the practitioner as a 'user' of supervision)

- ○ excitement at new roles and sometimes increased autonomy (e.g. 'Effective care management is dependent upon practitioners being given additional freedom to adopt a more entrepreneurial approach', Department of Health 1991d, para. 3:14).

Reduced by:

- ○ increased emphasis on the other two corners
- ○ uncertainty about identity and role (e.g. about social work role in care management).

The increased weight given to the supervisor's corner should not, of course, be taken to mean that supervisors have a greater sense of their power and authority; it mainly highlights the increased impact upon supervision of issues of agency requirements and accountability. To a great extent, indeed, this exacerbates the difficulty for supervisors in attending to all three functions of supervision.

We have been particularly struck by the very specific effects of some new developments on the supervisor's capacity to attend to the practitioner's corner. Many supervisors, involved in contracting with other agencies and organising packages of care, have become preoccupied not so much with their own staff's standard of practice as with that of other contributors to service-delivery – often finding themselves being approached anxiously by such workers (for example, family carers recruited through high street agencies) for informal consultation about work problems. Furthermore, where purchasing and providing are divided, the frequent concern about exactly who is supposed to be doing which task can deflect attention from looking at the work the supervisee is actually engaged in. As noted in Chapter 1, devolved budget-holding passes the needs–resources tension down to the first-line manager who, as supervisor, can be faced with a conflict between helping a supervisee to explore the needs of a case and holding in mind the financial implications of any decision and the needs of other, as yet perhaps unseen, service-users.

Anxiety about managing such new responsibilities has absorbed the time and energy of many supervisors, inclining them to cling to the supervisor's corner with less capacity to be open to other points of view. Some good supervisors have told us guiltily of the relief they feel when they do not have lively supervisees who ask questions or challenge. Meanwhile, now that supervisors probably meet service-users more frequently than in the past, they may develop an attitude of 'knowing the service-users' thereby finding it unnecessary to explore their workers' knowledge and experience. Thus, amid busyness, the supervisor may short-cut by leaving out the supervisee's corner. Alternatively, some supervisors may react to the increased weightiness of new agency requirements by abandoning their own corner, even welcoming supervisees' pressure on them not to be 'with management'.

Distortions in the functions triangle

The recent changes have also had a major effect on the balance of attention given to the three functions of supervision. The management of service-delivery has gained in weight (like the increase in the supervisor's corner just noted). The triangle of functions might now be experienced as depicted in Figure 3.4. This highlights the current emphasis on the service-delivery corner, and the low priority accorded to facilitating professional development. Focusing on the practitioner's work, moreover, is often put to one side, signifying the greatly changed relation between the managerial and the professional (or consultative) functions of supervision. We will discuss this change first.

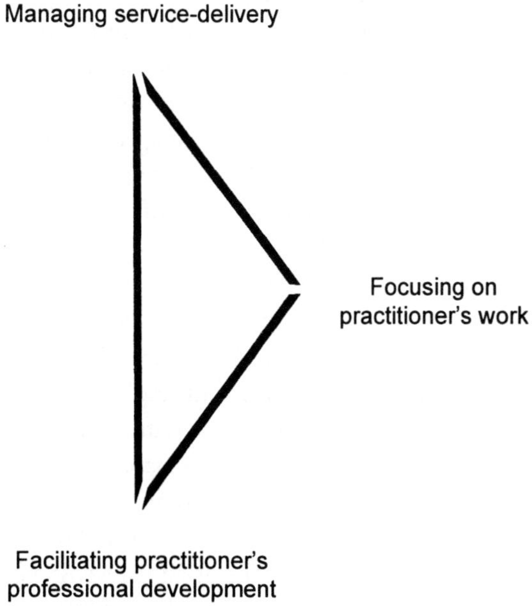

Managing service-delivery

Focusing on
practitioner's work

Facilitating practitioner's
professional development

Figure 3.4 Distorted functions triangle

FOCUS ON PRACTICE: THE PLACE OF CONSULTATION

Although the increase in specialism as the basis for organising services might mean that some supervisors will have greater specialist knowledge about their supervisees' work, on balance it seems less and less likely that this corner will receive adequate attention in the current situation. The development of new modes of work (for example, service-user participation, video interviewing in cases of child sexual abuse, work following major disasters) contributes to many supervisors feeling – and being – insufficiently skilled or knowledgeable to offer in-depth consultation to their supervisees' practice. Some of the changes in legislation, too, demand greater expertise in practitioners (for example, in sustaining partnerships with users or in the tasks of approved social workers), at a time when upward career progress is increasingly a matter of moving into management without much attention being given to developing expertise as a supervisor. There is also the growing phenomenon of line managers not being of the same profession as their practitioners, or not having any background in practice at all (as in many community care arrangements). More broadly, the mushrooming of managerial tasks (as described in Chapter 2) frequently leaves minimal time for a detailed focus on supervisees' practice.

For a range of realistic reasons, therefore, there may be more need for agencies to arrange for the supervisory function of focusing on work issues to be undertaken by someone other than the line manager. This is recognised, for example, in the government's guidelines for social services departments on work with child sexual abuse (Department of Health 1991b): 'Usually the supervisor will be the field worker's line manager, but the management and professional supervision aspects may be divided between two people. In this case, the separate responsibilities and lines of accountability must be made clear' (para. 6.1.2). The need for a clear line of communication between the 'supervisor' or consultant and the line manager is thus emphasised.

Of course, involving a consultant to supplement the role of the supervisor in focusing in depth on work is not new. Consultants internal and external have long been used to work in this way with individual practitioners or groups. Sometimes their use has been appropriate, sometimes a way for agencies to avoid confronting inadequacy in a manager or supervisor. We would suggest, however, that even when appropriate it has often been accompanied by a blurring of the respective responsibilities and accountabilities of consultant and line manager. Parsloe and Stevenson (1978) found a lack of clarity in the function and responsibility of internal consultants within social services departments – a conclusion not dissimilar to that reached by Rushton and Nathan (1996a) in recent research on the role of internal consultants in child protection work.

The latter authors highlight the danger that consultation will not be effectively integrated if the relationship between consultant and manager is not clearly defined. The role of consultant (especially if external) does not

usually carry accountability for ensuring that any suggestions are implemented, nor for assessing the competence of practitioners or making decisions about cases. Yet the consultant may have highly relevant information
which the line manager ought to know for these purposes, as well as for
thinking about the professional development needs of staff. It should be clear
when and how this information is to be communicated. We have noticed
that, however clear in theory a line manager, supervisee and consultant may
feel about this at the outset, in practice the implications are often not spelt
out and vagueness may develop once the work is under way. This blurring
of thought also appears in the frequent loose use of the term 'supervision',
even in statutory settings, for supportive work discussion between peers
(Atherton 1986; Loughlin 1992). Informal discussion with peers may be
extremely helpful, and may at times merit the term consultation, but it can
never be part of supervision within a line management structure. Some of
the confusion surrounding the terms supervision and consultation may come
from the therapy and counselling worlds where they are often virtually
synonymous, with no line management accountability involved. When
imported into an agency context, however, such confusion obscures crucial
questions concerning the tension between managerial accountability and
professional autonomy and discretion.

It is useful, therefore, to set a contract between the line manager and the
consultant (internal or external), clarifying respective responsibilities, confidentiality boundaries and lines of communication. Overworked managers,
practitioners eager for work discussion and consultants keen to help may
well recoil from the extra work this requires at the outset (and possibly extra
costs when employing an external consultant). However, avoiding the issue
may leave all three parties involved in unsafe practice. It is certainly helpful
when an organisation has contractual arrangements for consultants built into
its supervisory policies.

Three supervisory developments we have noted in this context deserve
attention. The *first,* in the field of child protection, concerns the growing use
of senior practitioners to carry some supervisory responsibility, in the face
of increasing burdens on team managers and as a way of employing their
practice skills more fully. Sometimes their role is specified in terms of the
supervisory functions triangle. For example, they may be clearly responsible
for all three functions of supervision, or only for that of focusing on
practitioners' work issues, but with clearly defined avenues of communication
with the line manager who carries responsibility for the other two functions,
including decision-making on cases. At other times, however, the senior
practitioner's role may be confused, anomalous, contradictory or simply

unsafe, with no certainty about communication between the three corners of the triangle of supervisory functions.

Second, Faugier and Butterworth (1992) address the dilemmas in nursing when the development of 'peer supervision', that is shared consultation about work issues, is totally split off from line management accountability, to the detriment of both. This allows for a scenario to develop whereby a peer 'supervisor', bound by an agreement of confidentiality, may feel trapped in an impotent position when, for example, seriously concerned about an apparently depressed 'supervisee' who is either unable or unwilling to seek help, and the consequent effect on his work performance. Such an arrangement would not allow for line management authority to be invoked, in order to act on concern about the supervisee's practice and confront him about the need to seek help if necessary. An initiative arising out of a laudable professional wish to fill a managerial gap thus runs the risk of disintegrating into secretiveness, fragmentation and unsafe practice if the question of supervisory accountability is not confronted in the contract-setting.

Third, we would suggest that using the triangles to think about the formal relationships required between manager and consultant may actually help to highlight the importance of consultation that has gone on informally in a hitherto unrecognised way. For example, the role of approved social workers in offering consultation to colleagues on mental health issues (Wiltshire 1995), or of a skilled worker in providing informal guidance to a new recruit (Kahan 1994), might gain more recognition from formal structures for feeding back to managers. The need for such consultation may well increase. Currently, for example, most supervisors in social services departments are likely to have a generic background but, with the divide between adult and children's services, supervisors in future may have little knowledge of any specialism other than their own, and may need consultation for themselves and their practitioners on cases that cross boundaries.

MULTIDISCIPLINARY TEAMS

Settings such as child psychiatry units, especially where staff are employed by different agencies, have always produced complexities in the relationship between the three supervisory functions. Joint structures that have developed more recently, for example in community mental health teams, are liable to show the same tendency. Øvretveit's (1993) admirably clear definitions, and his outline of alternative structures of accountability in community care, are relevant to the tensions between the three supervisory functions that we have been discussing in relation to other settings. Equally, our supervisory triangles are a useful supplement to thinking about the tensions in multidisciplinary teams. Øvretveit suggests that some flexibility in the line management role is necessary to allow multidisciplinary teams to function effectively. We would add that perhaps such settings require practitioners not only to be skilled in direct work, but also to be confident about their role within line management accountability rather than having a false view of themselves as totally independent professionals. This would enable the necessary flexibility in line management definitions to work effectively rather than become a vehicle for blurring.

FACILITATING PROFESSIONAL DEVELOPMENT: THE PLACE OF TRAINING

This corner of the triangle of functions has in recent years received even less attention from busy supervisors than consultation to work issues. Where professions have given special emphasis to the development of training, as in nursing, it has often been removed from line management involvement altogether; the use of experienced nurses as 'mentors' to newcomers in the area of professional development can raise the same dilemmas as we noted above with peer supervision (Faugier and Butterworth 1992). In social work, a study of supervisors' responses to practitioners returning from specialist post-qualifying training revealed little appreciation of how to use their new skills, and little interest in their experiences (Rushton and Martyn 1993). Although government publications about child protection and care management extol the importance of drawing up training profiles or training audits on staff (Department of Health 1991b and 1991d), and although the initiative in setting up training courses increasingly lies with commissioning managers rather than training departments, in practice the professional development of supervisees still remains fairly peripheral to the total supervisory enterprise.

Structures that require more joint discussion between managers and trainers at least give the possibility of a better link between the professional development function of supervision and the other two functions, rather than training and development choices being mostly a response to the practitioner's individual wishes (as so often in the past). Dynamically, however, there may be distortions here too. For example, focusing on a supervisee's need for further training may be a way for supervisor and supervisee to avoid facing concerns about the latter's general functioning or about specific aspects of his practice. As one trainer suggested, there 'could be a danger of investment in specialist knowledge as a panacea for anxiety about process issues' (E. Cooper, personal communication 1994). Training courses, like practice consultation, may be a valuable supplement to the activities of a supervisor but cannot be a substitute for supervisory attention to all areas.

As with consultants, in fact, a clear contract is needed about the boundary and line of communication between trainers and managers.

The triangles as supervisory tools

Our two supervisory triangles provide dynamic working models for supervisors in their struggle to achieve an effective and appropriate balance between the three corners according to the needs of the work, their own and their supervisees' capacities and the specifics of agency setting and professional role. We have emphasised how, in any supervisory relationship, the balance to be maintained in managing the tensions may vary considerably over time. We find it helpful to envisage the linking lines between the corners as having something of the quality of strong elastic, capable of being pulled in different directions and then returning to their original shape – though we are also aware of the danger of this image, which might suggest a capacity to stretch to everything rather than face the fact that stretching into one corner involves neglecting another.

The supervisory triangles can be used as a way of discussing and clarifying the purpose of supervision at the point of initial contracting. They are then available as a reference point for periodic evaluation of what is happening in supervision; supervisor and supervisee can each contribute their different perspectives about which corners have received more, or less, attention. One of the values of the triangles is the simplicity of their impact, despite the complexity of what they convey. This enables them to be of more practical use than many more sophisticated ways of analysing supervisory functions.

CHAPTER 4

Assessing and Developing Professional Competence
Stages and Styles

The supervisory function of facilitating professional development (which also implies assessment of a supervisee's level of functioning and learning needs) is probably the most consistently neglected corner of the functions triangle described in the previous chapter. It is, however, integral to the other two functions. Without some evaluation of a practitioner's work capacities, a supervisor clearly cannot avoid the risk of giving staff tasks well beyond their ability, cannot assess whether or not an adequate service is being delivered, cannot know what weight in decision-making to give to information and opinions provided by a worker and cannot consider what help he needs to become more effective.

In courses we have run for supervisors, participants will often present a pressing supervisory dilemma in such terms as 'I've got this worker that I'm not sure what to make of. I don't know how worried to be about his work. Sometimes it seems all right, and nothing disastrous has happened. Is it just that I'm expecting too much, or that I haven't found a way of getting through?'

The dilemma highlights the frequent difficulty of disentangling what is a worker's stage of professional development, individual style of work or personal limitation; distinguishing these from the supervisor's own stage, style, standards and personality; and also considering what issues arise, not from one or the other as individuals, but from their interaction as a pair. Many supervisors are predisposed to assume the competence of their workers, since they need to feel they can rely on them to get the work done. Equally, many supervisees feel inhibited or defensive about revealing gaps in their skills.

For those supervisors who rely almost totally, in their decision-making, on second-hand accounts of cases from workers (having little of the direct evidence of workers and service-users in action that is available in, say, a group care setting) the experience of beginning to doubt the worker's competence can be very worrying. The worry is exacerbated if the supervisor also feels that any attempt to explore evidence of the level of work might be perceived as negative criticism, liable to depress staff morale and cause problems in, for example, allocating work. What is sometimes overlooked is that assuming competence and avoiding exploration in this way may also prevent informed recognition of a worker's high level of skill.

The fact that any attempt to disentangle must take place within a close relationship between two people both aids and complicates the task. The advantage is clear, in that the relationship at best provides a trustworthy context in which exploration can take place; but this is also an area where individual personal and professional factors may be most powerful and most sensitive.

We shall address some of the emotional and contextual influences on supervisors' and supervisees' stages of development and styles of perform-ance later in this chapter (and more fully in succeeding chapters), but first we wish to focus on applying to supervision some ideas developed in the field of adult learning theory. Many of these ideas have long been implicit in discussions of supervision and training; those that have been more explicit may be sharpened by considering some of the relevant adult learning research. Our intention is to extract the ideas most pertinent to staff supervision; readers interested in exploring the theory and research on adult learning more fully are referred to such texts as Knowles (1973) or Gardiner (1989).

The two main topics we shall consider are, first, *the learning contract* and, second, *stages and styles of learning and working.* Under each heading, we shall summarise some key contributions of adult learning theory, consider their application to staff supervision, and then explore some other relevant issues. We shall give most space to the second heading, which covers many of the concerns that most preoccupy supervisors. At the end of the chapter we shall look briefly at *the learning organisation.*

The learning contract

The concept of learner-led training lies at the heart of adult learning theory. With its emphasis on learning from experience, on the impetus of the 'the need to know' in order to cope with real life tasks and problems, on evaluating learning by its effect on behaviour, on a clear learning contract and on the interactive process between learner and teacher (where the teacher is not the expert with the answers), its application to the supervisory context is clear. Though developed in the training context, the learning contract with its principle that goals, process and outcome are closely interconnected has important implications for supervisory contracts. Gardiner (1989), surveying the research in adult learning, quotes studies by Saljo (1975) that show in detail how different ways of explaining a task to a learner, and of assessing performance, will influence both her/his approach to learning and its outcome. The learner's previous experience of being taught will also influence how the learning task is perceived. Pottage and Evans (1994) give a vivid illustration of this in the development of a new course for mental health workers, where the curriculum was designed in close response to consultation with the workers.

Clearly, however, it is not the prime responsibility of a staff supervisor to train her supervisees, nor can she ever focus solely on their learning needs. Even in the supervision of social work students, Gardiner (1989) points to the inherent tension between a hierarchical organisational structure (with its ideological affinity to a teacher-led pedagogic form of input) and the self-direction at the heart of adult learning theory. Knowles (1973) acknowledges that the learning contract of a professional working in an agency needs to address the question of accountability; the diagnosis of learning needs must include those given priority by the organisation as the competences required to deliver the service. Such accountability would also require a supervisee to ensure that his real level of practice is made known to his supervisor; this needs to be met by the supervisor's 'capacity to "allow" into supervision information from practitioners when they are not able to undertake tasks in line with departmental procedures' (Department of Health 1991a, p.30).

The idea of a supervisory contract has a history independent of learning theory, and includes a wide range of matters already mentioned in Chapter 2. We would argue, however, that research into adult learning can usefully sharpen our thinking, especially about that part of the contract which concerns the supervisor's task of facilitating the supervisee's professional development. The following example introduces some of the relevant issues.

EXAMPLE 4.a: INEXPERIENCED SUPERVISOR AND EXPERIENCED WORKER

> Six months into his first supervisory post, a senior social worker responsible for supervising two members of a duty child-care team in a social services department began to feel that he ought to know more about the work of one of his supervisees. She was a highly experienced social worker, twenty years his elder, who had been redeployed to this

team a year earlier on the disbanding of the specialist family placement team where she had worked for many years. The senior social worker found she was a supportive influence in the team, but though she responded pleasantly to his questions in supervision she herself brought almost nothing for discussion, and he felt he did not know her cases. For some time he put this down to his lack of experience as a supervisor; perhaps she needed little from him and he had little to offer her. He had omitted to establish an initial supervisory contract with this worker, though he had done so with his other (less experienced) supervisee.

As he shared these concerns with colleagues on a course, he reflected that something about her age, her experience and her self-contained manner had inhibited him, exacerbating his lack of confidence in his new role. He had been preoccupied with proving himself rather than exploring her situation and the task they shared. He began to see that he did not know what she expected of supervision. For the six months before his arrival she had been virtually unsupervised and, from his distant knowledge of her previous team, he thought it likely that she had received little supervision there. As he stood back from the situation in discussion with his own supervisor he also wondered whether, despite her general experience, she was relatively inexperienced in child protection investigation, the main task of her current post; perhaps he was not the only one of the two who felt ignorant and unsure in their interaction. He felt he needed to know more about her past experience and her current view of supervision.

He resolved to discuss with his supervisee his failure to set up a supervisory contract with her and his wish to do so now. He decided to focus particularly on her expectations of supervision, her experience and training in child protection investigation and her feelings about being in the team.

Such a discussion, whether at the start of the supervisory arrangement or at this point, might or might not lead to open exploration and a clear supervisory contract. Contract discussions are not, of course, panaceas for all supervisory problems, but they can provide a useful reference point to return to at later stages, as we discussed in Chapter 2. In our experience, initial contract-making and exploring expectations of supervision are often bypassed, not just by inexperienced supervisors as in this example, but often because of unchecked assumptions of agreement as to the arrangements and basis of supervision. The existence or otherwise of a clear agency policy on

supervision contracts is, of course, highly relevant. Example 4.a also highlights two of the important aims in contracting:

1. to locate the present supervisory arrangements in the context of the
    supervisor's and supervisee's previous professional experience

2. to ensure that supervisees know they are expected to take some
    responsibility for identifying their own strengths, weaknesses and
    learning needs.

These points are further illustrated in a particular way in the next example.

EXAMPLE 4.b: EXPERIENCED SUPERVISOR AND INEXPERIENCED WORKER

> A very experienced senior probation officer was concerned about the
> unsatisfactory work of two untrained probation service assistants. Her
> difficulty in managing them was exacerbated by her feeling that their
> tasks were unrewarding and frustrating. These included considerable
> contact with users at points of crisis, but usually with a focus only on
> their practical needs which, the senior probation officer said, 'it's such
> a relief not to be dealing with any more myself'. She was afraid these
> two new recruits to the service would be put off from continuing by
> the preponderance of such work.

This supervisor was clearly well-intentioned in her interest in her supervisees'
development, but she was also making assumptions about how the two
workers actually experienced their situation. Instead of exploring this with
them, and considering the learning potential for new workers of dealing for
the first time with users in high stress – and having to cope with their own
feelings about either giving or being unable to give practical help – the
supervisor had put herself in their shoes. As Westheimer (1977, p.47)
reminds us, 'it is hard for experienced supervisors to forgive/remember their
early selves'.

Stages and styles of learning and working

Supervisors struggling with 'problem' supervisees often voice their concern
in terms of the difficulty of sorting out what is a supervisee's stage of
professional functioning and what is a matter of style or personality. Closely
allied is the question of how these are like or unlike the supervisor's own.
Adult learning research has also wrestled with the distinction and interaction
between stage and style, with results that are helpful though not conclusive.
Researchers in Sweden (Marton and Saljo 1976a and 1976b; Saljo 1975)
and in Britain (Pask and Scott 1972 and 1973) distinguish levels of

complexity in learners' conception of the learning task; the Swedish 'surface learning' and 'deep learning' are broadly equivalent to the British 'serialist' (operational) and 'holist' (comprehensive) learning. Surface or serialist learning refers to a focus on content, with the expectation of being given some certainty in a rather passive experience of being done to. Deep or holist learning focuses on principles, links and meaning – valuing uncertainty, with the learner as an active explorer. The detailed findings, however, highlight the need to be wary of allocating an individual to one learning style, though that may be appropriate in some instances. The emphasis is rather on these approaches as developmental stages in learning, and on the choice of learning approach being tightly related to context and to the interaction with the teacher. Nevertheless, those who have reached the more advanced stage of holist learning have a potential versatility not available to those at the earlier serialist stage, with the possibility of choosing the style of thinking and learning relevant to the situation.

Adapting style to stage

These stages in the development of learning (analogous to those of human growth and development in general) are closely related to several models of how competence develops in the course of a professional training and career. Table 4.1 broadly illustrates the definitions of a number of authors (summarising the work of others), which seem to us roughly comparable with each other though they emphasise different aspects of development.

Our diagrammatic summary cannot do justice to the detail of these categories, but gives some picture of the developmental issues involved in professional learning. It also highlights how supervisees at different stages of development will require different styles of input from supervisors – early stages requiring more didactic input and information-giving, later stages more conceptualising and exploration of uncertainty. The research of Pask and Scott (1972) on student learning found, not surprisingly, that performance is much enhanced when learner's and teacher's styles are matched. Gardiner (1989), discussing student supervision in social work, adds: 'the effect of mis-matching, though, is dependent on the level at which the mis-match occurs'. In Example 4.b, for instance, there was a risk of the supervisor's interest in more advanced levels producing a supervisory style beyond the comprehension of her untrained assistant staff. On the other hand, many experienced practitioners complain of supervisors so anxiously preoccupied with content that they do not (for a range of reasons) explore the more complex interactive processes in the work (Addison 1988; Waters 1992; Newburn 1993). It is thus extremely important for supervisors

Table 4.1. Stages of professional learning

Hawkins and Shohet (1989) (professional development)	*Level 1* Self centred. Dependent on supervision. 'Childhood' stage	*Level 2* Client centred. Fluctuation between dependence and autonomy. Overconfident versus overwhelmed. 'Adolescent' stage	*Level 3* Process centred. Greater professional self-confidence. Supervision more a shared experience. Adjustment to client at given point in time. Overview of client in context. 'Adult' stage	*Level 4* Process-in-context centred. Professionally autonomous. Able to conceptualise and generalise. Capable of supervising and teaching.	
Analogy of medieval guilds	*Novice*	*Journeyman*	*Independent craftsman*	*Master craftsman*	
Gardiner (1989) (professional development and social work training)	*Level 1* Predominant focus on content of learning. Acquisition and memorising of facts.	*Level 2* Focus on process of learning. Abstraction of meaning.	*Level 3* Meta-learning and versatility. Interpretation of processes.	*Level 4* Relative mastery of understanding and action.	*Level 5* Learning to teach.
Clarkson and Gilbert (1991), adapted from Robinson (1974) (any training)	From unconscious incompetence to conscious incompetence. 'Awareness'		From conscious incompetence to conscious competence. 'Accommodation'	From conscious competence to unconscious competence. 'Assimilation'	

themselves to have reached a sufficiently advanced stage of conceptualising learning, and their own role in it, to be able to exercise some choice of appropriate style.

Patchy or variable stages

On completion of formal training, professionals can probably be expected to enter their first job at somewhere around Hawkins and Shohet's (1989) level 2 or 3 (see Table 4.1), and some might already be approaching the transition from level 3 to level 4. Supervisors, meanwhile, would generally be assumed to be securely at level 4. As we know, however, professional (like personal) development is seldom so neatly and consistently organised. Supervisors' and supervisees' overall functioning may not necessarily correspond to the amount of their professional training, experience or grade of post. Perhaps more significantly, they may have well developed skills in some areas but not in others. The following are some of the issues concerning uneven stages of development in workers and supervisors that seem particularly prevalent:

1. Individuals may have *strengths and weaknesses in different areas.* In practitioners, for example, efficient record-keeping may accompany a more limited capacity to cope with the impact of feelings of users; advanced specialist knowledge or experience of a particular user group or setting may coexist with poor generic interpersonal skills; sensitivity in working with one user group may not preclude difficulties in responding to another. Such variations highlight the pitfalls of trying to distinguish between different stages, given the possibility of individual learning blocks or problems in specific areas. Similarly, supervisors may manage a team well, for example, but be poor at case supervision; or may cope well with stressful case material (drawing on their own experience as practitioners) but be poor at containing supervisees' anxieties. Difficulties can arise for supervisor and supervisee alike if either tends to use areas of relative competence to mask feelings of inadequacy in other areas of work.

2. The stage of *understanding of supervision,* and the capacity to use or provide it, may not correspond to the level of general professional skills. These capacities are often all too easily assumed, but in fact there is little formal thinking in most professional training about the use of supervision, and simply 'having supervision' may be the only contribution to professional development in this area. As

discussed earlier, therefore, expectations will be highly influenced by the level and range of previous supervisory relationships – as well as personal factors such as attitudes towards giving and receiving help and acknowledging limitations.

3. Assumptions are especially easy to make about *experienced workers*. The term 'experienced' is often used vaguely and interchangeably to mean both 'having been in the work for a long time' and 'competent'. As in Example 4.a, the concept of stages can be particularly useful in supervising experienced workers who are competent in many areas of their work but may need help in others – easily overlooked when a pressurised work context fosters a supervisor's wish to have reliable workers who do not require much attention. Such workers may be pushed into 'expert' roles by peers and supervisors, and even those who are generally competent and conscientious may feel unable to share their vulnerabilities for a variety of well-meaning reasons. The burden on such staff may be considerable. Newburn (1993) describes vividly the way some experienced staff working in the aftermath of the Hillsborough disaster desperately wanted to be challenged, and experienced a lack of care in the degree of autonomy they were given by their supervisors – who themselves felt deskilled.

In a different vein, some recent inquiries into child deaths (e.g. London Borough of Wandsworth 1990) have illustrated the dangers of placing unquestioning reliance on workers who have been around for a time. 'However experienced a worker, it is possible to get stuck, confused, frightened or bored' (Department of Health 1991a, p.30). More extremely, inquiries into child abuse scandals in residential settings (e.g. Levy and Kahan 1991; Kirkwood 1993) have highlighted the reluctance of agencies to question the apparent certainties of long-serving staff, especially when they are senior. Similar assumptions may, of course, apply to supervisors who have been in post a long time. Additionally, it may be assumed that competent practitioners automatically become competent supervisors, with little attention given to the range of skills required by a supervisor or the inevitable period of feeling deskilled in the transition to a new role (as illustrated in Example 4.a).

Doubts are currently being expressed in some departments and settings as to the need for detailed supervision of long established workers. It is notable, for example, that the Ritchie (1994) Report, despite its careful examination of the many factors that contributed to the breakdown of adequate community care for Christopher Clunis, referred to the need for supervision only in relation to inexperienced social workers. We would suggest that this tendency represents, at least in part, a wish to turn a blind eye to the inevitable variation in stages of skills and knowledge in every practitioner, and to avoid the challenge this poses to agency accountability (quite apart from agency responsibility for the professional development of staff). The paucity of active supervision of first-line managers' supervisory work is further evidence of this hesitation by agencies.

Recognising and addressing difference in style

Let us return to the question of individual style, which we have so far discussed only in relation to stages. Yet style may become an issue in itself. Some features of style are readily apparent, for example use of humour versus seriousness. Others may be more covert or take longer to recognise, for example attitudes to authority, family relationships, the meaning of work, expectations of being a success or a failure, and so on. These less obvious influences on style may be particularly powerful in supervisory interaction, because they are so open to misunderstanding. For example, a supervisor with considerable emotional investment in work may view a worker who leaves the office at closing time as uncommitted, not appreciating that (quite apart from possible family responsibilities) the work may play a less significant part in the worker's life than in the supervisor's without reducing his efficiency and serious commitment during working hours. When considerable stylistic differences are linked with personal and social circumstances such as age, class, disability, ethnicity, gender, race or sexual orientation, trying to explore their meaning in relation to working problems may feel (for both supervisor and supervisee) like questioning the worker's whole style of life in a discriminatory manner. Failure to explore their meaning, of course, could equally be a discriminatory avoidance of difference.

Regardless of specific problems, however, basic personal characteristics such as these may have a major but unacknowledged effect on the style of supervisory relationships. For example, in a thoughtful paper describing research into the impact of gender differences on supervisory relationships in a social services department, Conn (1993) notes 'the lack of connection between thinking about gender and power in the client system, and in some instances in the worker/client system, and thinking about these issues as an important aspect of the professional system itself' (p.48). This was despite (or perhaps partly because of) the noticeable difference in the way female and male supervisors described their roles, in terms of style: 'supportive', 'advisory', 'empowering', etc. on the one hand, 'co-ordinating', 'organising' and 'monitoring' on the other. Conn, like others, attributes such differences to the tendency for male development to be 'positively reinforced by a sense of control and power coming from maintaining difference and separateness, and female development...by a sense of control and power coming from closeness and intimacy' (p.43). While Conn carefully distinguishes between male or female attributes and absolute categories of maleness and femaleness, her findings highlight clear differences between men and women in her small sample of supervisors.

Adult learning situations reveal our distinctive individual characteristics more clearly than most. There are individual differences in style that are not indicative of the worker's achieved stage of professional development. However flexible and adaptable we may be, we each individually have some consistency in the style of learning in which we are most comfortable, and which is especially likely to be salient in new or anxiety-provoking situations. For example, on a continuum between 'head' and 'heart' (or ideas and feelings), some supervisees will be more likely to come to supervision pouring out feelings – so the supervisor's task is to abstract key issues and help to structure thinking from the experience – while others will present work in an orderly, summarised, even 'buttoned up' manner – when the supervisor has to try to 'get in' to broaden the field and explore the evidence of feeling and observation on which the summary was based. On a similar continuum between doing and thinking, some supervisees may best be helped by thinking through a situation in advance of intervening, while others think more clearly after having taken some action. Such differences will appear whatever model of learning is used, though some models allow greater freedom to attend to different styles. For example, in Kolb's (1984) model of experiential learning, which postulates a recurring cycle of concrete experience, reflective observation, abstract conceptualising and active experimentation, practitioners' styles might determine at what point they are most likely to enter the cycle. In our experience these differences of style, often associated with different theoretical approaches or models, are rarely acknowledged and explored openly in the supervisory context.

Example 4.a showed how it can be helpful to think of a supervisory difficulty in terms of a mismatch in stages between supervisor and supervisee. Questions of match or mismatch may be considered in relation to style also, though here they may have a different meaning. Recent literature (e.g. Inner

London Probation Service 1993) increasingly emphasises the need to be alert to differences in style if the supervisory relationship is to avoid being a discriminatory experience. At the same time, there may be a comfortable, unthinking and collusive avoidance of examining practice when the styles of supervisor and supervisee are very similar. This may be one factor in the failure, mentioned earlier, to explore the practice of experienced workers.

Questions of stage and style remain difficult to disentangle. Even at the most simple level they can be vexing – for example, the common dilemma for supervisors of how worried to be about supervisees' poor spelling, especially when supervisors may know that spelling matters a lot to themselves. Though there may be no all-purpose answers to such vexations, ignoring them rarely works since the suppressed irritation will only pop up in other areas. We would suggest that it is important for the supervisor, at the very least, to admit to herself the extent of her frustration and, eventually, to decide whether or not to take up an issue such as spelling.

Stages and regression

Any assessment of a worker's or supervisor's stage of competence, particularly in their capacity for learning and change, needs to allow for the possibility of regression under stress to an earlier stage of functioning. As we have indicated, stress may arise from personal factors, from work contacts and events or from difficult supervisory interaction. Two other possible sources of stress are important to consider if we are not to 'confuse problems with features helping towards future learning and survival' (Westheimer 1977):

1. *Response to new learning itself.* To have mixed feelings about the need to change and develop is a normal human response; giving up old ways and experiencing the uncertainty of facing the new can be threatening as well as rewarding (Salzberger-Wittenberg, Henry and Osborne 1983). Patterns of response may also become more rigid under stress. The degree of unlearning required in experienced practitioners may increase anxiety about change, and probably contributes to the adult learning pattern often referred to as 'plateaux, peaks and troughs'. Assessment over time is therefore needed to obtain a true picture. Newly-trained workers, on the other hand, may deal with the anxiety of coping either by identifying with the user (and becoming flooded with feeling) or by retreating behind impermeable boundaries into pseudo-competence (with mounting hidden anxiety) (Simmonds 1984).

2. *Response to working environment.* Burgess (1994) vividly describes the way individuals can be pathologised when their apparently 'regressed' performance may well be an adaptive response to a temporary or long-standing dysfunctional work context. An apparent 'troublemaker', for example, may in part be carrying a function on behalf of others in a troubled but outwardly compliant work group (Obholzer and Zagier Roberts 1994). Supervisors, themselves part of the same context, may understandably have extra difficulty in 'seeing the wood for the trees', especially if new to their supervisees. Some capacity to stand back and develop an organisational 'meta-perspective' is thus a competence required of supervisors; this is explored more fully in later chapters.

Evaluating the work of supervisees

Westheimer (1977, p.138) quotes from Robinson (1936): 'evaluation implies a judgement based on a standard'; in Westheimer's own words, 'evaluation is a judgement based on evidence' (p.140). It is clear from these contemporary-sounding quotations that the issues involved in evaluation have changed little over the decades. While we have shown how some understanding of the concepts of stages and styles is essential, the questions remain: what are we measuring and how do we know?

A review following a child death (London Borough of Wandsworth 1990) stresses that 'we simply do not know enough about generally accepted norms of good practice in the country' and, further, that 'we do not have a meaningful standard of comparison which takes account of the very different working conditions' (p.60).

Such dilemmas of defining meaningful criteria apply in all the caring professions. Nevertheless, in the past two decades major developments have taken place across the professions in setting standards, formulating essential competences and translating these into measurable performance indicators. These developments have been driven not only by professional concern to raise standards and accountability but also by political attempts to control the content and meaning of professional activity. It is beyond our scope to survey achievements and limitations so far in this complex area, with its core problem of defining outcomes specific enough to be readily identifiable without reducing the 'artistry' (Schön 1983) of what professionals in fact do (exercising judgement and integrating knowledge, practice experience and values) to a list of fragmented, discrete and mechanistic behaviours. These issues, especially as they relate to social work and management, are thoroughly and lucidly discussed by Lawler (1994), Jones and Joss (1995) and Yelloly (1995).

Meanwhile, this complex and rapidly changing national context highlights the difficulties supervisors face in trying to assess the day-to-day competences of their staff – clarifying what knowledge and skills are relevant for which tasks, determining what weight to give to different elements and deciding what standard it is reasonable to expect. The uncertainty is exacerbated if a supervisor is uneasy about how her own priorities are viewed by senior managers. However, the widespread political and professional preoccupation with seeking ways of assessing performance may at least serve to make assessment a more openly expected part of supervision.

At the heart of the emphasis on occupational competences is 'a move towards greater employer participation in defining training objectives and their implementation' (Yelloly 1995, p.56). This national trend has had repercussions for the tasks of first-line managers. For example, the development of National Vocational Qualifications has involved many manager/supervisors in assessing staff members' performance for purposes of qualification. It is generally true to say that managers have, at least in principle, taken on a much more explicit responsibility for professional training and staff development outside the traditional supervisory contract. In many social services departments, for example, the new business culture has meant that managers now commission training for their staff; or they may have become responsible for undertaking a training audit to establish current levels of staff knowledge and skills, as a baseline for further training needs in new areas of work (Department of Health 1991b and 1991d). Quality assurance systems have meanwhile attempted to link issues of individual performance to organisation-wide standards, providing much fuller information to all about required and actual standards.

At this stage, despite the newness and relative lack of sophistication of defined competences and performance indicators, it can be said that most staff supervisors have a more structured framework today than two decades ago in which to assess the capabilities of their staff. There is, however, a danger that some organisational measures focus more on quantity than quality, content rather than content-and-process; as was suggested to us recently (E. Cooper, personal communication 1994), they may end up measuring output under the guise of measuring outcome. It is to be hoped that this concern with what are clearly Stage 1 learning preoccupations (i.e. content and certainty) is a product of the relatively early stage of development of these approaches, and that the means will not become the end.

Nevertheless, however relevant and clear the measures might be, the supervisory task of assessing what is 'good enough' practice (like the practitioner's task of deciding what is 'good enough' parenting or self-care) will always require professional judgement amid some uncertainty. This raises questions of how to get the evidence of supervisees' actual functioning with service-users. Trainees of many disciplines are increasingly familiar with having their direct practice observed, but this training technique is not readily transferable to most work settings. Supervisors will have direct evidence of supervisees' functioning in supervision itself, in the team and in case conferences and the like; there is also the evidence from record-keeping and (increasingly) information from users' evaluation of the service offered to them. Group care settings clearly allow for greater opportunity of direct observation, though here the difficulty for a supervisor may be that her own experience with a particular service-user may at times distort her observation of a staff member's interactions.

It may be helpful to many supervisors to ensure that the initial supervisory contract includes an option of direct observation, so that introducing it later need not imply that there is a problem. Probably, however, the commonest difficulty for a supervisor is the inhibition she may experience in pushing a supervisee for details of his work, and in finding the skills to explore areas of uncertainty. Different aspects of such inhibited interactions will be looked at in later chapters.

Supervisors: which competences?

The widespread confusion or ambivalence in many agencies about the role of supervisors and the place of supervision – highlighted in various forms in this book thus far – makes it more difficult to consider the skills and competences necessary for effective staff supervision. We know of some agencies that have produced careful guidance in this area, and we commend the broader relevance of the list of supervisory competences in child protection developed by Richards and Payne (1990). Such specific thinking is rare, however.

A trawl through the literature on supervision could easily produce such a long list of essential skills and knowledge that any supervisor would be found wanting. Many of the skills mentioned by different writers are especially apt in today's conditions: for example, an ability to cope with uncertainty (Jones and Joss 1995) and with ambiguity and contradictions (Kakabadse 1982), a systemic understanding of organisational functioning (M. Pietroni *et al.* 1991) and certainly a firm anti-discriminatory stance. It is not, however, our intention here to assemble (let alone add to) a catalogue of all the desirable qualities of a supervisor. Instead, we shall highlight a few attributes which we consider core, and build on these in the course of the remaining chapters. We shall focus particularly on a central question that divides contemporary opinion: whether supervisors need to be skilled and knowledgeable in the specific area of work undertaken by their practitioners (for example, the user group or the method of intervention), or whether it is essentially management skills that they require. We shall come to our own view by way of looking at some of the arguments for these positions.

With increasing complexity in the role of first-line managers in most settings, the proportion of supervisors who retain any significant amount of direct practice is greatly reduced, as is the time they spend on it even when (for example in group care settings) it does remain a feature of their work. Dearnley's (1985) insistence that supervisors should maintain a practice caseload would nowadays be seen as detracting from the real importance of other management tasks and blurring the necessary separateness of the supervisory stance (London Borough of Greenwich and Greenwich Health Authority 1987). Rapid changes in legislation and local procedures, and the intensifying of the way problems present, mean that supervisors may now feel out of touch with their past experience of practice more and more quickly. Realistically, therefore, practice skills may seem less and less relevant, even though (in a report on post-qualifying training needs) M. Pietroni *et al.* (1991) continue to argue that supervisors of advanced social work practice need to understand practice themselves and to have been advanced practitioners. Meanwhile (as we have previously noted), in the field of community care staff supervisors may increasingly come from different professional or agency backgrounds from those they supervise, may not necessarily have experience of the user group or may be more preoccupied with their low stage of competence in new tasks such as budget management than with the full range of skills required for supervision.

There may be no absolute answer to the question of what knowledge of practice supervisors require, but it seems clear that a supervisor's sense of having some specialist knowledge or expertise related to the supervisee's practice must greatly enhance her confidence in her own authority, and in her ability to identify the evidence on which to assess a supervisee's practice. As one specialist supervisor told us, 'it helps that I automatically have some of the relevant questions in my head'. The Warner Report (Department of Health 1992a) on the management of staff in children's homes raises a related issue for the next tier of management:

> where the manager of a head of home does not have the experience
> of residential care their credibility with the home's staff can be

diminished. This may make it difficult for them to take decisive action if things start going wrong. (p.92)

The Report nevertheless concludes that 'the line managers of heads of homes should be recruited primarily for their management competence' (pp.92–93). Two studies of supervisors' and supervisees' experience (Nixon 1982; Waters 1992) both found that, while supervisees ascribed credibility to supervisors' practice experience, supervisors themselves (perhaps preoccupied with agency concerns) were less aware of this as an issue. In any case, as we said earlier, competence in one area can be used to mask insecurity elsewhere; a supervisor without specialist expertise might actually have less need to prove her 'superiority', and be more ready to acknowledge her areas of relative incompetence and learn from supervisees whose knowledge in those areas is more advanced than her own.

Although we would argue that the skills of a good practitioner are indeed highly relevant to the work of supervising, we are equally sure that no amount of specialist knowledge of practice or areas of work will of itself produce competence as a supervisor. Other perspectives are necessary. For example, Carpenter and Wheeler (1986) usefully describe how supervisors may make an important contribution to the effective and appropriate use of family therapy in social services departments even if they are not themselves family therapists. They argue that in that context a supervisor's broad knowledge of relationships between families and agencies, and a stance based on looking at outcome in terms of agency task, may be more appropriate than sophisticated knowledge of therapeutic techniques.

This brings us to the issue of how a supervisor's practice awareness can be related to her knowledge and skills as a manager in a particular agency context – how she combines these different capacities so as to address the tension of managing the three supervisory functions described in the last chapter. Good management, like good practice, requires skills in listening, exploring, formulating, decision-making and using authority to confront and enable. Kahan (1994) spells this out: 'in supervision and appraisal the skills are similar to social work but the responsibilities are different' (p.298). Kearney (1994), lamenting the frequent denial of this similarity, argues eloquently against what she sees as a tendency (across specialisms and user groups) to regard first-line management as a quite separate function with its own language, skills and ethos quite unconnected with those of practice.

Clearly, such a tendency may ignore all the interactive aspects of man-agement, and especially of supervision. Lawler (1994) points out that the emphasis on generic management skills at the expense of valuing the practice context is partly a response to the escalation of technical management tasks.

He suggests that the distinction now made between supervisory and management skills in post qualifying social work education (CCETSW 1992) might not have been made a few years ago.

The core attributes

For our part, we would argue that neither managerial nor practice skills *per se* will necessarily ensure good supervisory skills, though clearly both will help. Fundamental to our approach is an emphasis on the capacity of the supervisor *both* to get closely involved in a supervisee's situation *and* to draw back to a 'meta-perspective' in order to think. This capacity is in turn linked with 'the ability to know about, tolerate and handle three-person relationships' (Mattinson 1981).

Adult learning theory contributes much to conceptualising the competences a supervisor needs in maintaining this 'in and out' position. Table 4.1 highlights how a teacher or supervisor needs to be able to stand back from practice and conceptualise – to have a conscious sense of 'knowing what she knows' in order to impart it. Gardiner (1989) links this to the supervisor's need to be able to conceptualise about the process of learning and development itself. Westheimer's (1977) criticism of the persistent myth that those with knowledge can automatically teach remains relevant twenty years on, as does her interesting comment that this idea is itself rooted in a content-centred, lower stage view of learning.

Finally, a supervisor needs to have enough professional authority to acknowledge the inevitable gaps in her competence in some areas, and ensure that appropriate consultation is available to herself and/or her supervisees. Dearnley (1985) suggests that sustaining this capacity to face and acknowledge not knowing is a core difficulty for first-line managers, who experience pressure from all sides (not least from within themselves) to appear to 'know it all'. However, the supervisor who can admit her ignorance is also free to believe in her own potential for change and development – a prerequisite of being able to help others to change (Rushton and Nathan 1996b). This capacity for self-assessment and openness to learning offers the supervisee, too, the model that acknowledging ignorance can be a sign of strength – a model many professionals may not have encountered.

Supervision outcomes

Little work has been done on the effectiveness of staff supervision, and little thought given to how its outcomes can be defined and measured. We referred in Chapter 2 to the glaring contrast between the key place of supervision in many agencies and the lack of serious attention to its effect – between the significance attached to it by many practitioners and the paucity of relevant training in how to use it.

Nixon's (1982) research found disagreement between supervisors and supervisees as to the effectiveness of supervision on a number of scores but agreement about its impact on improving the service to users. A small American study in a mental health setting (Harkness and Hensley 1991) found that adult outpatients reported significantly greater satisfaction when their social workers received client-focused supervision than when supervision had a mixed focus. Whilst these studies raise as many questions as they answer, therefore, they provide a taste of possibilities and highlight the need for more broadly-based research.

The learning organisation

Professional performance and development, and the outcome of intervention, can no more be understood without considering the professional, team and agency context than can a child's development without thinking of the influence of the family or other caring environment.

Knowles' (1980) comment, in the context of adult education, is equally applicable to service-delivery agencies:

> No educational institution teaches just through its courses, workshops and institutes; no corporation teaches just through its in service education programs; and no voluntary organization teaches just through its meetings and study groups. They all teach by everything they do, and often they teach opposite lessons in their organizational operation from that which they teach in their educational program. (pp.66–68)

However comprehensive its supervisory policies and system of quality control, an agency whose senior managers fail to explore differences in a non-discriminatory way, fail to value creative questioning, fail to appreciate that rapid change may lead to deskilling and regression, fail to allow uncertainty, fail to acknowledge mistakes with confidence that they can be learned from, will be unlikely to sustain the practice of supervision as an effective and enabling resource. Supervisors will inevitably find it almost impossible to be thoughtfully enabling of their staff if they are not so treated by their own supervisors and not given a clear expectation that they will do so in turn. In organisations increasingly working on the assumption that human problems can be managed by prescription, 'failure is then interpreted as a problem of non-adherence, or as a need to realign existing guidelines, or produce yet more' (Pottage and Evans 1992, p.13).

By contrast, one of the main features of the notion of the 'learning organisation' developed by Senge (1990) and others is the willingness of senior managers to learn from the information front-line workers can provide about the consequences of decisions made at senior level. Pottage and Evans (1992 and 1994) coin the term 'the competent workplace' to denote agencies that are purposive, flexible and truly participative in approach; they highlight the connection between effectiveness and such a learning perspective, in which 'improvement is continuously being worked on through learning from day to day experience, by management and staff working in *partnership*' (1992, p.13).

Only in the competent, learning workplace can the full range of individual competence and incompetence be accurately assessed, and the impact of supervision accurately evaluated. This theme will be developed further in Chapters 7, 8 and 10.

CHAPTER 5

Feelings as Potential Evidence
Countertransference and Mirroring

EXAMPLE 5.a

> A community psychiatric nurse made a home visit to assess a young man whose neighbours had complained of his threatening and bizarre behaviour. The young man appeared self-contained and politely denied any problems, but the nurse found himself relieved to get out of the house and was surprised at how frightened and shaken he felt afterwards.

EXAMPLE 5.b

> A probation officer interviewed a quiet, withdrawn middle-aged woman accused of shoplifting. She was co-operative though said little about her situation, but as the interview progressed the probation officer began to feel overwhelmed by sadness and hopelessness.

EXAMPLE 5.c

> A young mother arrived at a social services office in a distressed state. The night before, she had been physically threatened by her former co-habitee, who had discovered her new address; she wanted to see her social worker urgently. When told she would have to wait, she started yelling and being verbally abusive to the receptionist. After she had stormed out, the receptionist felt tearful and shaken.

Projective identification, transference, countertransference

In the above (imaginary) examples it is not difficult to think that the feelings the workers were left with provide some information about what was going on inside the service-users. Clearly, in considering how much weight to give to these feelings as 'evidence', it would also be important to take account of the workers' current state of mind and how they usually felt with service-users. The exact meaning of the feelings would need further thought and exploration too. For instance, in the first example, it is not clear whether the young man had simply passed on to the nurse some sense of his own fear, as it were by 'contagion', and was not himself a threatening figure, or whether he was indeed potentially dangerous to others, making them experience the fear he could not bear to know about.

These encounters are the professional parallels of common human experiences. The psychoanalytic term *projective identification* refers to the unconscious processes whereby vulnerable, hostile or otherwise difficult feelings may be disowned by an individual and attributed to another, who may then (as a result of the interaction) actually experience the feelings as his or her own. The concept has received much attention and definition in psychoanalytic literature (for example Klein 1946; Bion 1959; Ogden 1979), but it is sufficient here to highlight two key purposes involved in projective identification. They are interrelated and usually unconscious. The first is simply to get rid of difficult feelings that cannot at that time be tolerated, by expelling them into another. The second is to communicate the importance of these feelings by getting another person to experience them, in the inarticulate hope that this person will be better able to tolerate, struggle with and give meaning to the feelings, in the interaction between the two people involved. Thus, an essential feature of both these modes is that the projected feelings are actually aroused in the recipient, who then becomes identified with them in the mind of the 'projector'.

The term *transference* is used to denote the range of feelings, conflicts, defences and expectations of relationships projected unconsciously into a current relationship (classically, with a professional helper) but originating in other, mostly earlier, relationships. The corresponding term *countertransference* (Heimann 1950) refers to the feelings, thoughts and behaviour unconsciously stimulated in the professional by the experience of relating to the service-user, especially in response to the latter's transference. Professionals in turn may bring unconscious transference issues from their own lives into their interactions with service-users. In systemic thinking, such processes might be spoken of in terms of people's attempts to draw others into expected ways of behaving, feeling or thinking – to play a part in a fixed family script or myth (Byng-Hall 1988) – thus maintaining a *status quo* of familiar experience and interaction.

Communication by impact

The power of some countertransference experiences cannot be overstated. The term 'communication by impact' (Casement 1985) perhaps conveys this better than the technical language of psychoanalysis. At the heart of the difficulties of many disturbed service-users (and others at points of crisis) is their inability to tolerate the experience of painful and intense feelings, which are expelled as soon as they threaten to surface by means of 'action' such as violence, delinquency, abuse or self-harm – or excessive helpfulness or intellectualising. Figure 5.1 depicts the 'jumping over' of the unwanted emotional experience, straight into 'action' of this kind.

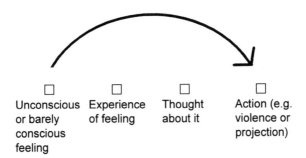

Unconscious   Experience   Thought   Action (e.g.
or barely   of feeling   about it violence or
conscious   projection)
feeling

Figure 5.1 Jumping into action

A worker confronted with such 'action' may feel shocked, invaded or taken over, as the 'jumped over' feelings appear to pass (by projective identification) from one person right into the other. It is no coincidence that we commonly use bodily metaphors to describe such experiences: she got under my skin, he got up my nose, it got right inside me, I felt I was being forced to swallow..., she makes me sick, I have a gut feeling about him. In Example 5.c, the receptionist felt physically shaken and tearful; in comparison, the professionals in Examples 5.a and 5.b might have found it easier to think about their relatively less extreme experiences. When practitioners are assailed by real somatic sensations, such as headache, weariness or nausea, which may be the first sign of unbearable feelings having been lodged in them, it can be very difficult to think about the possibility that what is happening is an intense countertransference response.

The complexity and speed of this kind of communication also has to be taken seriously. The common view of transference, in such terms as 'he treats me as though I were his mother', has a relevance but is too static and one-sided. What are projected are more likely to be core fears and self-pro-tective defences against relating and intimacy; who occupies what role may change rapidly. 'The aim often seems to be to produce a state of mind in [the practitioner] which closely resembles the state of mind [the service-user] feels burdened with' (Steiner 1976, p.69).

Three arguments

Implicit in our discussion so far is the assumption that workers are emotionally affected by their experience with service-users. Our first argument in this chapter is that this is unavoidable (despite many professionals' attempts to 'keep their distance') and that these feelings will inevitably find their way into supervision in a variety of ways.

Our second argument is that if practitioners can tolerate experiencing and thinking about their countertransference responses they will find in them a rich source of information about the core issues in the lives of their service-users.

Our third argument is that such an approach is a prerequisite of safe practice and decision-making.

Ambivalence about tangling with feelings

The value of considering the impact of feelings in this way has been increasingly recognised in recent years, especially in the field of child protection. The Department of Health (1991a) has emphasised the importance of helping social workers to

> recognize the effect achieved by the emotions being beamed out from the family. It is also a process which enables practitioners to know themselves... The method of supervision must identify how perceptions and feelings may be affecting work done, whether between field worker and family, or field worker and supervisor. (p.30)

In our experience, however, feelings easily valued on paper are regularly devalued or lost in everyday work. Agass (1992) suggests that 'we spend so much time with the damaged and distressed that we no longer question the effect our clients have on us' (p.13). Moreover, many front-line staff work in organisations whose stance conveys that emotional involvement of any kind with service-users is an unprofessional weakness, indicating a lack of objectivity and judgement. In such a climate it takes courage to expose feelings and argue for their status as potential evidence; detachment may appear a safer and more externally valued option. Professionals may also have their own reasons for choosing, consciously or unconsciously, to 'forget' their feelings. Believing in theory in the informational value of countertransference feelings can be easier than struggling in practice with the perhaps shame-inducing experience of having strong feelings of fear, despair, attraction, envy or hatred toward someone who is dependent on their professional care. Facing the feelings without confidence in their being understandable to oneself or understood by others may also raise fears that they will become overwhelming. Difficult practical implications may emerge. For example, taking seriously feelings about the potential dangerousness of a service-user might mean having to mention this in a referral for a hostel place, thus risking rejection by a scarce resource. We shall return later in the chapter to the central importance of supervision in valuing and 'decoding' the impact of practitioners' work-related feelings.

Mirroring

Mirroring, also known as *reflection process* (Mattinson 1975) or *paralleling* (Wilmot and Shohet 1985), is one aspect of countertransference that merits discussion in its own right. These terms have passed into common professional parlance (though *reflection process* is often confused with the use of 'reflecting' to mean either thinking carefully or, in counselling, feeding back to the client what s/he has conveyed to the counsellor). All three terms are often used loosely, and with limited value, as catch-all terms to suggest a causal connection where any similar dynamic issues appear to exist in different parts of a service or system. For example, workers who feel badly treated by their organisations may speak in a general way of this 'abuse' mirroring the abuse in the families with whom they work – though this may merely mean that there are experiences of ill-treatment in both areas. Even when the terms are used more accurately, it is sometimes implied that mirroring is an unhelpful phenomenon that should be corrected as soon as possible (Ash 1995). We shall attempt in this chapter both to look back to clearer definitions, notably to Mattinson's (1975) seminal book *The Reflection Process in Casework Supervision*, and to explore the potential usefulness of the concept in a constantly changing supervisory context.

Mattinson, adapting Searles (1955), establishes the thesis that in social work supervision 'the processes at work currently in the *relationship between* client and worker are often reflected in the *relationship between* worker and supervisor'. The core idea is that dynamic interactions that belong and originate in one area of relationship are acted out in an adjacent area as though they belong there, being carried from one area to the other by a 'player' common to both. (The term *paralleling* seems to us peculiarly inapt for a process whose essence is penetration and blurring between two distinct areas; hence our decision not to use it.) These dynamic issues, usually seen as originating in the service-user and projected (by transference) into the relationship between the service-user and worker, may then in turn be imported into the supervision session where they are unwittingly replayed by the worker and, sometimes, the supervisor. Mirroring is thus a secondary effect of countertransference that is not fully known about, but enacted; the practitioner, like the service-user, is compelled to act rather than feel or think, and may then (by a further projective identification) draw the supervisor into joining the enactment in supervision. The next example shows both worker and supervisor caught up in a mirroring interaction.

EXAMPLE 5.d

A social worker and supervisor, based in a child and adolescent psychiatry setting, discussed in supervision a case that had been preoccupying them for some months. It involved Nadia, a girl of thirteen, who had been admitted in crisis to a young people's psychiatric unit. On admission she had been in a serious physical state, having refused for some time to eat or drink. She was assessed as being severely depressed. Nadia lived alone with her mother (Mrs D), a refugee from persecution in her country of origin, who was viewed by her compatriots in the local community as a strange woman with whom it was impossible to communicate. Mrs D led an isolated life, focused on her one child, whom she treated physically and emotionally as an infant and whom she had protected from the 'dangerous' outside world by often locking her in the house alone. After admission to the psychiatric unit (following her mother's sudden panic at her physical state), Nadia had blossomed dramatically, gaining inches in a few weeks and for the first time enjoying being playfully naughty. Her mother, visiting regularly, had great difficulty in coping with the changes in her and in her relationships with others, and had quickly made a range of complaints to various bodies about staff mistreatment of Nadia and herself, so that a series of investigations was under way. The (experienced and gifted) social worker, alongside colleagues of other disciplines, had worked sensitively with Nadia and her mother together and separately, highly mindful of the pain of both, and had taken steps to involve a psychiatrist who spoke Mrs D's language and members of Mrs D's church community to act as advocates for her.

The supervision session in question had focused on the impending care proceedings. Immediately after the session the supervisor was taken aback to realise that she had quite inappropriately volunteered to draft the court report for the social worker, and the social worker had raised no question about this unusual offer. The ostensible reason the supervisor had given – that the social worker was very busy providing the extra reports required for the investigations into Mrs D's complaints about the case – made no real sense. The supervisor was even more puzzled as writing court reports was something she particularly disliked. Clearly some interaction that was hard to understand had taken place in the session.

Gradually the supervisor came to the view that she and the social worker might be blindly enacting the key dynamics of the case, an understanding confirmed and developed in her next discussion with the social worker. They saw they had been caught up in an interaction between regression (the social worker) and overprotection as the only means of helping (the supervisor), an interaction that mirrored the relationship between the daughter and her mother. Though the social worker and supervisor had previously been thoughtfully aware of the importance of this core dynamic in the case, their experience of its so 'getting under their skin' gave them a new conviction of its power and control, especially the pressure to regress that would continue to undermine Nadia's progress.

Mirroring may also take place in a less noticeable way around the fringes of supervision, or in behaviour connected with it. For example, a supervisee might 'forget' (or find plausible reasons to postpone) a supervision session where a particularly elusive or resistant service-user was due to be discussed – or might omit to present such a case for discussion at all (Vincent 1995).

Information about the case or blaming the user?
The use of the concepts of mirroring and countertransference to explain difficult feelings or behaviour in professionals is sometimes criticised as a way of blaming the service-user for the professional's mistakes or emotional problems. It clearly could be so used. Mattinson (1975) stresses the need to think of the behaviour in question in the context of the usual behaviour (and relationship) of the worker and supervisor, in order to disentangle what comes from where. An intense, 'out of character' response, or a sense of being compelled or taken by surprise, increase the likelihood that the practitioner is being powerfully 'controlled' by feelings from outside. In Example 5.d, it was comparatively easy for the supervisor to identify that something outside their usual experience was going on and to look to an explanation beyond the supervisory pair. Clearly this might not always be so easy, especially if

the behaviour involved felt quite comfortable to the supervisor – unlike offering to write a court report here.

The difficulty is compounded by the fact that any countertransference experience relies on there being related 'hooks' or 'host areas' (Symington 1985) in the professionals for the projected dynamic to latch onto. In this illustration, for example, there was little doubt that the anxiety of both professionals about the case itself, and about its high political profile locally because of the complaints, provided hooks for the social worker to regress and for the supervisor to 'cover herself' by taking on more tasks. At other times, it may be personal issues that provide the hooks that make workers more available to certain projections. In Example 5.b, the hopelessness that the probation officer picked up from the middle-aged woman might have resonated with, for instance, an experience from his childhood of living with a depressed mother, or a current experience of despair at his marriage breaking down. Stratton *et al.* (1993) point out that different members of a team observing an interview through a one-way screen may be attuned to different aspects of a family's dynamics, because of their different personal 'hooks', but that this does not nullify the relevance of their observations.

Mattinson (1975) makes two further important points, from her work with groups of experienced social work supervisors. First, she warns against too quickly 'pathologising' the professional, through underestimating the powerful unconscious impact of case dynamics on professional behaviour. She found that good supervisors, confident enough to allow themselves to be open to the complexities of the work, would often present their supervisory issues in a training group in a manner that enacted core aspects of the case dynamics. So, for example, a supervisee who angrily challenges the supervisor when discussing a case should not necessarily be assumed to be anti-authority, but may be importing into supervision a dynamic that he had struggled well to manage when face to face with the service-user.

Second, she points out that even where a practitioner's personal issues may be making a major contribution to the enactment, exploring the mirroring dynamic may still be the supervisor's most effective approach to understanding the issues in the case and helping the worker with the task. Such exploration might also provide indirect help to the worker, since an understanding of issues in the case is likely to speak to his own linked problems, whereas direct working on these is not within the supervisor's remit. Skynner (1964) discusses a related aspect of this theme, that is that professionals' choice of particular types of work, setting or user group may be consciously or unconsciously prompted by their own core internal preoccupations. In some areas of work, this has in recent years become an increasingly explicit basis for choice. As long as the needs of the user remain the focus, and the worker is not caught up in undiscriminating identification, this linkage may provide a fruitful resource for sensitive work as well as contributing to the development of the worker.

If it becomes apparent over time that a supervisee's personal issues are seriously distorting his perceptions or behaviour, this needs to be taken up by the supervisor with, if appropriate, a suggestion that the supervisee seek help; the supervisor herself should not embark on further personal exploration, but remain focused on the acceptability or otherwise of the supervisee's standard of work. Some supervisees may appear to invite personal exploration, but to do so beyond the acknowledgement of a personal dimension can, in our view, only deflect the supervisor from her role, and may also be resented later by the supervisee.

Supervisory space: processing and assessing evidence

It will be clear by now that we consider supervision to be crucial in addressing the impact of countertransference, in whatever way it presents. This goes well beyond what Hawkins and Shohet (1989) call 'pit-head time', that is 'the right to wash off the grime of the work in the boss's time' (p.42). The significance of supervision lies rather in the search for meaning in the 'grime' of difficult work-related feelings.

Fears and possibilities

Before exploring the how and why of this, we should acknowledge how daunting the task may appear. Supervisors may be as affected as their supervisees by agency, personal or professional inhibitions on exploring work-related feelings. In a study of supervisors' views in child protection work (Rushton and Nathan 1996b), one supervisor said:

> 'If they tell you what they're feeling, what the hell can I do about it? Maybe some of my holding back (from the staff member) is because I think if they tell me all this, what can I do except say, well, you've got to carry on, hold on.' (p.364)

Bombarded with feelings by stressed workers while needing to ensure the work is covered, the supervisor's task is indeed extremely difficult. A defensive supervisory interaction may seem preferable to opening up the supervisee's potential shame, fear of failure, distress or anger. A mirrored pressure to act not think may also reinforce the supervisor's natural tendency to do so. In Example 5.d, the supervisor succumbed to the pressure to 'do something' in offering to write the court report. More often, action may take the form of premature decision-making or prescribing tasks; being too readily 'supportive' of the worker may also serve to avoid exploration, as Blech (1981) spells out:

> If a worker confesses to feeling no good, to having done something stupid or collusive with a client, it is all too easy to forget and excuse. These adjectives are the language of guilt whereas the misdeeds (if such indeed they are) are much more creatively used as information and indications of how the family experiences its own pain and problems. (p.12)

Such an argument may leave many supervisors feeling deskilled, anxious about how to manage an appropriate boundary between a worker's personal and professional feelings (as discussed in the previous section and Chapter 3); or not knowing how to explore the countertransference, having perhaps received little or no training in doing so. Often, however, all that is required is for a supervisor to give clear permission that feelings can be spoken about, that they are facts as relevant as any other, and like most facts need to be studied more closely in context in order to be understood. One question by a supervisor about what it felt like being with a service-user (for example, the experience of bathing an elderly person) may completely change the 'colour' of the other factual information that a worker has reported. Sometimes the task is more complex, and some supervisors may properly wish to involve a consultant. In our experience, however, supervisors who begin to accept feelings and interactions as a source of information, and who have some concepts to help them think, often find that they already understood more than they realised. Even if no immediate sense can be made of the situation, the experience for the supervisee of having a supervisor alongside him, struggling to try and know about the feelings, can have a powerful effect in 'detoxifying' them and freeing him from their control (a dynamic that supervisors are frequently more ready to recognise in work with service-users than in their own supervisory work).

However, supervisors who understand the value of exploring feelings and mirrored behaviour may also be reluctant to do so, for a variety of reasons. Finding oneself caught up in an enactment never ceases to shock, and the supervisor may sense that the worker would experience it as shameful and unprofessional. Clearly, it is easier for the supervisor to speak to the worker's enactment when she can also acknowledge her own involvement, as in Example 5.d. Searles (1955) goes so far as to say that the supervisor should probably not draw the worker's attention to his enactment but merely use the information it gives, but this seems unduly cautious and patronising. As Mattinson conveys, it deprives the worker of a valuable learning experience, and the opportunity to explore the concept and contribute to assessing its relevance.

Safe supervision: pulling together the threads

Having explored some of the difficulties and pitfalls, let us return to the arguments why countertransference and mirroring experiences should be explored in supervision.

First, the impact of feelings from a case may significantly contribute to regular neglect by a supervisor of particular corners of the supervisory triangles described in Chapter 3. In Example 5.d, for instance, the supervisor was in danger of abandoning her own corner and joining the social worker as the report writer, thus also failing to acknowledge the worker's competence or consult properly to the needs of the case.

Second, failing to assess the impact of feelings may also result in demoralised staff. Sickness and burn-out are not just responses to overwork, but can be a result of carrying around feelings whose weight may essentially belong to the service-user. Many authors (e.g. Kraemer 1983; Morrison 1991) testify to the deeply disturbing effect on workers of some countertransference experiences. Practitioners who are helped to think about the feelings, however, may learn to put them to use and lighten their load by understanding. In some contexts, for example distressing violent incidents, practitioners may in fact need repeated opportunities over a number of years to reflect on the impact, as their capacities for understanding deepen with distance from the events (Smith and Nursten 1995). Staff survival is thus at stake (Brown and Bourne 1996, pp.106–127).

Third, we come to the need for supervisors, one step back from the fray of direct contact with service-users, to consider the case information available from countertransference and mirroring. Example 5.d illustrates a creative use of such information that enhanced understanding of family relationships. In some situations, failure to use this information may exacerbate the initial problem and lead to ineffective intervention or dangerous practice. For example, the initial impact made by a service-user may become, unsafely, the basis for continuing decision-making if the supervisor does not challenge the supervisee in order to trace and understand the source of his views. Countertransference feelings that remain 'undigested' may propel professionals into action that pushes the feelings back at the service-user with a 'boomerang effect' (Moustaki 1981). Thus, projected anger might provoke a retaliatory or dismissive response, while depressed feelings might induce a sense of professional powerlessness leading to withdrawal – or flight into precipitate action. Such effects of neglecting work-related feelings can be cumulative and dangerous. For example, it is difficult not to connect the 'failures of the human heart' by professionals, that so shocked a recent inquiry into the suicide of a depressed man who had earlier killed his mother (City of Westminster *et al.* 1995), with another of the panel's findings, namely the absence of proper debriefing procedures following a serious incident.

Fourth, individuals and families may project different aspects of their conflicting emotions into different professionals or agencies. Between agencies, these can (if left unaddressed) become amplified into serious rifts, or collusions, over cases that most need co-operation (Reder and Kraemer 1980; Furniss 1983; Woodhouse and Pengelly 1991). Inter-agency issues will be explored further in Chapters 6 and 7. For the moment, we shall focus on the supervisor's role in cases involving a number of staff within the same agency, putting together the different pieces of the emotional jigsaw in order to build up a complete picture. The use of co-therapists in marital psychotherapy (Ruszczynski 1992; Vincent 1995), or of an observing team behind the screen in family therapy (Lindsey and Lloyd 1982; Andersen 1987), is deliberately designed to provide greater availability to a wider range of feelings, behaviours and beliefs in the service-user system.

Without built-in space for drawing the experiences together, however, professionals may merely battle over the 'truth' of their respective perceptions. Group care settings (in social care and nursing) provide particular challenges to staff and supervisors in that the conflicting projections are intensified and confused by the reality of close day-to-day living, often including physical dependency. Winship *et al.* (1995), for example, emphasise the role of supervision (in an inpatient drug-dependency unit) in ensuring that decision-making takes into account both the anger of staff subjected to negative and destructive projections and the sympathy of those encountering more dependent or health-seeking behaviour. In the classic paper on this theme, T. Main (1957) describes how 'special' patients may, by secretive pressures, cause major divisions among staff that can only be understood as mirroring the self-destructive conflicts within the patients.

Downward projection and mirroring

Most of the literature on mirroring focuses on the conveying 'upward' of dynamics from service-users to workers. Conversely, however, Mattinson (1975) also draws attention to the way in which dynamics originating within the supervisory relationship may become mirrored in a worker's behaviour with an individual or family. This would be more likely to happen when the feelings involved in the supervision sessions were not discussed or thought about. For example, an anxious supervisor with a 'check-list' approach, insisting on clear-cut responses from the supervisee, might contribute to the latter's behaving similarly in face-to-face work with users. It is probably useful to distinguish this form of mirroring from a worker modelling himself on the supervisor, which implies some conscious awareness and selection of the model adopted – together with a more healthy internalising as described in Chapters 9 and 10.

Of course, the supervisor's own supervision is highly relevant to her functioning in this respect. A supervisor who is helped to consider her feelings as relevant to the work will be in a better position to provide a similar service to her supervisees – both emotionally and in terms of having had experience of relevant techniques. On the other hand, a supervisor angrily told off (however justifiably) by her own supervisor about, for example, poor paperwork, without space for explanation, will be more likely to deal with her own anger unthinkingly by taking it out on supervisees in a similar way – or perhaps by colluding with a supervisee's poor paperwork in covert defiance of her own supervisor.

The context in which services are delivered has changed considerably since the concept of mirroring was first developed in the 1960s and 1970s, and most professionals today are probably affected as much, emotionally, by the impact of their agency structure and ethos as they are by the dynamics of service-users. Senior management style will often be developed in response to the primitive anxieties engendered at the boundaries of the organisation about maintaining its very existence (see Chapter 1). The behaviour of senior managers who attempt to deal with these anxieties only by instigating procedures, directives and restructuring will tend to produce a 'domino' effect down the hierarchy. Conversely, we have been impressed by the powerful impact a new director or head of an organisation, in particular, can have on poor staff morale if s/he is able to listen seriously to what employees say; this is a vital element in the development of a 'learning organisation' as discussed at the end of Chapter 4. In the broader context, professionals increasingly face a barrage of projections from society and the media. Valentine (1994), for example, discusses how public anxiety and revulsion about child abuse are projected into social workers, who themselves may then experience these devalued feelings to the detriment of their functioning – not least in supervision, where acknowledgement and thought are required in order to prevent increasing demoralisation. This is a negative aspect of greater public accountability.

The emotional impact of different kinds of work

The concept of mirroring began as a way of understanding uncharacteristic behaviour in a worker as a response to the specific dynamics of a particular case. It is harder to distinguish mirroring from other effects (including the downward mirroring we have just discussed) when worker, supervisor and the agency as a whole are being bombarded by the impact of emotional issues arising from certain sorts of work that occupy most of their time and energy. With the re-emergence of specialism by user group, and with statutory agencies focusing almost exclusively on severely disturbed users, the impact of recurring key dynamic issues may well become so much part of the way of life of an organisation that little thought is given to under-standing the mirroring involved and containing its effects (see Chapter 7).

It is crucially important, however, for a supervisor to be alert to the different dynamics that are most likely to arise in different sorts of work and their potential effect, through mirroring, on the supervisory process. We now illustrate this in detail in relation to work with child sexual abuse (especially intrafamilial abuse), drawing on material from courses run by colleagues (Oliver-Bellasis and Vincent 1990) and ourselves. We shall list *nine core dynamic issues*, describing each one first in the family context (FAM.) and then as it might appear in supervision (SUP.). The list makes no claim to be the definitive or most relevant one; readers may wish to supplement it with their own observations, in child sexual abuse or other fields of work.

1. Omnipotence versus impotence

FAM.   There is no experience of ordinary 'good enough' authority or vulnerability. For example, the child is an impotent victim but often has a sense of omnipotent, dangerous but secret power in the family. The perpetrator denies her/his own and the child's vulnerability by omnipotently controlling the child and claiming to know what s/he wants.

SUP.   Supervisors and practitioners may feel their 'ordinary' past experience is irrelevant and become paralysed by doubt, leaving all responsibility to 'experienced' or specialist workers – who in turn may feel isolated and weighed down but also act as though they 'know it all'.

2. Premature growing up

FAM. Adults fail to protect the child from knowing and experiencing too much too soon. There can be a precocious pseudo-maturity and premature loss of innocence and curiosity.

SUP. New or young workers have no 'easy' cases to begin on, and feel they have to cope with everything that comes their way. Their feelings swamp them or become blunted. Supervisors may regret this but feel unable either to question it or attend to the feelings.

3. The gap between suspicion and evidence

FAM. The child does not know what is normal or acceptable, and a carer may not know (or may be unable to face) what is going on. Both child and adults are unable to cope with love and hate towards the same person, or with confusion and uncertainty.

SUP. A strong suspicion but with little certain evidence leads to polarising, into either a false 'certainty' or a negligent wish to 'turn a blind eye'. The polarised terms 'disclosure' and 'denial' reflect this. Supervisors may inappropriately push workers to go on probing for evidence, denying the need to plan on the limited evidence available; or supervisors and workers may collude in not 'disclosing' their suspicions.

4. Perversion of appropriate interpersonal boundaries

FAM. Most obviously, the taboo on breaching the adult–child sexual boundary is defied.

SUP. Professionals may be overwhelmed with details of perverse intimate sexual behaviour and feel contaminated. Appropriate boundaries become difficult to maintain – for example, deciding when to end the assessment of evidence and make decisions; holding an appropriate personal–professional boundary when discussing intimate feelings engendered by the work; preventing the needs of cases from becoming insatiable and intrusively taking over professional and personal time.

5. Gender splits

FAM. Typically, men are the perpetrators while women are often categorised with children as victims in intrafamilial abuse. There remains a difficulty in acknowledging that women can be perpetrators.

SUP. Otherwise good cross-gender supervisory relationships may become strained, or even strongly mistrusting, as male–female difference predominates. 'For men, there may be a sense of collective guilt or alternatively defensiveness' that impedes effective functioning (Glaser and Frosh 1988, p.155); for women, there may be collusive supportiveness in opposition to men. Agency policies on male and female roles in sexual abuse work may deny any impact of gender; or they may collude with stereotypes of men as unreliable persecutors and women as either idealised or unable to look after themselves.

6. Authority as untrustworthy

FAM. The child has no experience of reliable adult authority that is able to look, hear and take responsibility for actions. There is no model of a co-operative parental couple acting together in the child's interests. Alliances are perverse and cross-generational, denying appropriate authority.

SUP. Authority may easily be seen as persecuting. It may be hard to sustain any belief that the supervisor's authority might be helpful, or that two professional adults (worker and supervisor) could co-operate to promote the welfare of a child.

7. Attacks on triangular relationships

FAM. Normal triangular family relationships are denied and replaced with secret, guilty 'twosomes' (child and one adult), excluding the rightful position of the 'third' (typically the mother) who may not let herself know of her exclusion.

SUP. Extra pressure is put on the struggle to keep all three corners of each supervisory triangle in mind (Chapter 3).

8. Disbelief that worries will be heard

FAM. The child may be threatened to keep silent. Attempts to speak may not be heard or believed. Belief that sharing worries can lead to improvement is destroyed.

SUP. Workers may only hint at concern about abuse, and supervisors may not quite 'hear' (or vice versa). Fears arise that investigation and taking statutory action will only damage the child further.

9. Accommodation to the impossible

FAM. 'Sexual abuse accommodation syndrome'. Summit (1983) delineates a typical five-stage sequence of concealment, disclosure and retraction by a child:

a) secrecy (the family ethos)

b) helplessness (because the child is dependent and needs to maintain the image of caring parents)

c) entrapment and accommodation (ensuring self-blame to please parents and avoid reality)

d) delayed, conflicted and unconvincing disclosure (as the child struggles with the need to share versus the wish to avoid the consequences of doing so)

e) retraction (when faced with sceptical professionals or a hostile family in crisis).

SUP. 'Professional accommodation syndrome'. Morrison (1991, pp.261–264) follows Summit's five stages in describing how professionals and agencies may collude to keep hidden the fact that good staff feel seriously affected by the impact of the work:

a) a professional ethos develops whereby staff do not tell, and agencies and supervisors 'covertly restrict permission to disclose'

b) a false expectation that good staff should cope and that 'uncomplaining staff are coping' promotes shame at feeling upset

c) workers blame themselves to preserve a view of supervisors as 'good' and accommodate the agency ethos – this split may feel intolerable and result in unpredictable behaviour

d) disclosure of stress may be delayed and unconvincing, perhaps through an involuntary display of volatile or depressed behaviour which, however, can then be used to deny the worker's competence – alternatively, evidence of continued 'capable' work may be used to invalidate the complaint of stress

e) workers may retract ('Oh, I am fine now, it was nothing to do with my work') – perhaps more acceptable to all concerned than complaining. This 'confirms that feelings are not to be trusted'.

Point 9 in particular places supervision in the middle of upward and downward mirroring, and the ethos and culture of the agency; in Chapter 7 we shall explore further the phenomenon of *socially structured defences* (Menzies 1959) against work-related anxiety which pervade a whole agency or professional group. Here we note that, while the detail of our nine points is specific to child sexual abuse work, similar dynamic issues will arise in supervision of any work that touches on deeply disturbing relationships or provokes very basic anxieties – for example work with violent offenders, psychotic patients or severely ill young people. In the next chapter we shall highlight the impact of one cluster of interactions relevant to all such work with severe disturbance, across all settings and user groups.

Mirroring or other kinds of link?

We began the discussion of the term mirroring by referring to its frequent loose and over-inclusive usage. Having explained many ways in which it is a highly relevant and useful tool, we repeat our warning against its misuse as a panacea to the problem of struggling to understand any interaction that seems puzzling or difficult. We end with an example where it was impossible to know whether certain processes were the result of specific mirroring even though some of the issues did seem to be linked.

EXAMPLE 5.e

The young deputy manager of a family centre presented his supervisory dilemma to fellow course participants. He had been in the agency six months, and was worried about his supervision of a middle-aged female staff member – especially about her failure to implement many case decisions, and her lack of concern about this. The most worrying situation involved a case neglected by a previous worker who had left 'under a cloud' six months before; the current worker was failing to make an appropriate contract and focus on the work of re-assessing the risk to the children. Both parents had learning difficulties, and their two children had been on the child protection register for years because of past neglect. The parents, supported by an advocate, had requested a re-assessment, asserting that they were now coping and that their children's names ought to be removed from the register. From what little information he had, however, the deputy manager was very concerned about the parents' capacities.

In the course of describing his sensitive attempt to be fair to the staff member – acknowledging her years of experience and her discomfort at being supervised by a man – the supervisor also sketched in some of the recent history of the centre. A year previously, serious parental injury to a child attending the centre had prompted an investigation, which had raised concerns about many aspects of practice in the unit and about the work of certain staff. Threats of disciplinary action had collapsed in the face of strong union backing for these workers (including the previous male deputy manager); they had nevertheless been redeployed. There was considerable anger in the agency that the female manager of the centre had survived while numerous other staff had appeared to 'carry the can'. On his arrival, the deputy manager had been told by the manager that the female worker in question 'needs to be phased out'. This had fuelled his wish to be fair to her.

As he expanded on the details of his dilemma, the deputy manager and his fellow course members became increasingly aware how several similar issues seemed to be emerging at all levels, from the case itself through the workers to the different layers of management. These were: the struggle to be fair in a current re-assessment of competence – not being controlled by past information, while giving due weight to relevant history; the neglect of responsibility in difficult situations; the failure of those in authority to stand firm under pressure and take responsibility for their opinions and actions, however unpopular; the scapegoating of those in more junior positions, especially men.

By the end of the presentation the group felt overwhelmed. The deputy manager's position appeared precarious and unsafe despite his seemingly excellent practice, and the issues seemed densely interwoven and enmeshing. It was tempting to try and force an omnipotent clarity by declaring that both case and management dynamics were being mirrored in the supervisory arena; but the truth was that, at least at this stage, the exact source or sources of the dynamic issues could not be clearly identified or isolated. The only certainty was that the similar issues at each level of the total situation served to exacerbate each other and magnify the problems of functioning effectively.

CHAPTER 6

Passing the Painful Parcel
The Drama Triangle of Persecutor–Rescuer–Victim

We shall now focus on one kind of dynamic interaction which is very widespread and particularly susceptible to mirroring. In the language of transactional analysis, the concept of *drama triangles* is used to describe how, in a highly-charged situation, complex feelings that are actually interrelated can instead be split off from each other and attributed to simplistic characters or roles in a 'dramatic' scenario. Karpman (1968) describes a drama triangle comprising the roles of *persecutor, rescuer* and *victim,* which can all too readily be resorted to when feelings are running high.

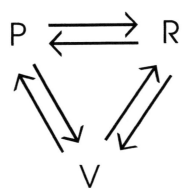

Figure 6.1 Drama triangle

The arrows in Figure 6.1 indicate how easily these simplistic roles can be assigned and rapidly re-assigned among the people involved, particularly in a persecutory climate where there may be greater resistance to grappling with the complicated and often confused dynamics that are actually present. Karpman uses fairy tales such as *The Pied Piper of Hamelin, Little Red Riding Hood* and *Cinderella* to illustrate this, pointing out that 'a person "living in a fairy tale" usually has a simplified view of the world, with a minimum of dramatic characters' (p.39).

The persecutor–rescuer–victim triangle is by now commonly used in thinking about intervention in situations of child abuse; especially familiar is the idea of the victim of abuse who becomes a perpetrator. The concept, however, is equally applicable to all situations of heightened emotions and disturbance, as we shall illustrate later. Before considering the application of the triangle to supervision, where it has been given less consideration, we shall explore more fully this deceptively simple concept. Karpman's first illustration brings alive the power of this interaction:

> In The Pied Piper, the hero begins as Rescuer of the city and Persecutor of the rats, then becomes Victim to the Persecutor mayor's double-cross (fee withheld), and in revenge switches to be the Persecutor of the city's children. The mayor switches from Victim (of rats), to Rescuer (hiring the Pied Piper), to Persecutor (double-cross), to Victim (his children dead). The children switch from Persecuted Victims (rats) to Rescued Victims, to Victims Persecuted by their Rescuer (increased contrast). (p.40)

Many in the caring professions will have little difficulty in identifying with the predicament of the Piper – the 'professional helper'.

Pass the parcel

The terms persecutor, rescuer and victim in this context signify not only what individuals actually do or have done to them, but more importantly the roles they take up *vis-à-vis* each other. Each of the three roles corresponds to a prevailing mental state, or position; while most individuals have some tendency towards one position more than the other two, it is very important to note that none of the three describes a complete person. The three terms can be conceptualised as follows:

1. A person in the *persecutor* position cannot bear to experience her/his vulnerability and has no sense that s/he or anyone can truly help, as all assertiveness is viewed as abuse. The 'persecutor' therefore seeks to project all vulnerability into a 'victim' – in whom it is then attacked, controlled and so kept at bay.

2. A person in the *victim* position cannot tolerate her/his own hostility and anger, and is unable to distinguish between destructive hostility and competent assertiveness. A 'victim' consequently seeks to get rid of any experience of her/his own anger and hostility

and find someone, the 'persecutor', into whom it may be projected, and who can then be perceived unequivocally in this role. Such a persecuting figure may thus be thought of as carrying a double dose of hostility – her/his own and that of the 'victim'. The 'victim' also abdicates any sense of responsibility for her/his actions and seeks a 'rescuer' into whom any competence the 'victim' has may be projected. The 'victim' thus avoids any real experience of ordinary vulnerability with its inevitable sense of worry and doubt about what to do.

3. A person in the *rescuer* position can bear neither vulnerability nor hostility in her/himself. A 'persecutor' is therefore sought who can be blamed for all hostility. Meanwhile the 'rescuer' projects all vulnerability into a 'victim', whom the 'rescuer' omnipotently sets out to save with panaceas that will remove both hostility and vulnerability from the scene – a project doomed to fail, leaving the 'rescuer' seeing most authorities as oppositional and persecutory.

Splitting

The process of passing the parcel described here clearly involves splitting off and redistributing different aspects of a dynamic situation in order that no one experiences the pain of the mixed feelings involved, with their attendant uncertainty. Instead of ordinary vulnerability, eased by some capacity to try to take responsibility for one's own care, and to assert one's needs *vis-à-vis* others, the false certainty and dramatic extremes of the persecutor–rescuer–victim triangle are espoused.

The term 'splitting', now widely used, grew largely out of the work of Klein (1946), within the psychoanalytic framework. While her reference to a splitting between the 'good' and the 'bad' breast can lend itself to cliché, it lies at the heart of much that we take for granted about the common experience of splitting. Klein argues that early on, a baby has to preserve the idea of the mother as being all good (the 'good breast') in order to be able to use what the mother offers. Any fury the baby experiences at the mother's not always being there is therefore directed elsewhere, as though at an absent 'bad breast'. The two 'breasts' are thus kept apart, for fear that the fury would overwhelm the 'good breast' and destroy it, thus destroying the baby's capacity to feed. In this initial *paranoid–schizoid* position, therefore, splitting is seen as necessary for the baby's psychic survival. It is an omnipotent, magical mechanism embodying the 'conviction that whatever trick the mind may play can achieve the desired effect – freedom from anxiety' (Herman 1989, p.12).

Later, feeling safer in the accumulated experience of contact with a 'good breast' and fortified by physical and motor development, a 'normal' baby is better able to tolerate the realisation that the good and bad breasts are different aspects of the same mother. In this important developmental step, the baby moves from a state ruled by the false certainties of a paranoid–schiz-oid view of the world to a *depressive position*. By this term Klein (1946) means not depression but a capacity to tolerate mixed feelings of love and hate towards the same person, and the ensuing feelings of guilt, grief, disillusion and concern.

This shift might also be seen as a move from a 'fairy tale' world of persecutor, rescuer and victim to one of recognising reality and having to act amid uncertainty. The early experiences of some infants, however, can block this growing confidence that the good can survive their omnipotent attacks; such interference with the capacity to reach the depressive position can persist throughout life. At the same time, it must be emphasised that no one is ever permanently established in the depressive position, and even the most emotionally mature adults will at one time or another revert, under stress, to the baleful certainties of the paranoid–schizoid position, portrayed so vividly in the persecutor–rescuer–victim polarisation.

Drama triangles and supervision

The tale of *The Pied Piper* has many echoes in supervision, as in the following imaginary but typical example.

EXAMPLE 6.a

> A social worker was called in to investigate a suspected case of child sexual abuse. As he became increasingly concerned that the child was indeed a victim of abuse, the parents felt victimised and the social worker was seen by the family as a persecutor. This increased his sense of needing to 'rescue' the child. As he removed the child, he began to feel the victim of comments by other 'persecuting' agencies, who tried to 'rescue' the parents from shame and the child from being removed from the family. The social worker turned with relief to his supervisor, hoping for rescue from his discomfort. When, after initial sympathy, she dared to ask for more details or to question something he had not thought of, he began to see her as persecuting and lacking in understanding of the situation; this made him retreat into the certainty

of his rescuing role, leaving her feeling kept out and persecuted by him.

This highlights how difficult it is for professionals amid great tension, criticism and anxiety to act thoughtfully and with caring authority, without either getting caught up in extreme and partial positions or being so perceived. The speed with which the roles can switch also contributes to the struggle for supervisors and workers in thinking about what is happening. We can readily imagine the drama triangle superimposed, in various guises, on either of the two supervisory triangles of Chapter 3, with a powerful influence on which corners receive attention at any one time and which are excluded.

The drama triangle and different theoretical perspectives

In courses for supervisors, we have observed that feeling caught up in a persecutor–rescuer–victim interaction is one of their most common experiences; this is often the concept they most quickly perceive as relevant. Part of its attraction is that it very easily crosses theoretical boundaries and can be discussed in family systems or psychoanalytic terms as well as those of transactional analysis. Its descriptive power is also invaluable for identifying that a split transaction is occurring, even before the source or reason has been fully understood. Thus, when a supervisor identifies such a dynamic in supervision, merely to acknowledge this may ease the situation and open up a joint exploration of what is going on. Many aspects of such interactions may be traceable to mirroring upwards from case dynamics, or downwards from organisational dynamics, as discussed in the previous chapter; the drama triangle concept could usefully be applied to most of the examples of mirroring given there. The persecutor–rescuer–victim triangle is probably the most frequently mirrored dynamic within front-line services today.

Denial of hostility

We would suggest that the wish of most people in the helping professions to deny their own hostility also contributes to their difficulty in confronting this powerful and abusive kind of interaction. It can be as hard and painful for workers or supervisors to believe that they are experienced as persecuting by service-users or supervisees (especially when they know they are also valued by them) as it is for most people to think of mothers being capable of sexually abusing their children. 'Helping' professionals are generally quicker to spot their own tendency to slide into the role of rescuer or victim (or recognise when they are so perceived) than to see themselves as persecutors. Certainly, the importance of acknowledging and thinking about hostile feelings towards service-users and colleagues is rarely taught in professional training. Failure to acknowledge such feelings, however, can lead to placatory behaviour and an inhibition on authoritative action, as energy is put into suppressing the unacceptable feelings. Presumably one reason for such inhibition is an anxious sense of guilt at having such feelings, and concern about their source. Winnicott (1949a), in his memorable paper 'Hate in the counter-transference', writes about having to face his own feelings of hatred before he could be free to take charge of a little boy who felt too hateful to be grappled with. Temperley (1979) describes situations where social workers, thwarted in their somewhat naive attempts to make contact with hostile parents, turn from would-be rescuers into masochistic victims of abusive behaviour. By failing to acknowledge their own anger, they fail to grasp the fury at the heart of the case. This can lead inexorably to unsafe decisions based on 'the rule of optimism' (Dingwall *et al.* 1983) rather than on the emotional realities.

In our courses, we have often been amazed at supervisors' apparently endless patience with difficult supervisees, which may eventually be revealed as a fear of being (or being experienced as) persecuting. Role-plays of supervision highlight how often supervisors believe they are being persecuting when observers can witness to their fairness and the care – sometimes almost excessive – with which they make challenges. Some supervisors, alternatively, deal with the issue of hate or aggression by abandoning all mediating care as merely 'rescue', taking instead a persecuting stance under the guise of 'being straight', determined that the supervisee is 'not going to make a victim out of me'. Thus the all or nothing dynamic still prevails. We pursue this issue further in Chapter 9.

The next two examples illustrate different ways in which two supervisors, in contrasting situations, sought to understand the strong feelings aroused in such drama triangles and in particular their own reactions of hostility and persecution.

EXAMPLE 6.b

> In a course for probation service supervisors in a particular region, the supervisor in a court welfare team presented her concerns about her supervision of one of her staff. The supervisor, a woman in her early thirties, had been promoted to this, her first supervisory post, a year ago. The older woman supervisee had also applied for the job; she had previously worked as a supervisor in another mainstream probation team, where there had apparently been considerable concern about

her competence. It seemed, though the details were vague, that she had been put under considerable pressure by senior managers to transfer to what was perceived as 'easier' work and to accept a demotion. The supervisor had received no formal handover or specific details of concern from the previous supervisor.

The supervisor had attended carefully to setting up a clear supervisory contract with her worker and had tried to acknowledge and address, within the limits of her information, the issues raised by the worker's demotion and her unsuccessful application for the supervisor's post. Over time, the supervisee had expressed her gratitude for the supervisor's care, attention and clarity, and had indicated her view that the previous supervisor had had no patience or interest in her. Latterly, however, the supervisor had come to experience the worker as clingy, lacking initiative and seeking advice on minor matters, and she found herself wanting to avoid the supervisee whenever she saw her. She was concerned that, despite her best efforts, she was failing to come to grips with something about this worker, but she was unclear what the something was. Many aspects of the supervisee's work were clearly good, but the supervisor slowly spoke of feeling uneasy about the worker's own mental state, her possibly paranoid view of service-users' responses to her and the reliability of her observations of others' behaviour. The supervisor was not sure, however, what solid evidence she had for these concerns.

As the supervisor told her story there were increasing noises of recognition from her colleagues on the course, despite her care to maintain, as far as possible, the supervisee's anonymity. It emerged that the concern about this worker's emotional state and reliability was widely known in the agency as a whole. Thus reassured (as she said) that she was not herself 'mad', the supervisor went on to provide more information – her worries about the supervisee's absences, and her suspicions on a few occasions that the supervisee had been drinking. She had raised most of these concerns with the worker at various times, only to feel they had just slipped away. By the end of her presentation, the supervisor herself was surprised at how many incidents and concerns she had listed, and realised that she had become more confident of her views and her information as she had set them out. When asked what she felt to be the main inhibition on her confronting the worker more clearly, she quickly replied that she now realised how concerned she was about the fragility of her worker's emotional state, and feared that any confrontation would tip her into a breakdown for which she, the supervisor, would (however irrationally) feel responsible.

It appeared that for a long time senior managers had avoided taking action on their concerns about this worker, perhaps similarly feeling that they would be persecutors and make her a victim, rather than that by using their authority they might help her in her vulnerability and, more specifically, attend responsibly to the weaknesses in her professional work. The detail of who contributed what to this dynamic is not relevant here. What is clear is that the court welfare service had been victimised by being seen as easy work where failing workers could be dumped, and a new supervisor had been used, perhaps quite unconsciously, by the senior managers as a potential rescuer to let them off the hook. The inexperienced supervisor, needing to prove herself and not in a strong position to make demands for information and a proper hand-over, offered a ready receptacle for such projections. Her rescuing role was perpetuated by the supervisee's response of gratitude and (for a time) dependence, as she presented herself as a victim of her previous supervisor. The supervisor had not colluded with the supervisee's wish to see the senior managers as persecutors (a common temptation). Now, however, the supervisor felt persecuted by the supervisee's demands, and came to fear that her own anger would cause the supervisee to be her victim.

The discussion helped the supervisor to become clear that she could use her authority to gather together her information and introduce a searching discussion without actually being a persecutor, however much she might be made to feel one. There was no guarantee how the worker would respond to being confronted; her personal and professional coping might indeed be threatened, or conceivably the supervisor's firmness might provide a sense of safety that would help her in both spheres. The supervisor was therefore encouraged not to rescue her senior managers by allowing herself to carry the responsibility alone and so putting herself in a vulnerable position. She concluded that she would discuss the matter fully with her own line-manager before proceeding and, if necessary, ensure that their communication was confirmed in writing; in this way, whatever transpired would be in a context where it was clear that some thought had taken place, and a sustainable exercise of authority would be made more possible.

We have given this illustration in some detail because it exemplifies a number of issues that present with disturbing frequency on courses for supervisors. Notable among these are the apparent 'misuse' of a new supervisor to rescue a department from past negligence, and the supervisor's lonely preoccupation with the fear that any professional challenge will persecute and cause emotional breakdown in a fragile worker. Inevitably, one major effect of this dynamic will be to obliterate any realistic attention to the service-user corner of the first supervisory triangle (Chapter 3). Whatever the sources of this kind of persecutor–rescuer–victim dynamic, the all too frequent lack of regular space for supervisors to reflect on their behaviour and face their unpalatable feelings in these complex interactions is a major contribution to unsafe practice.

EXAMPLE 6.c

> An experienced, able social work supervisor, based in a hospital where she had worked for many years, was shocked at having shouted down the phone at one of her more experienced supervisees, who worked mainly on a unit for chronically and terminally ill young people. The worker had been complaining on the phone to the supervisor (as she often had over the previous few months) about the impossibility of working on two cases where both social services and the health authority were failing to provide the necessary resources to help the families care for their ill youngsters. The two agencies, both with reduced budgets, were fighting over their respective responsibilities. The supervisor had been arguing hard for more resources, though with little success, and in fact shared the worker's concern that the service to this user group was being marginalised by both departments, but over the months she had increasingly felt she was the one blamed by the worker. She feared her explosion on the phone would serve only to confirm the worker in her view of being the victim of a non-understanding management (now including the supervisor), while she could remain the rescuer of the families. The injustice of the lack of resources and the rightness of the worker's advocacy for a time blurred the issue of how such a split had developed between the two people who in reality shared a concern about this area of work.
>
> With hindsight, it seemed that this worker might at the best of times have some difficulty in dealing with the families' inevitably mixed feelings, tending to address their sadness and vulnerability (as rescuer) while 'passing the parcel' of their fury and impotence to others, especially her supervisor. When this difficulty was exacerbated by the

real issue of a lack of resources, and her own grief and anger at the marginalising of the service she provided, she failed to take responsibility for being the department's representative to the families. For the supervisor, the fact that she was soon to leave the hospital added another imminent loss to the scenario, with attendant feelings of being an abandoning and neglectful persecutor. The supervisor hoped that by talking to the supervisee about her 'explosion' she could open up a discussion of their interaction, and of the dilemmas for the worker in coping with the intense mixed feelings aroused by this work.

Race and gender

In these examples, the supervisors and supervisees were all white women, and the service-users concerned were also white. It is important to consider how this affected the persecutor–rescuer–victim interaction, and what assumptions might be made had the configurations been otherwise (we remind readers of our invitation, in the Introduction, to consider their assumptions about race and gender in all the examples). In both examples, there was some indication that the supervisors were loth to be seen as persecuting because they also felt more linked to their female workers in situations where some of the senior managers described as unhelpful were male. Especially in areas of work where abuse and violence figure largely, it is easy for men to be automatically perceived as persecutors and women as victims; this is explored further in Chapter 10.

While gender and race differences will have a powerful impact in any working situation (varying according to the individuals involved, the balance in the workforce, and how institutional issues are handled), we would argue that they have a particular bearing on the way drama triangles operate. Since the purpose of the persecutor–rescuer–victim splitting dynamic is to keep the self and others in stereotyped roles and allow no mixed feelings, it lends itself to the distortions inherent in discrimination on the one hand, and rigid political correctness on the other. This is well addressed by Lousada (1994), who points out that the hatred and attack on thinking inherent in racism can all too frequently be replicated in the struggle against it; on either side, efforts to defend against the anxiety experienced can 'take the form of certainty, a moralistic condemnation of those who represent uncertainty' (p.159).

Black supervisors, still a minority in most agencies, may feel an added pressure to prove their competence and a heightened concern about taking action that might lead to their being seen as persecuting, or as needing to discuss problems with senior managers. Often too, in our experience, they describe being extra tough on their black staff because of wishing them to do well. Meanwhile, white supervisors of black supervisees who are sensitive to the power dimension of their situations can apply to themselves the warning given to white child-protection professionals working with black families by Baldwin, Johansen and Seale (1990): such workers need help to

> focus on the risks of operating only at the two extreme ends of the practice spectrum, for example, paralysed and inactive because of fear of being 'racist', or inappropriately 'rescuing' children. Middle ground courses of action and intervention need to be discussed. (p.30)

Good anti-oppressive and anti-discriminatory practice draws on the same basic skills as other aspects of good practice (Devore 1991) – in this context the capacity to tolerate and think about the feelings associated with all three positions in the drama triangle.

Drama triangles in teams and agencies

Our examples so far have looked at the function of the persecutor–rescuer– victim triangle in the context of supervision. The drama triangle is also relevant to much interaction within teams and agencies, and supervision can be indirectly affected via these channels. The following example illustrates one type of situation:

EXAMPLE 6.d

> Staff in a day nursery (with equal numbers of black and white personnel) had for a long time complained to the white head of the nursery about the work of one of their black colleagues. Her appalling time-keeping, record-keeping, insensitivity to parents and general unreliability constantly affected their own work. They felt victims of her persecuting neglect and quite appropriately looked to their manager for help, having regularly tried without success to sort out the issues directly with the worker concerned. After considerable groundwork and warning, the manager took steps that eventually led to the worker's dismissal. There was then a backlash of criticism from the majority of the team, who berated the manager, and her manager, for being racist and uncaring. Their sense of guilt at having contributed, through their information and criticism, to the dismissal of a colleague (especially one who was a single mother living in an area where work was hard to come by) led them to deny their previous professional assertiveness and to behave instead as though they had wanted their manager to be an omnipotent rescuer – whereas she had

now become in their minds a persecuting figure who might turn on them too.

This example illustrates the dilemmas faced by managers in the caring professions, where a proper use of authority in challenging difficult behaviour will seldom be widely welcomed and will often be seen as persecuting by staff who may readily identify with a victim. We would argue that this tendency is on the increase in departments where rapid organisational change and an often distant senior management leave staff very conscious of the vulnerability of their employment. However well managed, the triangular interaction of practitioner, supervisor and senior manager easily lends itself to splitting, with the most senior member of the triangle usually cast in the role of persecutor. Harding (1992), exploring the future of the personal social services, highlights this tendency: 'I heard managers say "management should communicate", reflecting a traditional failure to see themselves as part of the section of management that needs to communicate' (p.47). More specifically, Nathan (1994) points to practitioners' frequent difficulty in facing the inevitable gap between the needs of service-users and the available resources (including skills), and their temptation to diffuse or deny the discomfort by projecting blame onto a withholding, 'persecuting' management. The latter, of course, may only too often behave in a way that fits neatly with these projections. This represents, in microcosm, the split triangular interaction of government, services and service-users (citizens) described by Braye and Preston-Shoot (1993), who show how, in any confrontation between two of these (especially over the needs–resources tension), the third party may be invoked to deflect the developing conflict – that is, claimed as persecutor or rescuer by whichever of the other two is feeling most victimised.

Drama triangles and inter-agency work

The scope for splitting the three corners of the persecutor–rescuer–victim triangle between agencies and professions is vast, especially in work with individuals who project their own internal conflicts onto different workers or families who 'beam' various aspects of their own interaction into different agencies (Department of Health 1991a) – discussed in Chapter 5. Case conferences provide vivid examples of this; it is, of course, all too easy as a participant to perceive the stereotyped roles taken by others and the partial truth of their contributions, while assuming one's own contribution to be objective and whole. The dilemma is always how to maintain a perspective on the whole picture (including oneself), remembering that all corners of the triangle have to be considered together rather than superficially battling with each other.

The differences between professions and agencies provide ready hooks for such battles. In, for example, assisted housing projects for psychiatric patients discharged from long-stay hospitals, staff are inevitably prey to conflicting projections by residents – of, on the one hand, hope and excitement about freedom and rehabilitation and, on the other, fear at the loss of former routines and roles that were safe and familiar (however restricting). When such projects are jointly staffed by both residential social workers and nurses from the old wards, it is not surprising if the social workers identify with the former projections and the nurses with the latter – each profession perhaps seeing itself as rescuer and the other as persecutor of the 'victim' patients.

This tendency was vividly illustrated by the child sexual abuse crisis in Cleveland in 1987. Hawkins and Shohet (1989) trace how what began as a triangle of 'victim' children, 'persecutor' parents and 'rescuer' doctors and social services rapidly shifted into 'victim' families, 'persecutor' doctors and 'rescuer' local MP and media, before swinging again into 'persecutor' media and MP, 'victim' doctors and social services and 'rescuer' official inquiry report. Fortunately, however, the Butler-Sloss (1988) report resisted the rescuer role. Instead, it succeeded in 'bringing good supervisory under-standing of the whole situation, in which there are not "goodies and baddies", but in which there are well-intentioned people on all sides who have made mistakes or been misguided' (Hawkins and Shohet 1989, p.129) – in a context where, at the same time, some of those who made mistakes also discovered cases of child abuse that others might have failed to see. Woodhouse and Pengelly (1991, pp.241–263) also discuss the dynamics of the Cleveland situation in their study of collaboration between agencies.

We explore defensive interactions within and between professional groups more fully in the next chapter. Meanwhile, we emphasise our view that, in the caring professions, it is particularly the rescuer tendency – with its failure to acknowledge and speak to negative, angry or hateful feelings – that is most likely to contribute to dangerous practice based on splitting and partial truth. This leaves the hostility unthought about and so freer to operate unexpectedly in the professional system and control the action, whereas to face and think about it may be both essential and constructive, as shown in examples of supervision in this chapter. Bacon (1988), in a study of decision-making in child protection conferences, suggests that the unac-knowledged hatred of professionals towards some service-users (which in part mirrors the hatred emanating from the families) may result in inappropriate decisions to provide no further involvement with the families – totally against the tenor of most of the conference discussion. In the field of community care, reports following tragedies (e.g. Ritchie 1994) highlight the failure of agencies to pass on adequate information to each other about service-users' histories of violence. We would suggest that one reason for this is the operation of a rescuer mode, prompted by a misplaced fear of being persecuting and unfair, and the difficulty that many professionals have in facing the amount of hate and aggression in the case.

CHAPTER 7

The Invisible Organisation
Professional and Institutional
Defences Against Anxiety

In earlier chapters we have seen how supervisees and supervisors may unknowingly import into supervision some specific emotional interactions that have arisen in other working relationships nearby. We have also seen the importance of using supervision as a thinking space where the anxieties surrounding these 'imports' can be contained, and their informational value understood. In this chapter, by contrast, we shall explore the effects of more generalised anxiety about work to which a whole agency, team or professional group is exposed, and the collective defences which staff are unknowingly collaborating to maintain. These processes can be more difficult to recognise or deal with in the small arena of supervision. Most of the relevant literature is written from the perspective of external consultants or researchers. Nevertheless, it is important for supervisors to appreciate the influence of group and inter-group processes in which they and their supervisees participate. After introducing the topic, therefore, we shall offer some ideas to help the supervisor (and especially the supervisor–manager) read the situation she is in, and end by sketching in the wider societal context. We emphasise at the outset that although the processes we discuss go beyond the individual they are not impersonal; at every level, individuals can at least struggle to take their share of responsibility for the parts they play.

Anxiety and defence at the organisational level

Anxieties and defences are in themselves neither healthy nor unhealthy. Anxiety is inseparable from the human condition, and all individuals need to develop psychological defence structures to deal with it, in order to protect their own mental health. We discussed in the last chapter some of the ways in which the developmental struggles of early infancy can help or hinder this process. Mental ill health comes when defensive structures break down (so that the individual is swamped with unrealistic anxiety), when they become rigid and impermeable (so that even realistic anxiety cannot be felt or appropriately acted on) or when they are maladaptive (so that realistic and unrealistic anxieties cannot be distinguished from one another and dealt with accordingly). Mental health is, of course, a relative concept, and 'normal' people tend to revert to primitive defensive states of mind when under stress; on the whole, however, their relatively flexible and adaptive psychological defence structures enable them to tolerate painful and mixed feelings, take account of realistic anxiety and harness much of the energy inherent in irrational anxiety for constructive purposes.

Individuals do not live in isolation, however, but in relationships. They are constantly recruited and recruit each other, more or less consciously and willingly, into shared psychological defence structures which supplement, or reinforce, their individual defences. For any relationship system to endure, feedback mechanisms will have been instituted (some conscious, many unconscious and automatic) whereby its members try to keep each other from upsetting or stepping outside the shared defence structure in which they all have a psychological investment. It is no surprise that concepts of this kind, from psychoanalytic and systemic perspectives on couple and family dynamics (e.g. Cleavely 1993; Byng-Hall 1980), can also illuminate the dynamics of organisations; for the personal defence structures that individuals bring to adult work systems are formed in the matrix of the family system, transmitted down the generations through the intimate persuasiveness of couple and parent–child relationships (Shapiro and Carr 1991). Even though organisations may be less powerful and enveloping than families (for one thing, membership is more a matter of choice), we agree with the general hypothesis proposed by Jaques (1955) that

> one of the primary dynamic forces pulling individuals into institutionalised human association is that of defence against... anxiety; and conversely that all institutions are unconsciously used by their members as mechanisms of defence against these...anxieties. (p.496)

As with individuals and families, organisations too may have more or less 'healthy' (flexible and adaptive) defence structures for processing anxiety in order to carry out their stated tasks. One of our main aims in this book is to show the potential for 'health' of an established culture of supervision, where the enabling defence structure of space to think together about anxiety-provoking work is built in throughout an organisation.

What the eye doesn't see

We repeat, however, that the full scope of an organisation's defence structures can be difficult to recognise, especially since their less 'healthy' aspects are more likely to be unconscious. As the following example suggests, much may depend on where the observer is standing.

EXAMPLE 7.a

> Staff from a training organisation had for many years been engaged by a large voluntary agency to run seminars for team leaders on staff supervision. A succession of trainers had valued the continuity of this work, felt genuinely appreciated and in turn cherished the agency for its thoroughgoing commitment to supervision and training. One year, the planned programme did not attract enough members to be viable, and the agency, wishing to preserve the link with the training organisation, cast around for an alternative. The current trainer was rather hesitantly asked if she would do some similar work in the agency's residential care division instead. The request opened her eyes to the fact that supervisors from this division had never attended the seminars, which had been organised for fieldwork supervisors; none of the trainers had previously noticed or worried about this. When she began the work, she discovered that the group care managers of some homes did struggle to give supervision, but to very uneven effect as they had little training and only highly ambivalent support from the divisional management, while in other homes structured supervision was unheard of and regarded with suspicious incomprehension. Group care managers also complained that fieldwork staff seemed very pressing when they wanted to place residents, but tended to 'forget' about them once placed.

The trainer's field of vision had been confined to one sub-system of the agency – the fieldwork division, with its flourishing culture of supervision. When her encounter with the residential care division shifted her vantage point to a higher system level – the agency as a whole – her perception shifted dramatically. Some of the differences in the two divisions' attitudes to supervision probably had a basis in the different levels of training traditionally found in the two kinds of setting; others might have been determined by the idiosyncratic approaches of the two divisional directors. The significance for our purposes, however, lay in the way the overall system was operating. This seemed to ensure that when service-users who could not cope in the community (or could not be coped with by their families or fieldworkers) were placed in group care, the anxiety surrounding them was also 'placed' in the residential care division; there it was 'systemically' neglected and left unprocessed, perhaps sometimes by individual fieldworkers but essentially by the shared assumption – apparently pervading most of the agency – that the resource of supervision held indispensable in one division was quite unnecessary in the other.

Work-related anxiety and defences in care service organisations

We need to be more specific about the kinds of anxiety that typically arise in health and welfare services, and the characteristic *socially structured defences* (Menzies 1959) that tend to become built into the culture of a service agency or a profession. Menzies pioneered work in this field with her classic study of the nursing system in a large teaching hospital where teaching staff were concerned about the high drop-out rate of student nurses, including some of the most able. It is worth reviewing some of her findings, because of their seminal importance. She noted that many staff and students, individually, could identify how the rigid hierarchical regime was seriously under-utilising students' capacities but, collectively, all personnel seemed to perpetuate the system as if change was impossible. Menzies concluded that the system served a more deeply-rooted purpose, as outlined by Jaques (1955). She pointed out that, whilst primitive human anxieties were present in everyone at some level, they could be stirred up in specific ways for nurses by the task of caring for ill people in hospital. Nursing staff had to deal with distressing, disgusting or over-stimulating situations whose objective reality might come uncomfortably close to unconscious infantile fantasies and deeply-held adult fears.

Menzies describes the unconscious defensive use not only of overt structures (like the two service divisions in example 7.a) but also of less tangible shared assumptions, traditional informal practices and hallowed rules and procedures, all of which she saw as 'social systems' elaborated over time in the culture of the nursing profession, interacting with that of the hospital.

Although many of these systems were intended to facilitate work at the task, Menzies showed how nurses' task performance was impaired when their socially structured defences not only failed to reduce anxiety but actually increased it, by disabling their capacity to distinguish between realistic and unrealistic anxiety and to take responsibility for appropriate action. Junior nurses, not allowed to take responsibility for even the most trivial decisions, learned to see themselves as 'irresponsible' regardless of their individual capacities.

Menzies' work has been confirmed by subsequent studies and retains its relevance. In particular, though some of the social structures she described were specific to the time and place of her study, her analysis of their common defensive purpose can readily be applied to different structures in other situations. For example, she describes how the system of constant rapid redeployment of student nurses from one ward to the next, supposedly in the interests of gaining broad experience, diminished the opportunities for consistent caring relationships with patients, which many students had imagined would be a rewarding part of professional life; instead, nurses rapidly learned to avoid any feelings for patients, to refer to them as (for example) 'the liver in bed ten' instead of using their names and to regard both patients and themselves as interchangeable. The common defensive purpose here, Menzies suggests, was to depersonalise patients (and nurses' relations with them) so as to avoid the anxieties of personal contact; otherwise, nurses would have to deal with their own and their patients' painful feelings about illness, dependency and loss, which the nursing service had no built-in means of processing. But the quality and continuity of care offered to patients inevitably suffered.

The specific strategy of arbitrary redeployment has vanished from nurses' training, but the anxiety remains; other structures, for example the increasingly 'hi-tech' procedures of modern nursing, can readily be used for the same common defensive purpose of warding off anxiety by depersonalising the nurse-patient relationship. This phenomenon is not, of course, exclusive to hospital nursing. Innumerable labels and jargon ('your parolee', 'that schizophrenic', 'on the register', 'on a section') can be found in professionals' common usage, reducing the personal impact of the relationship with the service-user. Woodhouse and Pengelly (1991) describe the depersonalising of care relationships among general practitioners, health visitors, marriage counsellors, probation officers and social workers, each using different specific structures but for the same common defensive purpose.

Another common defensive purpose uncovered by Menzies (1959) was the avoiding, or diffusing, of anxious responsibility for making decisions. Clearly, safe and effective task performance does require rules about who is authorised to make certain decisions, for example in medical or child protection emergencies; and it may be a healthy defence to have procedures ensuring that crucial information is shared, so that no one person is left holding it on their own. The 'unhealthy' element lies in the habitually rigid, or habitually vague or chaotic, use of structures that in themselves are necessary for proper functioning. Mattinson and Sinclair (1979), in their study of a London borough social services department, describe how intake

Table 7.1. Task-related anxieties, defences and interprofessional perceptions

	Health visitors (under-5s)	General practitioners	Social workers (child protection)	Probation officers	Marriage counsellors
1. Raw material	The mother–baby relationship	Illness	Parents harming children	Crime	Conflict/breakdown in intimate relationships
2. Primary task	Education to promote child development	Diagnosis and treatment	Protection of child	• Stop people offending • Keep them out of prison	Facilitate change through insight
3. Service-user group	All new babies and their mothers	Everyone	Children at risk and their parents	Offenders	Couples in trouble
4. Access	All births notified	Open access	Referral and open access	By orders (courts, prisons)	Self-referral (app'te)
5. Core anxieties	• Dependency versus autonomy • Abnormal development	• Intimate contact • Uncertainty • Contact with illness	• Child abuse • Doing more harm than good • Guilt at hating clients	Conflict: • care/control • offender/society • autonomy/conformity	Oedipal: • exclusion • intrusion • rivalry
6. Characteristic defences	• Regress to dependency • Deny own competence • Keep relationship with client benign, 'normal'	• Boundary between doctor and patient • Confidentiality around doctor–patient relationship • Scientific reductionism	• Procedures • Excessive caution • Distancing • Using agency as citadel	• Rules and regulations • Categories of work • Fairness • Splitting	• No initial assessment • Confidentiality around counsellor–client relationship • Isolationism
7. Self image: (optimistic) (pessimistic)	Autonomous educators Dependent handmaids	Life preservers Death dealers	Carers Dustbins	Mediators Suckers	Special Fragile
8. Others' perceptions: (idealising) (derogatory)	Baby care experts Unthreatening stooges	Omniscient Arrogant	Saviours Withholding	(professionals) Moral authority Punitive (courts) Caring Soft	Marriage experts Amateurs
9. Caricature	'Mumsy'	'Omnipotent'	'Always in a meeting'	'A law unto themselves'	'precious'

and duty rota systems can both enable need to be assessed in relation to resources and be used by workers to reduce complex emotional problems to simplistic practical categories.

Woodhouse and Pengelly (1991) studied a large sample of cases contributed by fifty practitioners from five different services in one county. We have attempted to summarise their main findings in Table 7.1; items 1–6 list the different defensive structures and assumptions maintained by each profession or agency to try and deal with work-related anxieties specific to the 'raw material' of human issues encountered in carrying out its primary task (that is, the task it exists to perform). We shall refer to items 7–9 later in the chapter.

Whilst Table 7.1 is over-simplified and schematic, supervisors on our training courses have found it makes a useful framework for thinking about the current situation in their own services. As with other studies, some of the structures identified by Woodhouse and Pengelly as having a defensive use may be specific to place and time, but work-related anxiety and the use of socially structured defences are perennial. In particular, they found two defensive strategies that seemed universal: first (as mentioned above), the depersonalising of relations with service-users and, second, the tendency for practitioners in anxious situations to retreat to a narrow definition of primary task and apply it rigidly. The latter strategy was one that had serious implications for inter-agency collaboration as well as for workers' own practice.

It is also clear, from the studies mentioned, that the formal and informal cultures of whole professions such as medicine, nursing and social work include characteristic defensive structures which their members bring into the service organisations where they work. We shall refer in passing to some of these, but we mostly have the agency context in mind in this chapter.

In every organisation, as well as the *technical system* for managing work at the primary task (described in mission statement, management diagram, policies and procedures), there is necessarily a *social system* of human relationships through which staff operate the technical system (Trist and Murray 1993). The social system is fuelled by the dynamic motivation of staff, in part seeking the satisfaction of working effectively and co-operatively, but in part (as we have seen) seeking to control and reduce anxiety. Care agencies, where the task is entirely concerned with human 'raw material', where the main technical resource consists of the staff themselves and where the work must be carried out predominantly via relationships with service-users, are especially prone to be affected by specific anxieties stirred up by the work, and by the staff's need to defend against them. Mature, enabling defensive structures like supervision (properly used) can operate in the service of the task, but many aspects of both the technical and social systems can be turned to covert defensive purpose; their effect may be 'anti-task' (Menzies 1979). This covert defensive use tends to become institutionalised, by unconscious agreement between members of the organisation, and is highly resistant to change.

Reading the situation I am in

Clearly, it is not an easy matter for a supervisor as an individual member of an organisation to decipher its covert defensive system, especially since she herself will be participating in it. As we have already noted, defences against anxiety are inevitable; they are psychologically needed by staff and can facilitate as well as hinder effective work. When they are covertly hindering work, the resulting dysfunction will by definition be endemic, going far beyond the two individuals in a supervisory relationship and beyond any one piece of work they are considering. This is what makes it difficult to recognise.

Covert, or unconscious, defences can operate in supervision itself, as we have discussed (in different conceptual terms) in the last four chapters. When this is habitual and permeates a whole organisation or unit, the misuse of supervision can be seen as an unconsciously agreed defence that is seriously dysfunctional; for example, when supervision is dominated by a mechanistic, check-list approach, the procedures designed to focus anxiety can become instead a way of avoiding it. Widespread disuse or undervaluing of supervision can be seen in a similar light – for example, when elaborate policies about supervision have been formulated at senior level but little attention is paid to its actual practice or effectiveness.

At best, however, supervision can play a significant part in identifying and countering particular instances of 'systemic' dysfunction, noticing its pervasive patterns, its discrepancies and its confusion of ends with means, and paving the way for it to be addressed in the wider organisational context. As we have stressed, supervision includes not only ensuring the required service-delivery but also exploring the emotional impact on the worker – and, crucially, struggling to understand the relevance of one to the other. This makes supervision one of the best safeguards an agency can have against systemic dysfunction reaching severe or unsafe levels – a mature defence system and not merely a bureaucratic way of ensuring that 'the collective back is covered' (Moore 1995).

In the next three sections we look at some of the issues for supervisors in trying to read the situation they are in: within their own part of the organisation, in the relation of that part to the whole organisation, and in dealings with other organisations outside.

Inside the boundary

The supervisor who is also manager of a team of practitioners may seem comparatively well placed to consider the particular anxieties she and her staff are exposed to through their work, and the defensive strategies, mature and primitive, they together employ. She must, however, be prepared to recognise the part that she herself is playing. Her official role is, in fact, one of the most obvious structures available for covert defensive use by the team, including herself (Downes 1988).

As we noted earlier, the personal defences that individuals seek to reinforce through their shared defensive structures at work originate in the family group. A work team – usually a small, face-to-face group with a common identity and a 'home base' – is particularly apt to be structured unconsciously by its members as a 'family', with the manager as a 'parent' figure. This may only become salient occasionally, for example at times of stress, and can have constructive as well as dysfunctional uses. However, especially when the primary task concerns working with family issues, it may become a vehicle for wholesale mirroring of the troubled dynamics of the service-user group. Sometimes there is more than one role carrying official or unofficial authority, so a 'two-parent' structure is available – giving more scope either for co-operative use of authority or for power struggles and playing one off against the other. Some of these features are illustrated in the following example from a multidisciplinary team. We shall give the narrative in three parts, interspersed with commentary.

EXAMPLE 7.b

> The manager of a specialist psychiatric unit for eating disorders arranged to have regular sessions with a trainer in the same hospital with experience in organisational consultancy, in order to think about his role. The role was indeed complex, combining the responsibilities of line-manager of the nursing and administrative staff, budget-holder for the unit as a whole, and co-ordinator of the multidisciplinary team – which included separately-managed psychologists, social workers employed by the local authority and a consultant psychiatrist (assisted by registrars) who held clinical responsibility for the patients' treatment. The manager (who also took a share of direct nursing duties) was a thoughtful professional with a caring approach to his staff in their stressful work. The problems he brought mainly

concerned his doubts about his effectiveness, linked with uncertainty about his authority. He sometimes wondered if this was just an indication of his personal problems, and at other times pointed out how difficult or unsupportive some of his colleagues could be. The trainer, however, encouraged him to see the problems in their organisational context as well.

The manager had particular difficulty in defining his proper functional relationship with the consultant psychiatrist. Although his view of nursing went well beyond the stereotypical 'handmaid' role, he found it hard to escape from the traditional assumption that the doctor's authority was paramount. Looking at the way this unit had been structured, however, he began to see that in all three of his areas of responsibility he had authority that was separate from the consultant psychiatrist's. It seemed to follow that the most effective way of running the unit as a whole would be for the two of them to work as a partnership, but he felt very uncertain about facing the struggles this might entail. The need was underlined, however, when one of the nurses, ostensibly on a day's sick leave, rang in to confide to the manager her worry that she herself was suffering from eating problems (having always previously denied the half-concerned, half-derogatory rumours circulating among the team). The manager was taken aback and tried to be sympathetic but the consultant psychiatrist, overhearing this, said the nurse should be seen by a colleague at another eating disorders unit and without further ado telephoned to make the arrangements. Whilst admiring such decisiveness, which so contrasted with his own feeling of helplessness at that moment, the manager also felt displaced and increasingly angry. Thinking about this incident with the trainer, he realised that it was not just a matter of the consultant psychiatrist being high-handed, but also of why it had not occurred to him to say 'hold on a minute, I think we should discuss this'.

The technical system was clearly not working as designed; while individual factors played a part, the social system operated by the team as a whole must also be considered, especially its covert defensive aspects. The main dynamic issue for the unit was how it managed the characteristic anxieties and conflicts associated with the 'raw material' of eating disorders, to which all staff would be exposed through their work. For patients, these included the fear of being overwhelmed by painful feelings of empty worthlessness, with compulsive eating for comfort followed by compulsive evacuating; or the fear of growing too big – or growing up to physical and sexual maturity at all – with compulsive refusal to eat. Interacting with these anxiety-driven behaviours, relatives could be drawn either into equally compulsive 'caring' – only to find themselves perceived as coercive and their efforts subverted – or into collusive neglect. Either way, their relationships could be fractured, their authority attacked and their belief in their nurturing capacity undermined.

A working hypothesis can be made. First, that some of these dynamics (always active in the direct work with patients where practitioners were liable to be cast in 'parental' roles) were not being processed by the treatment team but blindly re-enacted in their relationships with one another as a 'family', where the manager and consultant psychiatrist were the 'parental' figures. Second, that the two 'parents' had become split, into caricatures of 'collusion' and 'control' respectively. This split not only mirrored the service-users' dynamic, but also followed the 'lines of least resistance' provided by 'real professional vulnerabilities' (Will and Baird 1984) between nurse and doctor. As well as the obvious differentials of prestige and pay (and often gender, though not in this instance), the traditional professional cultures of nursing and medicine socialise their members into automatic, and interlocking, defensive responses – for nurses, giving up power; for doctors, taking it.

With all these complexities, the unit's unconscious agreement to structure itself as a 'family', in order to manage the work-related anxieties, appeared to become seriously dysfunctional at the point when the possibility of a staff member actually turning into a patient brought the anxiety too close to consciousness for comfort. Example 7.b continues, with the question: what thinking spaces were available for processing the anxiety arising from the 'raw material' of the work, and attending to the connections between dynamic interaction at the clinical level and at the staff group level?

> The manager next reported that a junior nurse had complained about criticism by the experienced nurse designated as her 'mentor'. She had been accused of being over-sympathetic and protective in her work with a particularly worrying young woman on the in-patient treatment programme, undoing the work of the community psychiatric nurse (CPN) who had been trying to maintain a tougher stance before the patient's admission. The nurse had defended herself by claiming the support of her 'supervisor' for her own approach. This referred to a regular meeting for the in-patient programme nurses where their work was 'supervised' in detail by a child psychotherapist from another department. The mentor did not attend these sessions. Nor did the manager; he and the consultant psychiatrist had both inherited them

as 'part of the structure of the unit from its inception'. He could not remember the two of them ever reviewing with the child psychotherapist how these time-honoured 'supervision' arrangements were related to his managerial responsibility or the psychiatrist's clinical responsibility. He also realised that the function of a mentor had never been clarified in these respects either; it was apparently being treated as though it was individual supervision. Reflecting on the series of events involving the junior nurse, the manager recalled that the problems had actually started when the patient in question had managed, by her behaviour, to by-pass the normal admission procedures.

This graphically illustrates how the vulnerable staff 'family' could be blown apart – apparently by one desperate service-user, but in fact by their own unprocessed response to her. To add to our hypothesis: the available thinking spaces had become fragmented and non-accountable; instead of processing anxiety, therefore, they could be used for the defensive purpose of trying to disperse it in bits around the unit. This, however, only provided more 'lines of least resistance' along which mirroring could occur. The dynamic of persecutor–rescuer–victim (Chapter 6) can be clearly seen pursuing its inexorable cycle, as the 'victim' patient was shielded from the 'persecutor' CPN by the 'rescuer' junior nurse, who in turn felt persecuted by her mentor but rescued by her supervisor, leaving the manager to try and restore sanity. However, he had to recognise that he (as well as the consultant psychiatrist and other staff) had shared in the original impulse to rescue the patient by waiving the normal procedures for admission. He had also played his part in maintaining the defensive system that the team as a whole was using to ward off work-related anxieties, with such dysfunctional results. In particular, he needed to think about how his own supervisory responsibilities had become diluted in the general fragmenting of thinking spaces, and how his 'caring' stance could be ineffective and unsafe if it were merely 'permissive' and not allied with some appropriate use of authority – which he had tended to leave to the consultant psychiatrist.

Thinking with the trainer about how to tackle these issues, the manager spoke despairingly about the likelihood of ever getting his own manager's backing for a more authoritative stance. The trainer subsequently realised, with shock, that she herself had no very clear idea of whether, or how, their consultative work together had been authorised. She resolved to get this clarified with the manager, especially as it seemed to provide further evidence of the very problems they had been discussing.

Looking back over the story, indeed, the reader may see at how many points (the fragmenting of thinking space, the invoking of rescuers, the avoiding of proper authorisation) it could be echoed in the manager's use of consultation with the trainer, and the trainer's willingness to be used. The use of organisational consultants is subject to provisos about accountability in a similar way to clinical consultants, mentors and the like, as discussed in Chapter 3. Otherwise, these roles can be used defensively to avoid facing management problems, with the likely result (as here) that 'the basic situation remains unrealised and unchanged whilst new versions of it proliferate' (Britton 1981). At the same time, it is partly because consultation, like supervision, has this capacity to mirror the troublesome dynamics within the bounds of the thinking space that it also has the potential for understanding, provided the uncomfortable truth of the mirroring can be faced (as discussed in Chapter 5).

Across the internal boundary

Any internal boundary in an organisation can be used for defensive purposes, by those on one side of it splitting off their feelings of anxiety, blame, helplessness etc. and pushing them into those on the other side. A familiar example of this is the 'us and them' attitude frequently adopted by staff towards management, and vice versa. The 'boundary' here is marked by an obviously visible difference. Other common examples are the depositing of unprocessed anxiety by professional staff onto administrators, secretaries or domestic staff, or by specialist clinical staff onto nurses (Shapiro and Carr 1991); gender and racial differences may frequently be involved as well. Between professional staff, too, just as an individual may take up, or be assigned, a role in the team's defensive system, so may a whole team (or other grouping) in that of the wider organisation. The manager or supervisor concerned is less well placed to perceive this, partly because of her limited vantage point (as in Example 7.a), but more crucially because she and the team may have their own vested interest in it.

Collusive interactions and manoeuvres abound between sections of an organisation, and between one section and the organisation as a whole. Example 7.a illustrated a common split between fieldwork and group care sections. Sometimes working units can be defensively marginalised, especially in areas of work which seem peripheral to an organisation's mainstream task, and to which its commitment may be ambivalent. These areas can attract individualistic staff who feel impatient with the mainstream work and zealous to tackle the 'real problem'. Units such as bail hostels (in probation services) or outreach projects for drug addicts or runaways (in health or social services) can provide constructive ways of harnessing such workers' energies, but unless a team of this kind is firmly connected to the centre through line management it can become dangerously dysfunctional. The temptation for the workers may be to identify more and more with the service-users, take on increasingly unrealistic tasks and progressively deny their own account-ability (Zagier Roberts 1994b). The organisation's ambivalence may be expressed in initial enthusiasm and generous funding, rapidly giving way to exasperation and censure of the 'deviant' team. Such a scenario can give a spurious boost to morale all round, by 'proving' the workers' view that society (personified by management) does not care, and the management's view that the 'problem' (personified by the workers) is greedy of scarce resources. Both can feel justified, but meanwhile the service-users' predica-ment may not be receiving any sober, realistic attention.

Groups such as crown court teams in probation, psychotherapists in mental health settings, family placement teams in social services, teams in any setting specialising in child sexual abuse issues, may undertake very skilled work that is indispensable but arouses much anxiety in others who would feel, by comparison, ill-equipped to attempt it. Such groups are particularly liable to envious attack, and any mistakes they make may be fiercely seized upon in an effort to make them carry not only the anxiety but also the lack of competence felt by their colleagues. They may be suspected of allegiances elsewhere. For their part, such groups may indeed come to regard themselves as elite. Their boundaries may become closely guarded, and their links with powerful outside groups in their specialist fields can seem to offer more *sentience*, that is emotional significance (Miller and Rice 1967), than those with their own fellow employees and managers. They may arrogate for their special knowledge more certainty than it realistically warrants, whilst undervaluing or ignoring that of others; mistakes will then, in fact, become more likely. If their interaction with other parts of their organisations develops, collusively, into this kind of two-way negative feedback, their value both in their own work and as a resource for others will be greatly reduced.

A manager or supervisor may become worried that some such defensive process is occurring, but find it hard to define in the face of the entrenched attitudes of all concerned. We would suggest that some of the concepts mentioned in this book can provide frameworks for understanding and change. Even though the dysfunction may be widespread, particular instances can be identified through, for example, careful consideration of the *supervisory triangles* in Chapter 3 to see whether the exclusion of one of the corners, or the neglect of their interrelatedness, has a hidden institutional significance. Other signs may be a general *laxity* or *denial of accountability*, either to agency objectives (including quality measures) or between colleagues when a case is referred from one part of an organisation to another (or held simultaneously in both); the agency, via managers, may collude with lax accountability. Clear data on whether or not the technical system is working as designed may be gained from applying Lawrence's (1977) concept of the *normative, existential* and *phenomenal primary task*, mentioned in Chapter 1. As Zagier Roberts (1994a) points out,

> analysis of the primary task in these terms can highlight discrepancies between what an organisation or group says it sets out to do and what is actually happening. It can thus serve as a tool for individuals and groups within an enterprise, as well as for consultants, to clarify and understand how the activities, roles and experiences of individuals and sub-systems relate to each other and to the enterprise as a whole. (p.30)

In these ways what has developed unthinkingly may be exposed to consciousness. However, to move from changed awareness to changes in behaviour is no easy matter, especially since personal defensive needs will be so bound up in the institutionalised defence structures. The process will test supervisors' and managers' capacity to persist in exploring different points of view, to tolerate often bitter resistance without undue retaliation, and to distinguish when planning for change is negotiable and when not. Above all, they will need a mature capacity to own and exercise authority; we discuss this more fully in Chapter 10.

Across the external boundary

Much of what we have said about dynamic processes between parts of an organisation can also be applied to those between different organisations. In this section we focus on some additional factors that need to be considered, bearing in mind the supervisor–manager's increasingly active role at the organisation's local boundary in today's rapidly changing environment.

In terms of some of the concepts we have been using, the first point to notice is that in a network of services provided by separate organisations there is no unified technical system or centrally defined primary task, despite official guidelines about collaboration and however close it may in fact be. A service network is therefore an incoherent system; this increases the scope for defensive behaviour between organisations, and the difficulty of achieving agreed understanding and change when dysfunction is occurring. Referral from one agency to another, for example, has been described by Woodhouse (1977) as frequently 'the point of maximum dishonesty'.

The defensive systems of the service agencies involved in a local network, and of the professional groups employed in them, are constantly in dynamic relation to one other, as we outlined in Chapter 6. Woodhouse and Pengelly (1991) describe how this operated in practice in the county area they studied. The social services department, for example, was expected by other practitioners to respond with immediate action if notified of concern about child protection – even though the notification might purport to be 'confidential' and 'not to be disclosed' to the service-user family. In this way, the department's proper statutory role could be exploited by referring not only the case but the anxiety surrounding it for the social workers to bear, while the referring practitioner hoped to preserve a 'good' relationship with the family. Of the other four services in this study,

> doctors were invariably treated as omnipotent and omniscient (notwithstanding their disagreements with each other) whenever illness was at issue. Health visitors were deferred to, if not to the same degree, on matters of abnormal infant development and could be exploited in their role as 'normal' visitors to clients' homes. It often seemed as though marriage guidance counsellors alone held the key to intimate couple relationships, behind a veil of secrecy. Probation officers were credited with moral authority, correcting delinquents either by care or by punishment. (p.232)

Such perceptions by practitioners of each other were always ambivalent, 'idealising' when another service's help was wanted, 'derogatory' when the idealised expectations were not met. Practitioners' perceptions of themselves were similarly split into 'optimistic' and 'pessimistic'. Returning to Table 7.1, we have tried to summarise in items 7–9 the main mutual perceptions and caricatures found by these authors in the course of their study. It will be noted that probation officers were perceived in almost opposite ways according to context; among other professionals it was their 'control' function with offenders that was seen (in a good or bad light), whereas in the courts their 'caring' function was to the fore. Such contextual variation may apply to other professions and agencies.

Other studies have investigated interprofessional stereotypes (and the possibility of modifying them), for example in shared programmes for medical and nursing students (Carpenter 1995), or for these two groups plus social work students (Pietroni, P. 1991). Despite the hope that attitudes might prove more malleable at this early stage of professional life, Carpenter notes that nurses' prejudices shifted only slightly as a result of the shared programme, those of medics not at all. On the other hand, Pietroni uses similar findings to argue for the value, and inevitability, of difference; instead of futile attempts to iron it out, he calls for leadership that understands the dynamic meanings ascribed to different professions by the wider culture of society, and the realistic function and limitations of each discipline, as a means of bringing about more creatively integrated services. Whilst his analysis is important for multidisciplinary settings, however, it is more difficult to apply to service networks of separate organisations where no overall leadership is available. In the latter situation, as Woodhouse and Pengelly (1991) point out,

> ...each agency, as we have seen, is subject to specific anxieties related to its task; but at the network level it also has channelled into it the anxieties about its area of competence that other agencies cannot contain. This incessant projective redistribution of unmanageable anxiety between agencies can only serve to rigidify the structures and practices through which their members attempt to ward it off. (p.232)

Thus, in their study, the social services department could sometimes behave like a 'citadel under siege', its members inclined even more to fall back on rigid application of bureaucratic procedure and a narrow definition of primary task. As noted earlier, such rigidity was resorted to by staff of all five services in the study when faced with excessive anxiety. Thus, 'in the relevant service network constellated by a given case, the practitioners involved may be impelled to use institutional defences not only internally against their own anxieties but externally against each other, to the detriment of collaboration' (p.232). Alternatively, workers from different agencies (especially those whose primary tasks and defence systems were relatively congruent) might form collusive coalitions against other workers with opposing views, or against service-users.

Inter-agency groups are often established to deal with specific issues, notably in the field of child protection. In a case conference, for example, there is certainly the opportunity for the kind of leadership envisaged by Pietroni, but also formidable difficulty since by definition such a conference is convened out of mounting anxiety for the safety of one or more children. The task is to clarify the evidence for concern and decide on an appropriate and co-ordinated response. In order to achieve this, however, it is necessary to enable the participants to contain and manage their anxieties, so that they can think together, it is also necessary to monitor and (if necessary) address the dynamic process that emerges in the temporary structure of the conference itself. Several studies (e.g. Hallett and Stevenson 1980; Bacon 1988; Woodhouse and Pengelly 1991) have shown the capacity of case conferences for dysfunctional decision-making when 'defences against anxiety are at the same time defences against reality' (Downes 1988).

We noted earlier that some specialist groups in an agency may be suspected – not without justification – of allegiances elsewhere. This can happen particularly when an inter-agency team is established (for example a joint social services and police team for child protection investigation work, or joint assessment teams in other fields). Zagier Roberts (1994c) shows how the members of such a team can find their 'sentience' shifting imperceptibly from their own employing organisations to the team itself, as they become invested in working together on a shared task. They can begin to take decisions or initiatives beyond their delegated authority, and feel aggrieved when questioned by their 'home' managers – to whom their sense of accountability has become weakened. Such teams need to be staffed by workers who are firmly rooted in their own respective professional identities; as Trowell (1995) observes in the context of joint training courses at postgraduate level, 'considerable problems arise if professionals lack a grasp of the role and tasks of their own discipline' (p.193).

Changing organisations – changing defences?

In terms of this chapter's themes, the drive in the 1980s and 1990s to replace a national 'dependency culture' with an 'enterprise culture' represents an attempt to uproot the perceived socially structured defences of the population in general, and care services in particular. However, while there is merit in exposing unnecessary dependency (perpetuated by professionals as well as service-users), dependency as a fact of life can never be rooted out. It is inherent not simply in children and long-term dependent adults, but in everyone to some degree. Even those able to function 'independently' seek ways of getting their dependency needs met through, for example, intimate relationships and membership of groups and organisations; mature functioning entails a recognition of interdependence rather than a defensive 'counterdependency' (Stokes 1994). In illness, misfortune or loss, a sense of dependency is part of a useful defensive response, enabling one to acknowledge need and seek and use the help of others.

The ideas of Bion (1961) illuminate this issue. He holds that, in the life of any group, work at the given task may be either hindered or promoted by the 'basic assumption mentality' that is constantly active in the shared unconscious fantasy of the group. He distinguishes three forms of basic assumption. In *dependency*, the fantasy is that group members are there to have all their needs met; in *fight–flight*, an enemy is identified, to be attacked or escaped from; in *pairing*, salvation lies in some future event, hopefully to be brought about by two people getting together. While a group dominated by basic assumption mentality can distort or completely avoid the work task, nevertheless each basic assumption is potentially conducive to certain kinds of work provided reality is not lost sight of; Bion stresses this constructive or 'sophisticated' function of basic assumptions. Using Bion's model, Stokes suggests that different care professions necessarily mobilise different basic assumptions in support of certain tasks (e.g. dependency for nursing sick people in hospital, fight–flight for social work tasks of advocacy or removal of children from danger, pairing for counselling or psychotherapy); when needing to collaborate, however, they may find each other's assumptions strange and even repellent. This underlines Bion's view that each basic assumption serves partly as a defence against anxieties associated with the other two.

Seen in this light, as Halton (1995) suggests, the dismantling of the welfare state in recent years may represent a national revulsion from the anxieties stirred up by dependency, and a defensive resort to fight–flight mentality – embodied in the market values of competition and devil-take-the-hindmost. Halton concludes that the market model is fundamentally inappropriate for care services, which function best through a mobilising of the 'sophisticated' form of dependency basic assumption.

Dilemmas connected with these overall issues constantly arise in daily practice – for example, how to marry up the requirement to compete and the requirement to collaborate in partnership, without overemphasising either as a defence against anxiety aroused by the other; or how to make constructive rather than defensive use of outcome measures and audit. New structures like the separation of purchasing and providing functions readily lend themselves to covertly defensive use; all capacity for deciding what is needed can be ascribed to purchasers, while providers may be tempted to overload their staff or offer 'quick fixes' for fear of losing business. The epidemic of reorganisation itself may (insofar as change becomes compulsive and repetitive rather than flexible and adaptive) be a national defence against facing the realistic limitations and uncertain outcome of much service-delivery and the painful gap between needs and resources.

Exhortations to a 'seamless' model of multidisciplinary care in the community (Department of Health 1991d), though ostensibly for the benefit of service-users, may aggravate professionals' own tendency to avoid the anxiety of differentiating their proper roles and skills, with the kind of dysfunctional results we have already discussed above (and will return to in Chapter 9, in the context of supervision). We have certainly seen how boundaries that denote difference can be used defensively, but in our view this points to the need for boundaries to be managed thoughtfully, not abolished. Webb (1992) points out the ambiguity of the move towards 'convergence' in nursing and social work training (particularly in the learning difficulties field); whatever its value, it also involves 'a decomposition of specialist knowledge and…a collapsing of space between the two professions', as they are 'hustled, jostled, induced and obligated to become more collaborative and less protective of jealously held identities' (p.225). This can readily be seen in the employment of both nurses and social workers as 'care managers', a job title expressing the purposes of employers – and perhaps service-users – whilst erasing the holder's professional identity. Thus, convergence may lead to a healthy adaptiveness, or to increasing professional insecurity and the alternative defence of denying difference. The project of breaking down the established socially structured defences of care professions may serve only to breed new ones.

Finally, there is also much ambiguity in the wider processes of social change in Britain in the past two decades, especially as they have affected the relation of individuals to organisations. Miller (1986) points to a decisive shift in assumptions, from reliance on employers and the welfare state as providers of security to mistrust and disillusion in the face of rising unemployment and cuts in services. In a climate of 'failed dependency', there has been a 'psychological withdrawal from organisations', not only by the unemployed but also by those whose precarious employment increasingly demands compliance and over-work rather than the exercise of personal authority and skill. In many organisations, including care services, this has generated a collective defence of 'don't stick your neck out' as a strategy for survival. Although it is possible to remain employed under such defensive constraints, large numbers of individuals have become self-employed as a way of achieving greater autonomy albeit with greater risk. Many professionals, for example, do 'agency work' by choice rather than subject themselves to psychological 'conditions of employment' which they experience as antipathetic to their personal defence structures; experienced and skilled staff set up as independent trainers and consultants or migrate to the expanding professions of counselling and psychotherapy. Miller (1986), though not regretting the demise of the dependency culture, stresses the difficult challenge of developing more mature organisational defence structures that might encourage individuals to reinvest in organisations in a more autonomous and less dependent way. As already stated, we see supervision in its full sense as just such an enabling structure but, like Miller, we cannot be more than guardedly optimistic.

CHAPTER 8

New or Old Breed?
Dealing with Loss and Change

Without confidence in the continuity of our purposes and sense of the regularity of social behaviour, we cannot begin to interpret the meaning of any event. But unless we are also ready to revise our purposes and understanding, we may be led to actions which are fatally misconceived. (Marris 1974, p.15)

When supervisors have presented their work on our courses in recent years, the most pervasive theme has been the impact of change and how to manage it. Some supervisors, uncertain whether this impact – for them so much a fact of professional life – was worth discussing, would be taken aback by how strongly their feelings, usually of loss, welled to the surface when once they began to talk. Others could talk about scarcely anything else, illustrating precisely the struggle they faced at work in moving on and focusing on their tasks. Our experience in this seems similar to that described by Downes, Ernst and Smithers (1996) in their recent courses. We have therefore chosen to devote a chapter specifically to issues of change, even though they are present implicitly or explicitly in most of the other chapters.

Chapter 1 outlined some of the areas of dramatic change in the turbulent environment of health and social services since the mid-1980s, in the organisation and structuring of services, the definition of professional roles and tasks, the value orientation of service provision, the legal framework and the security of employment. Change may, on the one hand, pose a healthy challenge to the rigid resistances of some institutional and professional defences; on the other, reorganisation itself may be embarked on as an institutional defence against experiencing the reality of the needs–resources tension – a manic flight into 'solutions' to insoluble problems, without enough continuity for previous changes to be evaluated.

M. Pietroni (1995) thoughtfully explores these issues in the light of the post-modernist thinking that grew out of disillusion with the radical politics and socialist promise that were current earlier in the twentieth century:

> The loss of certainty, the acceptance of a relativist philosophy and the fragmentation of values, thought and beliefs...in relation to social work have been identified as normal features of post-modernism. So the nearest that there are to facts in the post-modernist world are the constructivist nature of knowledge, the dizzy pace of change, the babel of professional languages and the continuous erasure of categories of thought and formal structures of all kinds. (p.45)

Change and uncertainty are certainly facts of professional and organisational life; Pietroni concludes that professionals need to 'reframe their knowledge, skills and practice into new combinations and categories to suit a world where skill-mixes of a radically new kind are required and ethical dilemmas are often profound' (p.49). One of the greatest difficulties facing profession-als in this post-modern age, however, is the contradiction that lies at its heart, as relativist values which query all previous beliefs exist alongside the 'fundamentalist' ideologies underpinning much current service planning, with their dogmatic approaches to complex dilemmas. The danger in such flux is to deny the human and professional impact of rapid change and uncertainty. 'Because this splintered world is philosophically and structurally coherent with our age...it attracts little attention and raises too little concern' (M. Pietroni 1995, p.44).

Our interest here is not in the positive or negative aspects of the changes themselves, but in the impact on supervisors and practitioners of such major psycho-social transitions (Parkes 1971). In addressing this impact, we have found that the ideas of Marris (1974), however familiar, have a freshness and relevance that never fails to surprise.

Change as crisis: mourning precedes moving on

The literature on the impact of life events makes it clear that even change that is chosen and welcomed (for example, getting married, having a child, moving house, taking up a promotion) is not achieved without emotional discomfort (Parkes 1971). All developmental transitions inevitably entail some degree of loss; individuals, families and groups experience a pull towards 'homeostasis', reasserting the familiar balance that any change threatens to disturb. Marris argues that new experiences can be assimilated only when they are 'placed in the context of a familiar, reliable construction of reality'; resistance to change, or the 'conservative impulse' can then be seen not only as a rejection of the new and a wish to protect the old, but also as a holding on to a secure reference point from which it is possible to consider adapting to the new. In this, Marris extends and adapts to the context of organisational change the ideas about grieving and kindred personal experiences explored by Parkes (1971; 1975a; 1975b). He highlights two points in particular: that mixed feelings are inevitable and normal as a reaction to change; and that relationships and events before, during and after a loss will crucially influence the course and outcome of mourning.

Loss: a core experience

It is almost a truism to say that 'the management of change is the management of people in change' (Marris 1974), yet we need to understand why it is so difficult an idea to act on, as a senior or first-line manager or practitioner, when introducing or responding to change. We shall suggest three broad reasons for this before pursuing in more detail the issues for supervisors.

1. The centrality of loss in human development

Different strands of psychoanalytic thinking (e.g. Klein 1946; Winnicott 1953) agree in highlighting the importance for secure development of the infant's capacity to face – and mourn – the reality that his mother (or primary carer) is a separate person with a separate will, and the consequent loss of the sense of being able omnipotently to control his world. Finding a way to deal with this is experienced as a matter of survival. In his classic work on attachment, Bowlby (1969; 1973; 1980) emphasises that the infant's capacity to cope resiliently with disappointment and with upsetting, unpredictable events is closely linked with having a secure relationship as a base from which to explore.

The growing body of research extending Bowlby's work (Ainsworth, Bell and Stayton 1971; M. Main 1993) has established that the responses of one-year-olds to brief separation from their mothers are significantly linked with the mothers' patterns of interacting with them; this holds good when the same children and their mothers are observed at six years. Moreover, parents' representations of their own childhood experiences of attachment and loss (and the effect of these on their development) are reliably predictive of their children's attachment behaviour (Fonagy et al. 1993).

The children observed in these studies fall into four groups, according to the kinds of attachment behaviour they display. Group B (about half of most samples) present a *secure attachment*, capable of being upset and cross at their carer's absence but also of being fairly quickly comforted on her return.

Group A (*insecure avoidant attachment*) behave in a manner that conveys superficial unconcern, diverting their attention elsewhere even when the carer returns. In the home situation this group might sometimes be aggressive towards their carers. Group C (*ambivalent/resistant insecure attachment*) convey a heightened emotionality that undermines autonomous behaviour. They are often clinging, and unable to be comforted by the carer's reappearance. Group D (*disorganised/disorientated insecure attachment*) present contradictory, fragmented and changeable behaviour, as though they had never begun to develop an organised pattern of attachment.

This summary does no justice to the complexity and range of the research, which is still developing and which, though impressive in its results, needs to be approached thoughtfully (Rutter 1995); for example, the crucial question of what might enable attachment patterns to change has yet to be fully considered. Our purpose in describing this work is to highlight the centrality of attachment, separation and loss as formative early experiences, building up characteristic 'internal working models' that influence later responses and meanings in every individual.

The four kinds of infant responses will be readily identifiable in the responses of many adults not only to personal losses but to major changes in their work environment. Adults' sense of personal identity may, to a greater or lesser degree, be bound up with occupational identity. Freud, when asked to define mental health, is said to have replied, 'the capacity to love and to work', and our choice of profession may lie as close as our choice of partner to the heart of who we are and how we see ourselves (Daniell 1985; Ruszczynski 1991). The way we manage change reveals, and challenges, how we manage ourselves and our expectations of others, more perhaps than any other aspect of our working lives.

2. Loss as the core theme in work with service-users

While coping with loss is a universal issue, the experience of loss is probably the core theme in professional work across all user groups: loss of childhood innocence, of the hope of being a successful parent, of physical functioning and health, of the expectation of a stable marriage or family, of sanity, of employment or housing, of life. The list is endless. We would argue that the struggle of practitioners, supervisors and managers to deal with the impact of loss in their work with users becomes mirrored upwards into the organisation and affects professionals' capacity to manage their own organisational and professional changes (see Chapters 5 and 7).

3. Change hits staff at all levels

While junior staff in an organisation understandably see the managers above them as imposing change on them – as indeed they are – it is also clear that senior health and welfare managers themselves feel less than ever in charge of the changes they are introducing and more at the mercy of rapid financial, political and legal change – which they too feel is imposed on them. Managing the feelings of staff about organisational change is arguably more difficult than containing a service-user's feelings of loss; with users, as Downes and Smith (1991) point out,

> we can leave them and their disturbing dynamics, detach ourselves and reflect on what is going on and then return to them for the next session. Somehow it is harder to do this with staff with whom managers spend a good part of their time, especially where the manager constitutes a large part of the 'problem' by being the one who is imposing change. (p.37)

Managers are thus in a position analogous to that of a parent who, grieving the loss of a partner, has difficulty in coping with the reactions of her child at the same time. This might take various forms: being too preoccupied with her own grief to consider the child at all; identifying with the child and confusing her own responses with his; turning to the child for comfort; or denying the child's concerns in a misplaced wish to protect him (but also herself) from having to experience distress. Supervisors similarly preoccupied will find it hard to provide a supervisory 'secure base' from which their supervisees can move out with confidence to their tasks.

The management of change

This then is the backdrop to the struggle of supervisors and supervisees to continue to focus on delivering a service amid change. The following example sets out some of the supervisory issues that can arise from the impact of change.

EXAMPLE 8.a

> With only a few months' notice, the acute admissions role of a psychiatric hospital was transferred to a district general hospital in a town some distance away. The former admissions ward in the psychiatric hospital retained the care of the more chronic patients who required frequent re-admission. These patients were well known to the ward staff but had previously formed only a proportion of the patients in their care. About half of the ward staff, mainly the younger

ones, moved to the new ward in the general hospital; those who remained, including the nurse manager, did so largely because of local personal commitments.

On a supervision course, the nurse manager presented his concern about his deteriorating relationship with one of his longest-serving male nurses. The manager conveyed with energy and enthusiasm the considerable effort he had put into building up his new team of staff, integrating old and new, and the generally positive results. However, in staff meetings, whatever the topic, the nurse in question always seemed to find something negative to say and was often critical of the manager's functioning. His behaviour in supervision was similar; when the manager had tried to talk about this, the nurse interrupted and did not seem to hear. The manager had also failed to get through to the nurse his concern about some aspects of his work.

In our discussion it appeared that the manager too might be finding it hard to listen, as he could repeat little of the content of the nurse's complaints, except that he felt picked on and was not getting what he wanted from supervision. When asked about his previous relationship with this staff member, and about his own response to the reorganisation, the manager's demeanour changed and he became slower and quieter. He spoke of how he had worked with this nurse on different wards for about fifteen years, and had always got on well with him. He was a conscientious nurse and, though lacking skills in some areas, could always be relied on in a crisis. A bond had developed between them early in their careers, through the support they gave each other when a previous ward they had enjoyed working on had been closed at short notice. The manager went on to speak of his personal and professional disappointment at the loss of enjoyable work and valued colleagues and his annoyance at not having been consulted by his line-manager about the changes or given more warning. However, since he believed – as a manager – that the changes made sense in terms of improvement of service to patients, he had determined to take a positive attitude and help his staff to do so too.

The understanding that emerged from this discussion focused on the responses of the two men, one black, one white, to the ward changes in the context of their previous shared history and the current team environment. The nurse manager's frustration was seen as an expression of his sense of betrayal at his colleague's negative response – which itself suggested a similar sense of betrayal at finding the manager not only unwilling to share with

him the sadness and anger at loss, as in the past, but seeming to put all his
energy into moving ahead with new staff members.

Three principles

To explore further the issues for supervisors in managing change, we now
reproduce three principles set out by Marris (1974), with our own commentary (extensive for the first of the three).

> 1. The process of reform must always expect and even encourage con-
>   flict. Whenever people are confronted with change, they need the
>   opportunity to react, to articulate their ambivalent feelings and
>   work out their own sense of it. (p.156)

Even managers who, having worked hard on essential plans for change, try
to keep in mind the emotional impact on staff (and their own doubts and
fears) can find it hard in reality to believe that opposition by staff has any
justification, let alone merit. Despite Marris' warning that 'every attempt to
pre-empt conflict, argument or protest by rational planning can only be
abortive' (p.155), there is a wish that difficulties should be sanitised by some
rational means. Training is sometimes used by managers and planners in this
way. For example, the generally thoughtful Department of Health (1991d)
guide for community care managers states, 'It is important that managers and
practitioners do not feel de-skilled or daunted by the scale or pace of change,
so any training must recognise and build on existing skills' (para. 105). We
know of only one in-house training department that responded to major
changes by running courses not only about their content but also on 'loss
and change'. First-line managers, who (like the nurse manager in our
example) are more often called upon to implement the plans of others than
to initiate them, face the additional predicament of how to act with the
authority of their role while knowing about their own anger or anxiety at
the changes; how to remain loyal to their own managers and not collude
with their staff, while at the same time acknowledging the staff's feelings.

At the heart of the dilemma for managers at all levels lies the fear that
conflict and resistance, once given a voice, would overwhelm and paralyse
the organisation with hostility, despair and negativity, rendering progress or
any effective action impossible. Schorr (1992) notes the differing responses
to his sobering report on the state of the personal social services:

> some who are furthest from the front lines have found it depressing
> and fear that it may provide an excuse for giving up. On the other
> hand, line workers have seemed to find relief and encouragement in

the report. They had felt isolated and alone in their perception of the difficulties; nor are they so far disposed to give up. (p.52)

This suggests that many senior managers may in fact secretly fear their own despair as much as, or more than, that of their staff.

Marris (1974) describes how change provokes 'a conflict between contradictory impulses – to return to the past, and to forget it altogether' (p.151). At such times, any belief in the inevitability of mixed feelings and the possibility of surviving them can quickly disappear; splitting and the triangle of persecutor–rescuer–victim then prevails (see Chapter 6). In Example 8.a, the split was enacted in the positive versus negative approaches of the two men. We have heard of staff in some organisations being informally labelled by senior managers in such split terms: 'the old breed', referring to those who voice the resistance and are not moving with the times; and 'the new breed', meaning those who are positive and not stuck in the past. Here the split in attitudes that management tries to promote, devaluing the past and idealising the future, becomes personalised. Insecure employment, meanwhile, puts pressure on staff to be seen as one of the relevant 'new breed'. Moreover, the experience of 'survivor guilt' following the redundancy of colleagues can numb the capacity of staff to speak their minds.

This kind of splitting in an organisation where mixed responses to change are not welcomed (reinforcing everyone's individual propensity to split off difficult feelings) is likely to result in unsafe practice as well as under-use of the potential creativity of staff in contributing to the changes. Being 'positive' to avoid pain is essentially a mechanism of manic denial (Klein 1940). We would suggest that the frantic 'spinning plates in the air' way of managing that seems inevitable to busy supervisors sometimes owes as much to the fear of stopping to think about difficult feelings as to the realistic pressure of work. Priorities then become determined by crisis – not a recipe for safe service-delivery. Those on the negative side of the split may feel trapped in a hostile or depressed mode, while of course many may veer uncomfortably between positive and negative feelings. We are again reminded of how young children respond to being separated from their parents. In the poignant films made by James and Joyce Robertson (linked with Bowlby's work and described in Robertson and Robertson 1989), which were so influential in earlier decades in changing institutional policies on parental visiting, the unvisited children first protested vociferously (a life-affirming response directed towards influencing their circumstances by getting adult attention), then moved on to despair and eventually detachment. The professional equivalent in the situations of change we are discussing might be initial conflict and opposition, followed by passivity and despair, and finally a 'cut-off' cynicism.

Thus, to repudiate the response of mixed feelings (in oneself or others) is also to lose the capacity to influence the course of events or control one's circumstances even in a limited way. In Example 8.a, the nurse manager's determination that his task was to 'sell' the changes to his staff robbed them and himself of the chance of more fully experiencing and processing the issues involved, forging a truer integration of past and future and learning a deeper control over their own human and professional responses. His limited protest to his own manager about the inadequate consultation and information concerning the changes also did little for his chances of influencing the way he might be treated in future. Even simply acknowledging the experience of mixed feelings, without doing anything dramatically different, may enable staff to be better prepared to withstand the strain. Managers who fail to 'visit' their staff's difficult feelings (literally, by staying away from their workplaces or by cancelling meetings or supervisory sessions; or metaphorically, by disallowing any expression of feelings) run the risk of behaving like children's ward staff before Bowlby – seeing parental visits as disruptive and unhelpful because they left the children angry and upset, and failing to differentiate between their own preparedness to face upset feelings and that of the children.

We should be under no illusion, however, about the difficulty and discomfort of the task of managing change, and the near certainty of not 'getting it right'. In the example, the nurse manager was conscientiously trying not to succumb to one of the greatest temptations in such circumstances, namely turning to familiar team members for reassurance and comfort in a collusion against senior management. Nor was his supervisee inhibited from expressing his opposition by fears about the nurse manager being so vulnerable or isolated that he needed to be 'looked after' – a frequent occurrence, in our experience, where 'concern' for an overburdened manager becomes yet another way of avoiding mixed feelings. It is never easy for managers to gauge how much and when to share information with staff or consult them about what valuable features of the old to hang onto and what to let go of. Downes and Smith (1991) describe how consultation with staff that is too extensive and prolonged can result in a lack of impetus and focus, while inadequate and hasty consultation will provoke excessive hostility. The essential issue is whether the struggle to consider the mixed feelings is engaged with, including whether mistakes can be acknowledged and the resentment survived without rejection. This is part of the containing function of supervisors and managers, which we shall discuss more fully in Chapter 10.

The second of Marris' three principles takes the discussion a stage further:

2. The process must respect the autonomy of different kinds of experience, so that groups of people can organise without the intrusion of alien conceptions. (p.156)

We would add: and so that individuals may also organise their own confused feelings. We have discussed so far the difficulty of coping with colleagues whose mixed feelings about change may be similar to one's own but who have different ways of trying to deal with them (that is, different defences). It may be even more difficult, however, to cope with those whose feelings are actually quite different. Marris makes the important point that reactions to change naturally reflect the nature of the changes themselves. He suggests three types of change. First, 'incremental or substitutional' changes which pursue the same purposes as before, so that 'the pattern of expectations remain essentially the same'; second, those that represent growth, but again do not threaten the integrity of what has been learned; third, changes that represent loss, 'either actual or prospective, from death or from discrediting of familiar assumption – a crisis of discontinuity' (pp.20–21).

Any group or individual in an organisation might allocate a particular change to any one of these categories. The nurse manager and his supervisee and the rest of the ward team, for example, might all have held totally different views about which type of change was embodied in the ward reorganisation. This is often true of old and new staff in teams, the old understandably being more preoccupied with the sense of loss and discontinuity while the new, less wedded to the past, welcome the developments (the prospect of which perhaps attracted them to join the agency in the first place).

However, to distinguish between genuine difference and the kind of 'splitting' group process we described earlier remains difficult. Further discussion with the nurse manager, above, suggested the possibility that these two men, locked in the opposition of their own positive and negative views, were also enacting a struggle on behalf of the ward team – about whether old and new could truly be linked, and how both the hope and despair of working with chronic patients could be acknowledged. On that view, it seemed no coincidence that they were the two most experienced members of the team who knew each other best, and might be expected to be the most robust to take on the struggle. The fact that one (the nurse) was white and one (the manager) was black, added to the sense that the two of them were engaged in a representative task for the multi-racial staff team in its continuing struggle about whether differences could be acknowledged and become a basis for development not division.

3. There must be time and patience, because the conflicts involve not only the accommodation of diverse interests, but the realisation of the essential continuity in the structure of meaning. (Marris p.156)

'Time heals' is a familiar saying in relation to personal loss, and it can be true in organisations that, with hindsight, individuals and groups may recall with amazement their opposition to innovations that are now valued or at least accepted. A long time-scale, however, is not easily sustained in a 'sound-bite' generation given to short term contracts, goals and structures. While agreeing broadly with Marris' emphasis in this third principle, we would stress that 'the essential continuity of meaning' involves acknowledging actual discontinuity when diverse interests are not accommodated. This would mean, for example, avoiding euphemisms when major cuts are implemented or when there is a real clash between old and new professional values. Otherwise, a 'cognitive dissonance' (Festinger 1963, p.17) arises, as professionals experience a discrepancy between their beliefs and their prescribed tasks and behaviour – a source of disempowerment and alienation, largely ignored by senior managers, that may prompt 'a growth in cynicism, in anti-professionalism, and an inclination to define their jobs privately while avoiding accountability' (Schorr 1992, p.31).

As noted earlier, Schorr suggests that senior managers themselves may feel as undermined as their staff, or more so. Marris (1991), however, shows how the burden of uncertainty imposed on them may be pushed down the line to junior staff (Chapter 1), who may be the most likely to respond with 'resignation; withdrawal from long-term hopes, purposes, or commitments; feelings of depression and hopelessness' (p.86). In some agencies, one is confronted with the professional equivalent of numbed, disorientated, confused, shell-shocked refugee children. In others, change may be more clearly seen as a preparation for growth and innovation, liberated from old restrictions.

The struggle to find continuity of meaning can present specific difficulties when change is only partial; the failed expectation of familiarity produces a particular sort of disorientation. We can all imagine the confusion, to take a minor example, if the secretaries' office at work were moved to another floor, and the frequency with which we would keep on going to the old location. More seriously, the same staff may continue to be employed by the same organisation to deliver a service – but a different service; or a similar service, but under a different management structure. Parkes (1975b) points out that the process of distinguishing which 'world models' are still relevant and which redundant may be particularly confusing when the loss is partial rather than absolute and it is not clear what, or how much, has been lost.

Finally, the 'realisation of the essential continuity in the structure of meaning' is dependent on maintaining a sense of historical context. For example, we have heard supervisors speak of having to function as the 'memory' of their supervisees' pasts when the latter, deskilled by new titles such as care manager or by unfamiliar new tasks, lose belief in the relevance of their previous work and experience. Supervisors themselves may lose sight of the continuing relevance of their previous practice knowledge, in their anxiety at feeling unprepared for managing a budget or adjusting to new legislation. Where a sense of history is ignored in case management or staff assessment, through a flight from either the past or the future, unsafe practice will become more likely and service planners will continue to 'reinvent the wheel'.

If we return for the last time to our example of the nurse manager and his supervisee, we find another illustration of how change can distort history, by producing a crisis which then comes to be seen as the starting-point of all problems. It was only in passing that the manager mentioned the nurse's lack of skills in some areas in the past; he mainly spoke of his recent failed attempts to take up some of these concerns. It emerged, however, that he had done little in the past to address these same problems, having enjoyed a somewhat collusive relationship with his supervisee and finding it difficult to confront the reality, since his promotion, of their no longer being peers. The crisis of change, which had required the manager to assert his authority in the team in a new way in order to implement the reorganisation, had shaken up this old defensive pattern between the two men. The resulting discomfort also offered the opportunity for a new, creative response to an old problem – a clear example of the potential for growth in experiences of loss, provided the necessary emotional processes are understood and worked through.

The impact of identification

As we noted in Chapter 5, mirroring can work in either direction. Professionals' struggle to cope with major change and loss at work cannot fail to resonate (consciously or unconsciously) with their experience of working with loss in the user groups they serve. Identifying with the pain of service-users can take a number of forms. Some practitioners may be enabled by attunement to the issues to work more sensitively with service-users' feelings. Others may become dismissive of feelings in service-users that are too similar to those they are finding it hard to cope with themselves (Halton 1995), and cut themselves off from knowing about the painful aspects of attachment for either. Yet others may turn to working with these 'fellow victims' as a source of emotional sustenance not available from their preoccupied peers or supervisors, with a consequent loss of professional focus. To ground these arguments in experience, we end the chapter with an example of a supervisor and practitioner who, despite their best efforts, became paralysed by over-identification with the service-user.

EXAMPLE 8.b

> A sixteen-year-old boy was referred by his special school to an adolescent psychiatric outpatient service. He was due to leave school in six months' time, but the school was concerned about his immaturity and his difficulty in facing growing up. The clinical team met with the young man and his mother, head teacher and year teacher. The team knew the head teacher well as an optimistic and caring man who was highly focused on the needs of both pupils and staff and provided regular supervision to year teachers on the interpersonal aspects of their work. At the time of the referral, however, the school had been under threat of closure for a year. There was a sense of escalating anxiety about this, since no alternative plans for pupils or staff had been confirmed.
>
> The year teacher told the psychiatric team she had not talked to the boy or his mother about what he might do on leaving school, as she would normally have done, because the future of the further education college she would have liked to recommend was also unclear. The head also felt there was no point in saying anything until there was 'something definite to say'. In a session with the psychiatrist, meanwhile, the young man very clearly said that he had wanted to talk to the teacher about his future, but felt unable to do so because he knew she and all the staff were upset about what was happening to the school.
>
> It took very little discussion between the psychiatric team and the teachers to confirm that there had been a paralysing 'fit' between, on the one hand, the professional and employment crisis of a school whose staff and head teacher were preoccupied with the losses threatening them and the service to which they were so committed and, on the other, the personal crisis of a boy and mother reluctant to face the losses intrinsic in the move to individuation and separation.

It could also be seen how the head teacher's total identification with his staff had deprived them of the containing function he was usually so ready to provide.

It was largely because of their high level of commitment that these professionals had become paralysed; however, their commitment also enabled them to seek help and use it effectively to get free of their paralysis and move on from labelling the boy as 'the problem'. The contribution of outside consultation to such committed teams or supervisor–supervisee pairs may at times be vital to effective service-delivery, provided the hidden or denied agenda can be clarified (as here). Whatever the ostensible reasons, invitations to consultants may often be triggered by an impending loss – such as a threatened closure or the departure of a key manager – whose impact is felt to be too powerful and all-encompassing to be openly faced in a staff group (Cardona 1994; Mosse and Zagier Roberts 1994).

CHAPTER 9

Calling a Halt
Exposing and Naming Differences

Sooner or later a supervisor may need to say, in one way or another, 'it's time we stopped and looked at what is going on'. We have already indicated in previous chapters a range of troublesome situations that might require the supervisor to do this, and a range of concepts available for making sense of them. The idea of calling a halt links these supervisory problems together and provides the gateway to understanding them.

As we discussed in Chapters 2 and 4, an initial supervisory contract provides a valuable framework in which to ensure that regular review of supervision finds a place amid the busyness of 'doing'. By building in evaluation, it allows for strengths as well as weaknesses, progress as well as blocks, to be considered. No contract, however, will prevent the need at times to call a more urgent halt, when the supervisor (or the supervisee) realises that some difficulty either seems to have become insuperable or is being avoided altogether, to the detriment of one or more of the functions of supervision. In this chapter, we shall focus mainly on the supervisor's role in calling a halt; this is a prerequisite for exploration of difficulties, and we start by looking at some ways of recognising when this is needed.

Previous chapters have provided many examples of how supervisors and supervisees may become caught up in confused or unfocused interactions with each other; we have highlighted how important it is for the supervisor to get involved enough to run the risk of becoming caught up, but also to be able to extricate herself so as to address the issue. Sometimes, difficult supervisory interactions like these may appear only briefly, in relation to a specific case or type of work; at other times, they may raise much more serious concerns about a habitual and highly unproductive supervisory dysfunction, or about a worker's basic competence. The difficulties may be consciously known about but unacknowledged by one or both participants; or they may be out of awareness but unconsciously enacted between them.

'Compelled' interactions

Hawkins and Shohet's (1989) terms, 'collusive transaction' and 'crossed transaction' (p.38), provide useful and simple tools for recognising some of the complicated interactions we have illustrated and explored throughout the book. However, since (in our experience) both can involve collusion, we shall call them *collusive supportive transaction* and *collusive crossed transaction*. An example of the first might be that the supervisee, seeking reassurance not challenge, behaves in a way that encourages the desired response from the supervisor; the latter duly takes up the required role, perhaps because it also meets her needs. This produces an inappropriately comfortable feeling, and an avoidance of difficult issues and supervisory requirements. A collusive crossed transaction, on the other hand, might occur between a supervisee who seeks reassurance and a supervisor who instead delivers judgement; the one feels continually blamed or misunderstood and the other feels compelled to be unreasonably judgemental. At an unconscious level, the supervisee may be inviting this contrary response which, again, may fit the supervisor's needs as well.

The characteristic feature of both these interactions is that both participants find themselves trapped in a way of behaving, usually without having consciously chosen it. They feel *compelled* to act in a certain way. The interaction may be initiated by either, or be equally attributable to both, but for it to happen there must be some hidden resonance for both of them, whose origins might be personal, professional or organisational. It is harder for the participants to become aware of a collusive supportive transaction, because of its relative comfort. Collusive crossed transactions are more noticeable; both participants may feel irritated, and a 'judgemental' supervisor may be left full of self-criticism at having yet again been so intolerant.

We have identified a third kind of 'compelled' interaction, which we call the *collusive parallel transaction* (not to be confused with the 'parallel process' mentioned in Chapter 5). Its main feature is the 'pseudo' nature of communication between the supervisor and supervisee, while both sustain the myth that actual communication is taking place. Each talks as if seriously responding to the other, but the conversation would sound to a listener more like two monologues, acknowledging the existence of the other but taking care not to meet – just as trains on two parallel lines may seem to approach each other but in fact pass without contact. Any possibility of exploration, difference, conflict or understanding is thus avoided. A covert rule of 'keep your distance' is operating.

Hawkins and Shohet suggest that the remedy for these compelled interactions is a *named transaction*, which occurs 'when one or other of the parties names the patterns and the games that are being played, so they become a choice rather than a compulsive process' (p.39). In our view, this definition (though pointing in the right direction) makes the important task of calling a halt sound rather simple, whereas in fact it is often a very complex and difficult intervention, a beginning not an end in itself. We shall discuss this more fully after the following example of multiple compelled interactions.

EXAMPLE 9.a

> The senior care manager in a social services team working with the elderly (which had been in existence three months) varied between worry, irritation and satisfaction in her attitude to one of her staff. She had known him for many years and had a casual, friendly relationship with him outside the office. The supervisor had previously (in her first management position) supervised the worker in a generic social work team, where she had been somewhat in awe of his theoretical knowledge and energetic commitment to advanced training, and had not really got to know his work well.
>
> In recent months' the supervisor had been reluctant to trust her own observation that the worker frequently seemed intolerant and dismissive in his attitude to the elderly women on his case-load and liable to give undue weight to the opinions of their carers in assessing their needs. When she did manage to raise this with him he denied it. The supervisor felt hampered by her knowledge, obtained in social contact with the supervisee, that he had been brought up largely by an elderly grandmother whom he had disliked, and that he had a difficult relationship presently with his mother, who was in a residential home. The supervisor had in fact been surprised when the worker had opted to specialise in work with the elderly. The supervisor was also irritated at the worker's casual attitude to writing up his assessments, which were repeatedly delayed. When she had taken this up with him she had been told, in what felt to her like a condescending manner, that she 'should not worry so much'. The supervisee had recently cancelled a number of supervision sessions, claiming he was overworked, but the supervisor did not feel that the amount of work explained the situation. The supervisor feared that her irritation had made her inappropriately sharp with him at times over unrelated matters, and she remained appreciative of the quality of his face-to-face work and his written work, once completed.

The supervisor knew she had been sitting on her feelings but should not go on doing so. She sensed that the supervisee was under stress and, in her heart of hearts, felt he might be in the wrong job. However, she was also anxious not to appear to be intruding, in her professional role, into the personal area of his relationships with elderly women. At times she felt she should wait to give him a chance to adjust to the new work, but sensed that she might just be rationalising her wish to defer any confrontation.

This example suggests something of the complexity and intensity of interaction between a supervisor and supervisee who are caught up in 'compelled' transactions. Very strong feelings, both positive and negative, may be engendered in one or both parties – of rivalry, envy, failure, fury and hopelessness, or of closeness, respect, dependence, co-operativeness and gratitude. It is important, therefore, not to underestimate the amount of professional determination and courage that may be required in order to call a halt and try to put words to concerns, however clear the need may be. The transactions here did not fit straightforwardly into any one of our categories, but were mainly of the collusive crossed (with each participant at different times seeking reassurance but meeting a critical judge instead) and collusive parallel types. A collusive supportive transaction had operated up to the point where the supervisor became conscious of suppressing her concern and being 'nicer' to the supervisee than she felt. However the interactions are defined, the supervisor's task of calling a halt and trying to name issues was a difficult one.

Naming

The term 'named transaction' coined by Hawkins and Shohet (1989) usefully reminds us that the task is to put words to issues that so far have been expressed largely through compulsive action. We need to extend their somewhat limited use of the term, however, to encompass the complexity of the task. The following three points highlight this.

1. NAME THE ISSUE – NOT JUST INDIVIDUAL EPISODES

Naming may often involve grasping the nettle of difficulties continuing over time. Instead of individual incidents being tackled separately as they arise, what may have to be addressed is the accumulation of concern about unsatisfactory performance or some stuck supervisory interaction. This means calling a halt to the habit of addressing issues as though they were discrete (and so more easily dismissed by a defensive supervisee), and ensuring instead a process of overall review in which a pattern might emerge that links them together.

2. NAMING DOES NOT ASSUME UNDERSTANDING

A supervisor may understandably feel more confident in naming her accumulated concern if she feels she has some understanding of the cause of the problems, but this is not necessary and not always possible. The essential thing to be named is the fact of something needing attention. The first intervention may be as general as 'I'd like to stop and think together about what's going on between us at the moment'; or 'I think over time we've become stuck in supervision in some way that I feel we need to look at'.

What is necessary, however, is clarity of thought about what issues are to be raised. Supervisors need to have considered the nature of their evidence, to distinguish what they are certain of from what they only suspect and to be clear about how they know what they know. They need to distinguish situations where they have clear grounds for serious concern (even though more exploration is needed) from those where the concerns have to be explored first to see what weight should be given to them. A third category might be where a supervisor is concerned mainly because of not knowing something (for example how the worker speaks to a service-user) and so needs to find out.

For the supervisor in Example 9.a, preparing to call a halt would mean thinking over the sequence of incidents that had caused her concern, including her own possible contribution. She would need, for example, to consider how far she felt she had the evidence to challenge directly the worker's claim to be overworked, or if she simply had doubts that she wished to voice and explore. In this situation, with a number of difficult issues, the supervisor needed to find a way of expressing the fact that she was generally concerned and felt it was time to review the supervisee's work and their supervisory relationship.

Naming at the point of difficulty is greatly helped if the supervisor and supervisee have previously discussed the concepts each uses in thinking about supervision. The ground is then prepared for referring to these concepts when considering the meaning of the current concern. Even if there has been no previous discussion, introducing the relevant concept at the time of naming, as a possible way of thinking about the dilemmas, may help to shift the interpersonal fixedness between the two participants.

3. NAMING IS ONLY THE BEGINNING

Once a decision to call a halt has been made, a process is set in train that can never be forgotten or reversed. The fact that a concern has been named will remain a shared experience of supervisor and supervisee, for good or ill.

Most supervisors, preparing to take up an issue, are highly mindful of this. At best, they would be raising something that even the most thoughtful supervisee might not initially want to hear; at worst, they might be opening up a 'can of worms'. A decision to 'name' requires facing the fact that time and energy will be needed to sustain the necessary exploration of the issue. Understandably, supervisors often delay the decision to name 'until the time is right', which may embody the unrealistic hope that it can be achieved without risk.

On the one hand, time for prior thought is clearly essential, especially if the situation is long standing. On the other, it is also necessary to have 'the courage of [one's] own stupidity' (Balint 1957) in reaching the decision to act. The capacity to stand firm and yet listen appropriately to the other – even be open to influence – is not easily sustained. In Example 9.a, for instance, the supervisor needed to stand firm about her concerns in the face of what might at first be a rather contemptuous response from the supervisee, but also to recognise that she might hear some justifiable criticisms of herself that would be hard to cope with but would need to be acknowledged. In such situations, supervisors may fear that a persecutory interaction will develop. Some may seek false comfort in the thought that the supervisee will agree – perhaps indeed feel relieved to be confronted – and that naming will thus provide a containment that may facilitate shared exploration. This may, of course, prove to be the case even in the most unlikely situations, but there is no guarantee of such an amicable outcome.

The fate of attempts at naming

Most of our examples in previous chapters develop situations up to the point of naming. In our courses for supervisors, we have frequently used role-play at this point, to study the experience of attempting to call a halt to particular dilemmas. One imaginary but realistic scenario we have used is as follows:

> A supervisor feels she does not really know what the supervisee does when face-to-face with service-users. She suspects that nothing exploratory or useful happens, and experiences the supervisee as defensive in describing his work in supervision, but her concern about not knowing has not been named.

Role-plays of this scenario tend to develop rapidly into authentically intense interactions. The following examples illustrate the main types of reactions and interactions we have observed, which we believe to be relevant to functioning in real life.

EXAMPLE 9.b

> The supervisor has thought hard about what to say to introduce the concern and does this well, but then tends to give up, or merely repeat herself, all her energy having been spent in the preparation.

The supervisor is then at the mercy of the supervisee's reactions.

EXAMPLE 9.c

> The supervisor does not mention at the outset that she has an important matter which she intends to raise; she does not name the fact of having a concern. Instead she tries to slide her concerns in during the course of the session, as though merely responding to other issues that arise. The supervisee normally spots this manoeuvre, wonders what is going on and often becomes more defensive.

The concern of the supervisor and the suspicion of the supervisee then become undercurrents that are not named.

EXAMPLE 9.d

> The supervisee comes with a lively issue for discussion and the supervisor's concern gets either pushed to one side or not mentioned at all.

Deferring the supervisor's issue may of course be appropriate if the supervisee's issue really is urgent but, needless to say, 'urgent' issues can also be used as deflections from fundamental concerns.

EXAMPLE 9.e

> The supervisee quickly moves into challenging the supervisor's 'naming', often by overstating the concerns she has voiced (e.g. 'are you saying you think my work is no good?'); the supervisor then, in effect, collapses, reassuring with a rapid 'no, not at all' and not persevering with the specific concerns that do exist.

This is a powerful example of the persecutor–rescuer–victim triangle in operation. The supervisor fears being a persecutor to the victim supervisee; the supervisee indeed feels victimised and reacts by becoming a persecutor in turn; the supervisor, now feeling the victim, rescues herself and the supervisee from any further conflict.

EXAMPLE 9.f

> The supervisor introduces her concerns in a peremptory way, brooking no discussion. Inevitably, the result is either an angry conflict or the collapse of any self-defence by the supervisee.

No exploration can take place about the issues, which may indeed become aggravated.

EXAMPLE 9.g

> The supervisee becomes quiet, reacts passively or subtly turns the tables on the supervisor by asking lots of questions. The supervisor finds herself 'in the hot seat', doing all the work as though the problem is hers alone. She then either attempts to use persuasion, convinced that if she explains enough the supervisee will see the rightness of her concern, or speaks as if assuming the supervisee will of course have similar concerns.

This kind of interaction actually embodies and replicates the supervisory problem – that is the supervisor's difficulty in getting the supervisee to take responsibility for describing the work. Observers often comment on the *collusive parallel* nature of the transaction – a surface communication and agreement between a seemingly benign supervisor and a passive or compliant supervisee, with an undercurrent (later confirmed by both role-players) of increasing fury. The attempt to name has thus intensified the existing dilemma, but at least a first step has been taken towards exploring it. The first attempt is usually the most difficult for supervisors and, however unsuccessful it seems at the time, provides some groundwork which can be returned to in the future.

Despite all these pitfalls, many supervisors do display a skilled capacity both to state the case and to explore supervisees' responses; to recover their stance when dislodged from it, and to be open about their own failings without losing the ability to challenge those of their supervisees. When confronted by supervisees who say the equivalent of 'are you saying you don't trust me, then?', they will be able to pursue the matter along such lines as 'I don't know whether I do or not, because I realise I don't really know your work and that is not safe for either of us'.

Fusion versus differentiation

Commendations of a warm, trusting relationship between supervisor and supervisee as a basic foundation for supervision occur so frequently in the literature as to seem platitudinous. More importantly, they beg the important question of how trust is achieved and what happens when, as often, it does not seem to exist and yet the supervisory relationship has to continue. Without some exploration of what is meant by trust, there is a danger of confusing ends with means (as we said about 'support' in Chapter 3).

We are not, of course, questioning the value for a supervisory relationship of mutual respect, and trust in each other's professional integrity, honesty, goodwill and concern. We would argue, however, that trust has to be earned; it is never a 'given', and never achieved by avoiding difficulties. We have heard supervisors speak of focusing on 'building up a good relationship' with new supervisees as a reason for delay in taking up difficult issues; or, in long-standing relationships, of having to be careful how to raise concerns for fear of 'breaking the supervisee's trust'. Whilst timing is certainly important, these attitudes suggest that 'trust' and 'good relationship' may often be synonymous with collusive support, where the presiding preoccupation is the wish to maintain a myth of agreement and sameness and avoid the possibility of conflict. A more fruitful aim would be to achieve a relationship of honest respect. The dilemma for supervisor and supervisee lies less in understanding this distinction than in acting on it. In practice, the pressure to be 'at one' – to avoid all difference or (more precisely) differentiation – can be considerable.

Here we would emphasise that exploring the differences that inevitably arise from factors such as gender, race or disability, though essential (Chapters 4 and 6), is not enough. Other, less visible, interpersonal or professional differences may also affect the supervisory interaction. It is only too easy, where there are race or gender differences, and especially when the supervisor is white or male, either to address all kinds of differences as if they were solely attributable to these factors, or not to address any difference at all for fear of being seen as racist or chauvinist. Either response may be the result of misplaced anxiety not to breach anti-discriminatory principles, but both may have profoundly discriminatory effects (Brummer and Simmonds 1992). Conversely, there is the trap of thinking 'there isn't a gender issue in our team – we're all women'. Race and gender, indeed, are areas 'especially prone to defensive certainties or fears of disagreeing, where real difference in all its complexity is difficult to explore' (Hughes and Pengelly 1995, p.166). A serious commitment to anti-discriminatory practice, and to valuing the differences stemming from race or gender, is no protection against the difficulty of engaging with interpersonal or professional differences.

The childhood roots of the problem of differentiation

Let us consider some of the factors in human development that may contribute to the universal difficulty of acknowledging and exploring difference. Psychoanalytic theory sees the achievement of individuation and acceptance of difference as outcomes of the Oedipal phase of development; the conflicts of this phase confront the infant with the fact that her/his relationship to the mother is of a different order from that of the parents to each other, from which the infant is excluded (one of the early losses referred to in Chapter 8). Modern post-Kleinian writers (e.g. Britton 1989) emphasise less the specifically sexual aspect of this, focusing more on the infant's struggle to come to terms with the reality that the prime carer has other preoccupations, concerns and thoughts besides those directed towards her/him. This is a major developmental step for the normal, happy infant whose 'omnipotence' has had enough scope to flourish but who must now come to terms with its limits. At the other extreme, the infant who has not had sufficient opportunity to feel 'at one' with a 'maternally-preoccupied' carer, but instead has been confronted early on by one too preoccupied with her/his own concerns to be able to focus on the infant's need, is prone to experience all later differentiation as betrayal or persecution. There is then a constant pressure to avoid this, either by trying to fuse with others or by shunning any close, intimate contact that might lead to disappointment.

Professionals working with disturbed service-users will often have had the experience of being apparently viewed as benign, but then rapidly dismissed as useless or persecutory if they dare to express a view independent of the service-users' wishes. More difficult for competent professionals to face is that such infantile reactions may also re-emerge in themselves from time to time. Mature functioning, however, means accepting this; to deny it is to claim omnipotence, since in reality no one survives these childhood conflicts unscathed.

Professional problems of differentiation

What anxieties, then, may be aroused by differentiation in professional life? Some terms used to describe anxieties in the Oedipal drama could equally be applied to those in a supervisory relationship: shame at exposure; humiliation at feeling small or a failure; fear of isolation; envy of others 'having it all'; feeling at the mercy of powerful others who do not have one's interests in mind. Stressful work contexts heighten the pressure to regress. Supervisors may, for example, feel isolated within their management hierarchy and wish to compensate by feeling 'at one' with their teams. Supervisees,

feeling continually battered by their contact with service-users, may understandably long for peace and total agreement with their supervisors.

Supervisors who call a halt are essentially re-establishing their differentiation from their supervisees, stepping firmly back into the supervisor's
corner of the participants' triangle (Chapter 3), away from a collusive
huddling in the practitioner's corner. Even so, many supervisors are tempted
to believe that the purpose of calling a halt is to persuade the supervisee of
the rightness of the supervisor's views – that is, to become 'at one' – rather
than to establish a more honest discussion that might in fact open up the
extent of the differences between the two participants. If agreement is
reached, it will be a bonus rather than an aim. Supervisors who express a
fear in terms of 'if I say that, he won't feel safe and he'll hold things back
from me' are deluding themselves, and forgetting that they too consciously
(quite apart from unconsciously) reserve the right to be selective about what
they tell their own managers. When a halt is called, it may be painful for a
supervisee to acknowledge that he feels too angry or unsafe to share some
matters, but if that is the reality then it is an essential prerequisite for any
continuing honest discussion.

The 'third position'

To take a stance based on differentiation requires confidence and the capacity
to maintain a *third position*. This refers to the capacity of either supervisor or
supervisee to observe and think about her/his own behaviour in the
interaction, while remaining involved in it. It is the capacity that is absent
when supervisor and supervisee are locked together 'eyeball to eyeball',

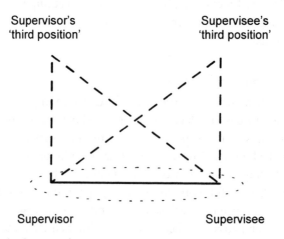

Figure 9.1 'Third positions' in supervision

struggling to persuade each other or to avoid facing difference. As Figure 9.1 indicates, each participant's 'third position' will give a different perspective; honest discussion comes from each recognising the validity of the other's perspective and trying to develop a dialogue, not from rushing too quickly to close the gap between them.

Returning for a moment to psychoanalytic theory, we note that finding a 'third position' perspective is a further achievement of negotiating the Oedipal phase of development more or less successfully. The adult's capacity for observing her/himself in interaction is founded on the infant's learning to tolerate the experience of observing interaction between others (e.g. mother and father) from which s/he is excluded, and the converse experience of her/his own interaction with either parent being observed by the other (Britton 1989; Wright 1994).

The capacity to maintain a 'third position' can also be compared to Casement's (1985) notion of an 'internal supervisor' with whom a practitioner may have an internal dialogue about the interaction in which he is currently engaged, when working with service-users. This grows out of the experience of having had an actual supervisor with whom such a dialogue could take place externally; in our terms, this self-observing function sets up an internalised version of the participants' triangle as a working aid to thinking about the situation one is in. Likewise, one of the arguments currently made for the increased use of child observation in professional training (Trowell and Miles 1991) is that it can enhance trainees' capacity to consider their own responses in emotional situations and to distinguish between themselves and the objects of their observation.

The supervisor on the line

However fortified a supervisor may be by such personal and professional learning experiences, calling a halt and taking a 'third position' is always liable to be a painfully anxious business, especially when she anticipates that the supervisee will not readily engage in honest dialogue. A brief example may focus our thinking.

EXAMPLE 9.b

> A supervisor in a voluntary agency, in post for one year, had taken up one issue of concern after another with a supervisee. The supervisee had usually responded irritably or patronisingly, providing an 'answer' which the supervisor felt unable to challenge, but which left her feeling dissatisfied and wrong-footed. She felt concerned but unable to produce solid evidence, especially as much of her information came

from other staff and she herself was based in an office some way from that of the supervisee. Her own supervisor (who was also the supervisee's previous supervisor) was generally supportive, recognising the pattern as a long-standing one. This middle manager was perceived by the supervisor as rather weak – kindly, and wishing things to be different, but unable to help the supervisor think about how to move on. They both felt inhibited by the fact that the supervisee was a close friend of a senior manager in the agency.

Presenting her work on a supervision course, the supervisor described how, in the supervisee's absence on leave just a few days before, she had received a phone call from an outside agency about a highly worrying situation, causing statutory concern, in one of the supervisee's most difficult cases. Unable to find the file in the locked filing cabinet where all case notes were supposed to be kept, she found it with a number of other files in the supervisee's desk drawer. She discovered that no recording had been done on this case and others, and also that apparently no action had been taken on a number of referrals allocated to the supervisee.

Relief at having at last got some clear evidence of negligent practice rapidly replaced the supervisor's anxiety about the case – only to be further replaced by shock at realising that, amid all her worries about the supervisee's work, she had omitted to check the files for some time. This was accompanied by shame and anxiety about how her own performance would be viewed. She belatedly realised that her failure to insist on seeing the supervisee's files (whereas she readily looked at those of other supervisees when the need arose) arose from her wish to avoid provoking another conflict. She quickly discussed the situation with her own supervisor, who supported her plan to confront the supervisee strongly on her return, and urged her to consider taking the first steps in the agency's disciplinary procedure. The supervisor did not feel confident that her supervisor would sustain this strong position if major conflict arose. However, she was determined to be firm the next week when the supervisee was due back.

In the supervision course discussion, there was a ripple of acknowledgement when one participant said 'then next week you'll have one of those "sleepless nights" beforehand'. Everyone present knew the amount of anxiety produced by the prospect of such a confrontation, and the amount of energy needed to sustain exploration of these issues and cope with the responses of the supervisee, other colleagues and managers.

This example highlights how taking up failures of a supervisee may draw attention to failures of the supervisor – in this case, not having checked the files. Even without such a specific omission, supervisors may often feel that to involve their managers in discussion about confronting problems with their supervisees will reflect on their own shortcomings as supervisors. The myth that a good supervisor ought to be able to sort everything out can be compelling in the behaviour, even if not in the rational thoughts, of hard-pressed supervisors (Dearnley 1985). Some supervisors, moreover, have actual experience of their senior managers not welcoming any discussion of problems with staff. There may be a pervasive organisational wish to 'turn a blind eye' and avoid confronting problems, as an institutionalised defence against anxiety (Chapter 7). This is seen dramatically in publicised cases of 'whistle-blowers' who try to expose institutional corruption or abuse, inevitably presenting managers with delicate and difficult staffing crises and usually receiving a highly ambivalent response.

Steiner (1985) argues that the key issue overlooked in most accounts of the myth of Oedipus is not the discovery that (as foretold) he had killed his father and married his mother, but the shocking evidence that everyone had in some way known all along what was happening but had chosen to turn a blind eye to the truth, so as not to have to take responsibility for what they saw. Twyman (1984) applies a similar insight from this story to child-protection work, likening social workers and foster carers to the 'whistle-blowing' servant and shepherd who had saved the infant Oedipus' life but who were vilified, when they eventually spoke out, by those implicated in his parents' attempt to kill him and in the subsequent cover-up.

In this perspective, it is arguable that the internal dynamics of many agencies leave professionals vulnerable to being caught up in mirroring a key fear of service-users – namely, that revealing worries that might reflect on their own functioning will provoke a persecutory rather than an enabling response.

Backing for the supervisor's authority

The supervisor poised on the brink of a serious confrontation with a supervisee, as in Example 9.h, is therefore well advised to explore first the backing she is likely to have from her own supervisor, and to clarify the extent and limits of her own authority to act. In that example, it might have been helpful for the supervisor to ensure that some written record was made of her discussion with her supervisor and the agreed plan of action. Clarifying the parameters of authority will usually help a supervisor to exercise it in the most enabling way possible, as well as providing a space within which she may be able to think and maintain the 'third position'. Our experience of running courses suggests that the first main task in this space is for the supervisor to have the courage to explore the fear of the 'worst scenario'. Facing this may start to generate some understanding of her concerns about the supervisee's work, and her own worries about the effects of calling a halt. It may also free up the energy until then caught up in the covert or scarcely voiced worries. In Example 9.h, the supervisor's worst scenario involved fears of being exposed to the supervisee's fury, abandoned by her own supervisor and blamed by the supervisee's senior manager friend while the supervisee was exonerated. Facing the worst scenario enabled the supervisor to prepare herself by recording for her supervisor a summary of their discussions, to think through how she would take up the matter of the files with the supervisee, and to expect to have to build on the process over many supervision sessions and so be less anxious about the initial outcome. Without ensuring time and space to manage the depth and range of feelings involved, to plan and 'rehearse' what needs to be done, and even to experience the anxiety of the 'sleepless night' before the confrontation, supervisors will run the risk either of rushing into precipitate action (perhaps authoritarian, perhaps disorganised), or of avoiding the confrontation yet again.

Backing for the practitioner's authority

Not surprisingly, the parallels in work with service-users are considerable. Long-standing supervisory concerns, as in the last example, are reminiscent of the kind of worry about safety and care in the lives of service-users which can preoccupy professionals over many years, with chronic uncertainty about what weight to give to accumulated, piecemeal information (as opposed to clear-cut evidence), and an ensuing lack of decisive action. In such situations professionals can vacillate endlessly between anxious concern and turning a blind eye. One of the clearest parallels is in the child protection field, where cases of child neglect often produce a response of worried impotence, out of a concern to balance the risk of harm against the need for continuity of care; in the end the professional response may itself be neglectful of the interests of such children, in contrast to cases of acute abuse (Minty and Pattinson 1994). The supervisor's response in Example 9.h, of almost welcoming a crisis in which the evidence at last became unmistakable, will be very familiar to practitioners in cases of child neglect.

Clearly, practitioners will be more likely to develop the capacity to call a halt in their work with service-users if they have experienced their supervisors doing the same with them in supervision, with constructive results. Indeed, in critical cases the two processes may need to go hand in hand. The key professional task in such cases is to survey the scattered history of incidents and interactions and think about how they may be linked together. Reder, Duncan and Gray (1993), in a thoughtful review of child-abuse inquiries, highlight the frequent failure of professionals to integrate available fragments of historical information that, fitted together, would have conveyed the potential seriousness of the situation. Inquiries into homicides by psychiatric patients (e.g. Ritchie 1994) have pointed to the same issue. In practice, however, this is often no easy task, with changes in personnel and in whole agencies as well as the constant pressure of work on the practitioner. It is the task of the supervisor, at one remove from direct contact with service-users, to ensure that the pieces derived from history and from different parts of the network are put together. Calling a halt in supervision may in this sense be the prerequisite for calling a halt in the case.

The hidden wish to call a halt

Our examples so far have referred to calling a halt by supervisors, but we conclude with a reminder of our earlier statement that it can be done by supervisees too. This applies most readily where a supervisee is concerned about problematic practice (his own or the supervisor's), or about the supervisory interaction, but it may also be a way of ensuring that good practice is sufficiently acknowledged.

Sometimes, however, the supervisor may pick up a wish to call a halt that the supervisee is hardly aware of, or has not consciously expressed. In particular, the supervisee's choice of (or way of presenting) case material to discuss in supervision may represent an implicit attempt to communicate to the supervisor a concern about some similar issue in the supervisory inter-action. Likewise, it is the experience of many trainers and consultants that the material selected for presentation in a work-discussion group may echo current issues in the dynamics of the group at that time. Langs (1994) takes the extreme stance of relating all case material to issues in the supervisory relationship, as the central pivot of his approach to supervision in psycho-therapy training. While we would not espouse such a dogmatic position (which minimises the often urgent need for attention to the case material in its own right), we nevertheless suggest that a supervisor who fails to hold this dimension in mind may overlook some of the supervisee's own attempts to review what is going on in supervision. The following example illustrates what we mean.

EXAMPLE 9.i

> The new manager of a child psychiatry day unit was undertaking a three-month supervision course, as part of which he was taping (both audio and video) some of his supervision sessions with staff for presentation to his course tutor. He had been thoughtful in drawing up supervisory contracts with his staff members, who had until his arrival had no regular supervision. He had also been thorough in preparing his supervisees for being recorded, and careful to obtain their written consent. Neither the supervisor with his course tutor, nor the staff members with their supervisor, had appeared concerned at having their work exposed in this way.
>
> In their penultimate tutorial, the supervisor presented to the tutor a recent supervisory session with one member of staff with whom (he had once commented) he felt he had a mildly competitive relationship. The audio tape began as usual with the supervisor checking consent to record; the worker expressed irritation at being asked every time about this, adding that by now it must be clear she had no problem with it. She went on to say she felt she had nothing she really needed to discuss. In response to the supervisor's questioning, however, she began to recount a session with a disturbed six year old girl on the unit. The girl's family seemed reluctant to have any contact with the unit and had given little information about themselves. The worker described what had been a typical, difficult session, with the girl rejecting her overtures and the worker having to make difficult decisions about when to 'follow' the child and when to insist on limiting her overactive behaviour in the room. She seemed to have handled the situation well up to the point when she had suddenly heard someone, probably a staff member, go into the room next door. She told the supervisor that she had immediately lost her confidence at this point, explaining that she always felt hypersensitive to being overheard and possibly criticised. In speaking of this incident, the worker's voice and tone became noticeably shaky and lacking in confidence. The supervisory session continued with discussion of the difficulties of engaging with this child.

In discussing this supervision session with his tutor, the supervisor said he was concerned about the degree of the worker's anxiety at being overheard, in a unit where there was a lot of shared work. He wondered how much this was a general problem for the worker, and how much might be the effect of a mirroring dynamic (from working with this child and family who seemed so secretive and resentful of contact). Further exploration in future supervisory sessions would clearly be needed, he thought, to understand and disentangle the issues. The tutor, however, focused on the worker's choice of this particular issue to present, out of others she might have chosen, at this point towards the end of the experimental recording of supervisory sessions. She pointed out the discrepancy between the worker's avowed unconcern about the sessions being taped (to be heard by an unknown person – the tutor) and her acute anxiety at being overheard by a colleague. The question the tutor raised was not that the issue of being overheard was not relevant in its own right, but that the worker's timing in referring to it might owe at least as much to issues in supervision as in her work with the child. Exploring the tutor's idea, the supervisor could see that it might be easier now for the worker to indicate misgivings about the recording or even about the supervision itself than at the start, acknowledging that he himself had been both so keen and so anxious in setting up the recording arrangements that, despite his careful attention to the detail of consent, he might not have been very open to considering his staff's misgivings; this worker might well have picked this up. Now that he felt more confident about the value of the experiment, and about his own supervisory work, he might be better able to listen to her need to call a halt.

Both tutor and supervisor then noticed the additional relevance of this discussion to their own working relationship, including the supervisor's choice of presenting this tape at this point to the tutor. The supervisor acknowledged just how unsure of his supervisory practice he had been when he first came on the course, and how painful it had been at times to expose it; but he now felt more confident about exploring his strengths and weaknesses. As in the supervision, so in the tutorial, the initial careful contracting, though important, could not remove difficult feelings. The inevitable doubt about a relationship that was going to require a high degree of exposure could not easily be explored at the start, but needed to be discussed at some point if an honest and thorough assessment of the supervisor's development during the course was to be made. The supervisor's choice of presentation could then be understood as his own totally unconscious attempt to call a halt, to ensure that a discussion took place with his tutor about his earlier doubts and his subsequent growth in confidence.

Supervisory interactions may indeed be very complex and take place, as here, on many interconnected levels.

CHAPTER 10

The Use of Authority
Challenge and Containment versus Persecution and Collusive Support

The use of authority in supervision has been a key theme underpinning the previous nine chapters. We have delayed discussion of authority *per se* until this last chapter in the hope that, following so many examples of the struggle to act with proper authority, we have by now established the need to avoid either a facile endorsement of its importance or a blanket dismissal of it as destructive of creativity. We go on to look more directly at the use of authority to contain the experiences of the supervisee within the framework of supervisory functions and organisational task, in order to enhance service-delivery; in this connection we also explore the analogy of parenting. Before concluding, we discuss supervisors' need of containment for themselves if they are to function effectively.

Authority

Authority can be understood only in the context of interaction; it is expressed in relation to someone or something. Moreover, it is seldom if ever true that one person has a monopoly of it. Although in this chapter we focus mainly on the authority of the supervisor, the supervisee's authority must always be in mind, and many of our comments refer to both.

The sources of authority

Not surprisingly, the question of where authority comes from has for decades been a key area of exploration in writing on supervision (e.g. Pettes 1967; Payne and Scott 1982), while distinctions between power and authority in organisations have also been defined in a number of ways (e.g. Grubb

Institute 1991; Obholzer 1994a). Drawing on these, we find it helpful to distinguish three sources of authority.

1. ROLE AUTHORITY

Within an organisation, this confers the 'powers over people, finance and resources which are delegated by higher management and employers. Authority is delegated to a position in order that the person in the position can do the work and meet the responsibilities of the position' (Øvretveit 1993, p.125). Therefore, the nature and extent of the authority need to be carefully related to those of the responsibilities. This authority does not have to be earned by the individual in the role; it comes with the job and includes, where applicable, aspects of the statutory authority and responsibility with which the organisation is charged. The supervisor's role thus provides the authority to oversee the supervisee's work, while the supervisee's role requires him to acknowledge this authority and provide the supervisor with the information necessary for her to fulfil her role.

2. PROFESSIONAL AUTHORITY

This is 'based on demonstrated competence, particular knowledge and skills and credibility' (Clare 1988). It may be gained through professional training, but is only manifested and recognised through being practised, and in this sense it is earned. This is not the same as mere attribution; authority may be more readily ascribed to some professionals than to others on the basis of status rather than expertise (for example, to doctors rather than social workers), with obvious dangers of abuse. Nevertheless, to be effective, professional authority must be sanctioned by those to whom it is directed (who exercise their own authority in doing so).

In supervision, it is professional authority that the supervisor uses in struggling both to differentiate and to integrate all the various sources of her authority; and that the supervisee uses to manage himself in a way that acknowledges his need for supervision and enables him to use it.

3. PERSONAL AUTHORITY

At one level this refers to the capacity of some people, by their demeanour and the way they manage themselves, to establish a natural authority and communicate it to others. More significant to our purpose, however, is the wider sense in which a person's attitude to authority permeates her/his own way of exercising professional and role authority and responding to that of others.

In the intimate arena of supervision there is no escaping the impact of the two participants' individual attitudes to authority. One of the arguments sometimes made against individual (as opposed to group) supervision is that it tends to encourage passive–dependent or autocratic attitudes to authority (Sproul-Bolton 1995); we would reply that, although authority issues may present in different forms in different supervisory structures, individual attitudes to authority will always affect any relationship that involves accountability, development and assessment.

Each individual has her/his own internal authority figures, models in the mind formed by the filtering of experiences with authority figures in the past – familial, professional and other (Dearnley 1985); these form part of the 'internal society' (Menzies 1970) referred to in Chapter 1. The individual's relation to these internal models 'is crucial in affecting how, to what extent and with what competence external institutional roles are taken up' (Obholzer 1994, p.41). In supervision, as we said in Chapter 2, conscious and unconscious expectations derived from past supervisory experiences will be particularly influential. The key issue is the extent to which these projections are fixed, how much they can accommodate to the reality – personal, professional and in role – of the current supervisor or supervisee, and whether they can adjust in the light of new experiences. 'Compelled interactions' of the kind we described in Chapter 9 may often embody attitudes to authority that are under the control of fixed projections.

Underpinning the exercise of any authority is the individual's capacity to manage her or himself; to know about her/his own strengths, weaknesses and anxieties; 'to manage the boundary between our inner world and the external environment, between our individual self and the group, in order to be the author of our own actions' (Zagier Roberts 1994d, p.190). This is a core personal attribute that has to be mobilised in any effective exercise of professional or role authority.

Managing the tensions

The complex connections between these three sources of authority lie at the heart of the supervisory examples we have discussed in previous chapters. Supervisors and supervisees who rely solely on the authority of role will tend to mechanistic implementation, characterised by coercion and compliance. Those who pursue professional concerns or expertise in a way that exceeds their legitimated authority of role put themselves, their supervisees and service-users at risk by abusing the power of their professional status. Sole reliance on personal charisma to influence others, ignoring the nature and limits of role and professional competence, results in the assertion of illegitimate power only.

Some tension between the three kinds of authority is inevitable if authority is to be exercised thoughtfully and non oppressively. For example, supervisors or supervisees may need to use their professional authority to question a decision made by someone above them, alongside their simultaneous recognition of the latter's role authority to make the decision. Those who, especially in today's climate, find the different forms of authority too much in conflict with each other may be faced with the difficult choice between resigning or having to accept what feels unacceptable. In the face of internal and external pressures to ignore one or more kinds of authority, managing the tension between the three is essential to effective supervisory functioning. This tension bears some relation to the tension between the three corners of the supervisory functions triangle described in Chapter 3.

Authority: factors that help and hinder

We need to respect the difficulty of the supervisory task of acting with thoughtful authority. All our examples of the work of good supervisors have highlighted the pressures on them to be either collusive or persecuting, 'suckers or bastards' (Mattinson and Sinclair 1979). Various ways of understanding these pressures have emerged through the chapters, but five key factors – some perennial, some more contemporary – need to be emphasised.

1. THE SOCIAL CONTEXT OF AUTHORITY

To place authority in its wider context we can do no better than quote from Zagier Roberts' (1994d) thought-provoking paper, 'Is authority a dirty word? Some dilemmas in idealistic organisations', which explores 'changing attitudes towards authority as evidenced by shifting patterns of behaviour in families, in organisations and in society generally' (p.185). Describing authority as a quality currently under attack, she notes that there is

> greater anxiety...about taking initiative, perhaps greater fear of being blamed, of raising one's head above the parapet. But there is also less consensus about the leader's inalienable right to executive action, including within managers themselves. Instead there appears to be only an inalienable right to dispute authority, without offering alternative leadership. (p.191)

She points out, however, that without a belief in the possibility of a good-enough authority 'there can only be stronger and weaker, the exercise of power: the parents who resorted to force, the "really tough" manager who was to whip the recalcitrant team into shape, the distant powers-that-be' (p.191). She suggests that the difficulty staff in care services may have in valuing authority is related to the conflict they experience when their motivating idealism is confronted with the harsh realities of 'market forces'. This is the context in which supervisor and supervisee meet.

2. THE PROFESSIONAL'S WISH TO BE LIKED

Within this context, supervisors have their particular difficulties in claiming authority. No matter how mature their attitude, most supervisors will sometimes find it hard to make overt the authority of role or expertise that separates them from their supervisees. We spoke in Chapter 9 of the supervisor's struggle to occupy the 'third position' in order to differentiate between herself and her supervisee; as Kadushin (1976) points out, in doing so she has to deny herself 'the sweet fruits of flattery, the joys of omniscience...and the gratification of being well liked' (p.252). Most people entering the caring professions are motivated to a great extent by a wish (indeed a need) to help others, and a corresponding expectation of being seen as helpful. The 'caring' or more obviously enabling side of authority may then be espoused easily; but combining 'care' with 'control', however acceptable in principle, is likely in practice to be uncomfortable. Some supervisors may escape this tension by abandoning the 'care' that brought them into the profession and concentrating only on the 'control'. Most, instinctively preferring 'care', are likely to become aware of their use of authority only when they are obliged to exercise it in pursuance of 'control'; this may simply reinforce their negative view of authority, and their difficulty in distinguishing between authoritative and authoritarian action.

The further fear that opening up differences in role and expertise might unleash powerful feelings such as anger, jealousy, envy and competitiveness is evident in the struggle to 'name', which we explored in Chapter 9. Zagier Roberts (1994d), drawing on the work of Miller (1990), vividly identifies the dread of some supervisors and first-line managers that to act in a way that differentiated them from their staff would be tantamount to abandoning the 'missionaries' (or 'blue jeans') committed to involvement with service-users, and siding with the 'mercenaries' (or 'grey suits') in the market place. The exercise of considerable authority of all kinds is required of such managers in order to look both ways (as discussed in Chapter 1), up and down hierarchical lines, and to hold the tension rather than enact the split.

3. MIRRORING NEGATIVE VIEWS OF AUTHORITY

Meanwhile, the 'missionary' practitioner is also exposed daily to painful issues of care versus control, which he may convey into the supervisory relationship. It is hard to overestimate the force with which professionals' belief in benign authority can be attacked through the experience of work with service-users in most front-line services. We would argue that a core dynamic incessantly available for mirroring is the perverse belief that care and control cannot co-operate with each other – that authority can be caring only if collusively denied, and if actually exercised is inevitably punitive and destructive. This corresponds to the rescuing and persecuting dynamics described in Chapter 6, and can leave professionals feeling powerless about their use of authority (the victim position). In the area of child sexual abuse, for example (as we discussed in Chapter 5), perpetrators and adults who allow themselves to be blinded to what is happening deny and abuse the authority of adulthood. Here, as in other areas (such as work with the psychiatrically or physically ill, or the elderly), practitioners may find it hard to know when intervening with authority is caring rather than oppressive and intrusive, when withdrawal constitutes thoughtful care rather than collusive neglect. The mirroring pressure on the supervisee to perceive supervision as persecuting is therefore considerable; even good supervisors and supervisees are likely at times, under such pressures, to behave in persecuting or collusive ways. We cannot repeat too often that understanding this intellectually does not remove the shock of being caught up in these dynamics, and especially of being experienced as persecuting when one is struggling to care.

Difficulties in 'marrying' care and control can also become entangled with gender-defined expectations. As touched on in Chapter 4, nurturing and enabling ('care') may be pigeonholed as the preserve of women, leaving decision-making, limit-setting and essentially depriving functions ('control') to men, with little regard to the need for these 'maternal' and 'paternal' qualities to be held together within each parent and every adult – including practitioners and supervisors. The mirroring effect upon professionals when their experience with service-users affords no sense of a benign co-operating parental couple, or other co-operative adults, is consistently underestimated, and can grievously interfere with their capacity to work together within or between agencies (Woodhouse and Pengelly 1991, p.254). Joint working between male and female professionals may at times be an invaluable way of heightening awareness of 'split' perceptions of authority and, through mediating these, offer the possibility of managing it with greater understanding (Conn 1993; Ruszczynski 1992).

There may also be a downward mirroring of senior managers' inadequate use of authority to hold together the twin concerns of caring for needs and controlling limited resources. At the same time, senior managers are always ready targets for projective identification by their staff as persecutors, however thoughtfully they use authority. Here, too, it is hard to address carefully the frequent reality of power differentials between the genders when stereotypes reign as 'truths'. Images of controlling men invariably in senior positions, with junior women doing the devalued 'housekeeping' and attending to matters of personal interaction, can be as much polemic as descriptive. The solution, sometimes proposed, that organisations should become more 'womanly', that is caring, and that women should combine caring with being more assertive (e.g. Grimwood and Popplestone 1993), comes close to perpetuating the view of 'male' authority as merely persecuting and negative (Reynolds 1994), while promoting 'female' authority as omnipotent rather than realistically limited. More helpful is the argument that a real increase in the number of women in senior positions might alter the balance of attributions and influence the way work is understood and managed (Hanmer and Statham 1988); this recognises the need to promote a partnership between 'male' and 'female' qualities in all managers.

This is clearly an area where it may be hard to tell what is a mirroring dynamic, what a feature of a persistent oppressive supervisory interaction, and what the influence of belief systems current in the social context which practitioners, supervisors, managers and service-users alike inhabit. Whatever the source, supervisors will find their personal and professional authority taxed as they struggle to manage these issues in themselves and in interaction with their supervisees.

4. SERVICE VALUES

The principles embodied in policies of empowerment, partnership and non-oppressive practice may easily be colonised by welfare organisations for the purpose of bolstering rather than challenging the existing power structures and relationships involved in service-delivery (Braye and Preston-Shoot 1993). Even where there is a genuine struggle to deliver services in a manner that aims to address power differentials and combat discrimination, the process may paradoxically lead to confusion about appropriate authority and a belief that to explore difference is dangerous (with consequent denial or stereotyping of difference as discussed especially in Chapters 4 and 6). The call to partnership with service-users, for example, can either help or hinder the thoughtful use of professional authority. At best, it clearly encourages professionals' respect for the authority of others, requiring clarification of different sources of power and authority and a willingness by professionals to question their assumptions. At worst, a debasement takes place, where partnership is falsely equated with sameness, and collusive avoidance of disagreement masquerades as respect. Professional and role authority then become denied in an atmosphere of unfocused idealism or unthinking political correctness, and authority is once again confused with abusive or discriminating power.

In their work on partnership with service-users in social services departments, Marsh and Fisher (1992) suggest that careful exploration of the sources of authority might provide a more empowering service. They uncovered

> problems arising from the lack of clarity about the boundaries of the authority to intervene where the two basic forms of authority for service, either users' requests or court requirements, are confused and conflated in social services' practice... We found that this confusion particularly applied to work in child protection where explicit legal authority is lacking but authority is nevertheless taken to impose intervention on users and little attempt is made to clarify to users their choice in receiving service. (p.21)

It is easy to see how such confusion and avoidance can also infiltrate professional relationships including supervision. Zagier Roberts (1994d) describes how, in a voluntary agency team committed to anti-oppressive practice,

> there was a growing body of unstated rules, the most powerful being that everyone was equal and the same. The team regarded interdisciplinary rivalry and abuses of power as the greatest threat to their objectives, and strove to obliterate all differences between individuals, disciplines, hierarchical levels, and even levels of expertise and competence. Although there was a designated team leader, she could not be allowed – nor allow herself – to have any power or exercise any authority. (p.187)

In similar vein, Øvretveit (1993) describes how a commitment to normalisation in services for people with learning difficulties may produce a covert side-effect of seeing all differences as divisive. 'Some of these teams are still able to value professional differences in skill and knowledge while also minimising power differences, but it is a difficult balancing act' (p.142).

5. INADEQUATE ROLE DEFINITION AND AUTHORISATION

Øvretveit, speaking of team leadership in community care, also brings us back to the definition of role as a source of authority.

> It is fashionable to emphasize leadership style and abilities rather than the formal position... However, there are limits to personal power, and for a team to work the formal leadership role must be defined and agreed by management and appropriate to the type of team. (p.121)

This was relevant in many of our examples in earlier chapters, where the formal authority the supervisor had to take up difficulties was not sufficiently clear, the role and responsibility of more senior managers in relation to poor performance by practitioners was ambiguous, or the supervisor was not given sufficient historical information to fulfil her task. Sometimes supervisors' professional and personal concerns could lead them to feel responsible for tasks that they did not have the clearly legitimated power to implement; the failure of senior managers to take up difficulties could easily be experienced as the personal or professional failure of the junior manager or supervisor.

More fundamentally, wherever agency requirements about the nature and purpose of supervision (as discussed in Chapter 2) are unclear, ambiguous or absent, the authority of the supervisor to make decisions is undermined; so is the capacity of the supervisee to complain (that is, use his authority as a consumer of supervision) when he is not getting what he needs from his supervisor. In this context, we have frequently been struck by supervisors' own vagueness about their agencies' disciplinary procedures. While some may take flight into procedures as an easy alternative to using supervisory authority to tackle concerns about practice, most supervisors would be surer of their role authority if they were more familiar with their agencies' procedures and their own managers' views about how, and at what point, formal disciplinary steps should be embarked on.

Role authorisation, moreover, is an even broader matter than this. It requires that agencies provide resources adequate to the responsibilities to be undertaken; otherwise role-holders cannot be said to have been fully authorised (Sutton 1997). The 'double-bind' message conveyed by unacknowledged contradictions between sweeping role definition and inadequate role authorisation is one of the major current sources of stress for first-line managers and supervisors. It causes particularly painful tension between personal and professional authority on the one hand and role authority on the other, and requires difficult decisions about when to compromise and when to make it clear that some responsibilities cannot be accepted.

Authority as empowerment

Clarity and confidence about the parameters of authority, from all sources, allow authority to be exercised in a more enabling way. Anxiety about the parameters tends to produce rigidity or fuzziness, whereas greater confidence encourages a less defensive or compliant attitude to the views of others. Many managers have drawn our attention to the fact that confident exercise of authority by senior managers is a prerequisite for clear delegation of tasks and responsibilities to first-line managers in a way that allows for creative variety, not fragmentation of service (as discussed briefly in Chapter 9). For first-line managers, such confidence from their seniors allows them a more flexible approach and more thoughtful risk-taking. It enables them to acknowledge their limits, seek help as necessary and use the experience of others, including their supervisees.

By the same token, we come to the somewhat paradoxical fact that, in order to empower supervisees, supervisors too need to exert more rather than less authority, be it by tolerating the anxiety of letting supervisees follow their own judgement, delegating appropriate responsibilities to them or confronting their questionable behaviour (a paradox familiar to any parent, as we shall discuss later). Thus supervisors, especially if appropriately empowered themselves, can provide powerful role models to practitioners about the nature of empowerment – essential if practitioners are in turn to work with service-users in a way that is truly empowering of them (Stevenson and Parsloe 1993).

Containment

Like authority, *containment* is a term so familiar that its meaning can be either taken for granted or misconstrued. Sometimes it is seen, even in relation to supervision, as synonymous with control, taking charge or putting the lid on a difficulty from outside, as the fire brigade might 'contain' a fire or the police a riot. Conversely, it can be debased to mean little more than collusive support (Chapters 3 and 9). We would define containment, however, as the process by which authority becomes translated into effective interaction.

An antidote for 'nameless dread'

The term as we use it derives from Bion's (1959; 1962) concept of the *container* and the *contained*. This refers to the mother's task of being open to the bombardment of her infant's inchoate emotions; of 'taking them in', processing them and trying to understand them. By her stance and response she can modify and transform the infant's terrors and fury, conveying to him the new experience of his powerful feelings being survived, 'detoxified' and made sense of. The infant is then able to take back into himself, not just the modified feelings, but the additional experience of a 'containing mother' – the foundation for his later capacity to contain his own experiences in a similar way. Bion (1959) contrasts the plight of the less fortunate infant, having to deal with 'a mother who could not tolerate experiencing such feelings and reacted either by denying them ingress, or alternatively by becoming a prey to the anxiety which resulted from introjection of the infant's feelings' (p.104). In the first case, such a mother may act as a persecutor or rescuer, to wipe out the feelings that need containing; in the second, she becomes the victim of them and loses any capacity to contain. In either case, the infant's terrors could only escalate with the experience of his feelings being uncontainable. In these ways, containment is conceptually linked with *projective identification* (Chapter 5), the earliest and most enduring form of human communication.

If we translate the concept of containment into everyday experience, for example in a carer's response to the desperate crying of a baby, we see the 'good enough' (Winnicott 1949b) carer as one who is capable, despite inevitable lapses, of being affected by the crying, of struggling to think what it means and what will help, and of continuing to know about the pain even if no immediate solution is forthcoming. On the other hand, over-identifying with the child's pain may render a carer paralysed by anxiety and unable to tolerate the child's cry. This can prompt a rush into action by, for example, rapidly providing a comforter or shutting the door on the sound to block out the experience; or it may produce a neglectful inaction. Physical child abuse often occurs when a carer feels overwhelmed by briefly 'letting in' the impact of the infant's cry, but then attacks to get rid of it.

Bion imagines the experience of the uncontained infant as one of *nameless dread*. It is a term uncomfortably pertinent to the experience of free-floating anxiety known by many front-line professionals today, and one that is instantly recognised by participants on supervision courses.

Containing the feelings in order to do the work

Though some aspects of Bion's model are not relevant to supervision, we can readily see some supervisor–supervisee parallels in the carer–infant interactions he describes. We now consider more specifically the application of the container–contained model to supervision.

The need for the supervisor to empathise with the supervisee's experience and be open to being influenced has been fully discussed, especially in Chapters 3, 5 and 6. In turbulent times, professionals' own experience of uncontaining environments frequently serves to escalate their anger or anxiety into almost speechless fury or despair – states of mind unlikely to provide containment for the feelings of service-users. The mental and emotional space required of supervisors struggling to provide containment for such workers is considerable; shortage of time for supervision, however real, may frequently be pleaded to avoid the anxiety of being unable to cope with the feelings if they were allowed to emerge (Nathan 1993).

Britton (1992), elucidating Bion's theory, describes the first quality of containment as the sense of being in a 'bounded, safe place', similar to what Winnicott (1960) calls a 'sense of being held'. In supervision, the consistency, regularity, clear boundaries and minimising of intrusion that we recommended in Chapter 2 contribute vitally to this. Nathan (1993) adds that clear, realistic agency procedures and guidelines may serve a similar purpose.

The originality of Bion's concept lies in his emphasis on the close relationship between thought and feelings. The container's second quality is the capacity to apply understanding to anxiety-laden experiences, in order to give them shape and meaning. They thus become 'contained'. The purposefulness of this activity is crucial to supervision. As discussed in Chapters 3 and 5, the aim in attending to a supervisee's feelings, as part of his working experience, is not merely to be 'supportive' but to explore them in order to discover the information they provide. This affords understanding not only about the worker but about the work itself, putting words to the situation to prevent the build-up of 'nameless dread' which would either paralyse the worker or catapult him into action as a means of avoidance. To take responsibility for seeking meaning may challenge the supervisor to face the anxiety of not knowing. It is often difficult for a supervisor to believe that the supervisee may be contained just by her capacity to name the problem and struggle alongside him to find meaning while acknowledging that she does not yet know. 'Sometimes, for the worker to understand the process is enough. As he comes to understand, he will be less of a victim' (Blech 1981).

The concept of containment highlights the intense interaction and interdependence, but also the essential difference, between the container and the contained. In order to be a robust as well as responsive 'container', the supervisor needs to be able to maintain the boundary of authority while tolerating being pulled by the supervisee into one corner or another of the supervisory triangles (Chapter 3). The fact that the container and the contained are not the same as each other is crucial; consider, for example, the difference between a supervisor who says 'I know exactly how you feel about this case, it reminds me of…' and one who, though holding her own experience in mind, remains focused on exploring that of the supervisee.

Containment thus provides a concept for the capacity both to be truly (rather than collusively) supportive and to challenge effectively. What supervisee really feels he can be reliably supported by a supervisor too weak to maintain her different position and face the discomfort of challenging him? One supervisor, thinking about this, described her experience of frequently feeling 'like a sponge', saturated by her supervisees' feelings and demands –

an image that vividly conveyed how she had lost the ability to distinguish her own feelings and thoughts from theirs, and with it the capacity to provide containment. Challenge will be reliable and non-persecutory only if it is based on hard thought about all the relevant feelings as well as other facts.

Containment therefore involves the supervisor in having her own internal dialogue between thought and feeling, as well as a dialogue with the supervisee, before deciding on action. This will be implicitly, and often explicitly, conveyed to the supervisee. As with the infant, it also offers a model for the supervisee to develop his own dialogue with an 'internal supervisor' (discussed in Chapter 9), that is the capacity to think about what is happening before rushing into action. It serves, too, as a model of appropriate self-care.

Supervisors themselves, however, are subject to the same impingements from their working environments as their supervisees. When even trainers away from the workplace have to struggle to contain the persecutory experiences that professionals bring (Foster and Grespi 1994; Hughes and Pengelly 1995), it is unrealistic to expect supervisors to provide containment unless it is also reliably available to them. We shall return to this at the end of the chapter.

Authority and containment: a parenting analogy

So far we have been applying aspects of child development theory and research to the supervisory context directly and formally. We now take a different (and more playful) approach, exploring some of the images that arise when supervision is compared to parenting. The analogy can be pushed too far – and sometimes is, by those who cherish the fantasy of the supervisor as idealised parent. Conversely, it is sometimes vehemently rejected by those who (personally or professionally) regard all parents as suspect. What seems inescapable is that supervisor and supervisee bring to their adult work relationship many issues about parenting absorbed from their personal and professional experiences, which may be colouring their interaction helpfully or unhelpfully. In our training courses this analogy has often sparked off in supervisors images and associations that they find illuminate their own supervisory predicaments. Picturing some family situations in the context of supervision has helped some supervisors to understand aspects of their intensive interactions with supervisees. Our purpose is not to cast the latter in the role of children, but to examine how the 'parental' associations of supervisors can influence their approach to supervisory responsibilities. Many of the following ideas come from supervisors we have worked with.

Collusion and persecution

The usefulness of the analogy lies in the way it can help supervisors uncover some of their unconscious enactments of common parenting dilemmas. For example, some supervisors (perhaps those who most object to the analogy) may go to great lengths to avoid infantilising their supervisees for fear of making them dependent; they may be caught up in the current contempt for dependency as weak and parasitic. They might wonder, however, if they are acting like parents who neglect their responsibility for what is done under their roof by even the most grown-up offspring, and their authority to decide what is and is not acceptable. This might hold good regardless of the relative skills and knowledge of the 'grown-up' practitioner and the supervisor.

Other illuminating parental analogies are more readily accepted. The collusive parent who seeks support in long discussions with a child while failing to send him to school, or identifies with a child's delinquency against authority, can be echoed by a supervisor who abdicates authority by stances such as 'I'm really the goodie; it's the senior managers who are bad'; or, 'I'm glad you felt you could tell me that' (while doing nothing to help with whatever 'that' is). Alternatively, the authoritarian parent who over-disciplines and has no capacity to relate to a child's emotional needs is paralleled in a supervisory stance of 'remember who's the boss'; or, 'surely professionals don't get upset?'.

Developmental stages and needs

The normal work of parenting involves struggling to mediate between what the parent wants, what the child wants or needs and what the social context requires – not dissimilar in some ways to the task of mediating between the three supervisory functions. Some qualities desirable in supervisors are readily parallelled in normal parenting capacities: to enjoy seeing the supervisee develop; to acknowledge having negative feelings towards him at times or different feelings towards different supervisees; to have a sense of self-worth that does not depend wholly on the supervisee's success in the eyes of others (especially senior managers).

Many supervisors, like parents, struggle to develop their own autonomous style rather than simply repeat – or reverse – their early supervisors' patterns; many are well aware of the difficulty of trying to give to the next generation good experiences they have not known themselves. Hesitations about the parenting analogy may indeed spring in part from its reminder of the awesome responsibility of supervisors and their influence for good or ill (as discussed at the start of Chapter 2). Supervisors have told us, with hindsight, that it was easier for them to 'play' with the analogy before they became supervisors; nowadays it only underlined the weightiness of the task and their fear of not being up to it.

In Chapter 4, we touched on the developmental approach to stages of professional functioning; these provide further analogies. Some supervisors find newly-trained supervisees (the 'younger child') easiest, with their need to be told how to do things and with the locus of decision-making being more clearly in the supervisor. Holding back as supervisees 'grow up' professionally may be difficult for these supervisors. On courses, supervisors often present problems with 'adolescent' supervisees, with all the difficulties of knowing what is the appropriate authority to exercise as they agonise about how and when to insist on control and when to allow independent action, in a context of continuous risk assessment. 'Young adult' supervisees may be experienced as a support and joy, bringing in fresh ideas and new skills, or as resistant and competitive; in either case there is the danger, already mentioned, of the supervisor losing sight of her role authority. Almost inevitably, supervisees who 'grow up' well will 'leave home' as part of their career development and many supervisors know the sense of sadness and loss that accompanies such success. As one supervisor said, joking at the parental analogy, 'they've just become good company when they go'.

As professional development proceeds, it often becomes harder to distinguish between a supervisee's stage and style; in any case, as we said in Chapter 4, progress through the stages is seldom clear cut. Many supervisees present dilemmas parallel to those of children with specific or general developmental delay, or suffering serious ill health, and the supervisor has to assess the nature of the problem and the areas where remedial help is needed. Persistent problems of this kind may cause anxiety in the supervisor about the supervisee's capacity to cope 'in the outside world', or anger at having to confront such problems, plus worry about the long-term future of a supervisee who seems unable to exercise reliable independent judgement. It should also be expected that supervisees, like children, may regress to an earlier mode of coping when under stress, which may be very difficult for supervisors who are under similar stress themselves. In this connection, Sutton (1996) makes the interesting point that issues in the (professional) developmental stage of the supervisee may be intensified if they reverberate with the (personal) age or stage of a particular service-user.

Different 'family' constellations

Many of the difficulties supervisors present on courses are bound up with the recent history of supervisory or team relationships. Playing with images of different family histories and structures can open up understanding of the areas of difficulty. Here are a few examples.

Locum supervisors or those acting up in the absence of the permanent supervisor may have feelings familiar to carers in short-term family placements. They face the dilemma of making a real, involved contact that gives full consideration to previous experiences, while at the same time constantly having an eye to preparing for the end of the 'placement'. The temptation is either to deny the temporariness or to use it as an excuse to remain detached. The situation is often complicated by the way short-term arrangements often drift into long-term, while remaining officially temporary.

Turbulent times produce turbulence in supervisory histories, and we have been struck by how many new supervisors face supervisees or teams whose recent experience has been of frequent change-over of supervisors, many having departed under considerable stress. This may have left the supervisees feeling as though they had 'killed off' their supervisors. The parallel with permanent carers or adopters taking over the care of children with disrupted placement histories helps to clarify the feelings. The new supervisors may be faced with suspicion and hostility, or denial of anxiety about the breakdown of previous arrangements, and – full of hope about putting things right at last for the supervisees – may resent the fact they are not readily welcomed.

Other teams with powerful shared histories, especially where the previous supervisor had been there a long time, or where a period of extreme difficulty has just been survived, may be fiercely loyal to the old ways as part of their sense of identity. A new supervisor appointed from outside may well feel very uncertain about the basis for her authority, much as a new step-parent might. This will be exacerbated if her appointment follows a period when a team member was temporarily acting up – one of several situations that reverberate with the dynamic of the oldest child who becomes 'parentified', carrying responsibility without proper authority, perhaps after the death or departure of one parent. There can be similar reverberations for supervisors who are promoted from within their teams and have to struggle to maintain the 'generation' boundary of authority, or for senior practitioner supervisors in teams led by team managers.

Supervisors often feel guilty about the different feelings they have for supervisees whom they 'inherited' and those whom they were involved in appointing – echoing the distinction some parents feel between step-children (or others placed in the family) and their own biological children. Supervisors have referred to the closer bond they feel with their 'biological children', together with greater commitment, higher risk of collusion and increased sense of failure at difficulties.

The supervisor as single parent is the most powerful image of all. Two kinds of reaction are common when this analogy is evoked. The first (embodying a just determination not to pathologise single parents) is to insist that the competent supervisor is able to combine 'maternal' and 'paternal' functions. This reaction often rapidly gives way to the second, which is to stress the amount of pressure and hard work that indeed confronts a single parent. Similar links can then be seen between the supervisor's plight and that of many single working parents (and non-single working mothers too) – taking on more and more, being pulled in all directions, never feeling that they do enough of anything or do anything properly, having to farm out certain aspects of their 'parenting' responsibilities but then having to find the time and energy to maintain good relationships with the 'child-minders' (reminiscent of our discussion of supervisors' relationships with consultants in Chapter 3). The temptation is to turn to the 'children' for inappropriate support amid the isolation and busyness, especially when 'extended family' or 'grandparents' seem remote. How hard it is to keep an eye on what the 'children' are doing, let alone devote proper time and attention to their developmental needs.

Containment for supervisors

Many supervisors feel keenly the isolation of being in effect 'single parent' supervisors, with their own supervisors increasingly removed from any engagement with the details of service-delivery. In most agencies, despite the Department of Health's (1991b) recommendation (specifically to social services departments regarding child sexual abuse work), there is a startling lack of arrangements for supervisors to meet and consult each other about their work; again, the parallel is with single parents who rarely get out and meet other adults. The reasons for this must be various, but the consequence is that most supervisors miss out on the additional strength they would have if they co-operated, and have little sense of the cardinal importance of their role throughout the agency. Even though some senior managers clearly do pursue a 'divide and rule' approach, many supervisors are also reluctant (as discussed earlier) to expose their own doubts and uncertainties to each other, especially in what they feel is a competitive climate. In our own experience, one of the most important features of an in-house supervision course is often the trust that can develop between first-line manager colleagues who had been virtual strangers; this can provide containment for their work after the course has ended.

To continue the parenting analogy, we know that children grow up most happily if they sense that their parents' lives are relatively contented, or at least that the parents can take care of themselves and are not dependent on their children's presence, or success, for their well-being. We also know, from the classic study of depression in single mothers by Brown and Harris (1978), that one reliable preventive factor is a confiding relationship with another adult. For the sake of her own professional health and that of her supervisees, therefore, a supervisor needs to ensure that she has for herself a professional confiding relationship, an adult 'partnership' that can provide containment; this is important regardless of the supervisor's capacity to have a dialogue within herself or with an 'internal supervisor', as we discussed above.

There is no doubt that supervisees are more likely to be contained if they feel their supervisors are contained and taking care of themselves (Brown and Bourne 1996, pp.26–7). Yet the task is formidable. Halton (1995) speaks to supervisors as well as practitioners when he asks, 'How can providers of care working in this disabling atmosphere keep themselves in a suitable frame of mind to look after others?' Some ways of doing this are suggested; however difficult, most are essential to safe practice.

- Supervisors need to value their supervisory role enough to give themselves *adequate time to think* about it, whatever the pressures on them. We suggest that when booking supervision times they also book in time, before and after sessions, to gather their thoughts and clear their minds in preparation, and reflect on the session before something else intervenes. In the post-session time, or soon afterwards, they also need to provide themselves with space to write up their supervisory notes, and not unthinkingly assume that the time will somehow appear (or else that this task will inevitably have to be fitted into 'overtime').

- If *supervision of her supervisory work* is not available, a supervisor needs to raise this with her manager as a matter of concern. This can seem difficult, particularly when she feels the issue is her manager's inability to provide appropriate supervision. Reluctance may also be fuelled by resentment at having to ask for what should be an essential resource, or by anxiety about revealing need. However, having once exercised their professional authority to take the matter up, some supervisors have been surprised at the professional competence and authority they have re-awakened in their managers, resulting either in better supervision or in appropriate alternative arrangements being made. Even in situations where resources are unlikely to be brought forth by such a professional request, supervisors able to express their needs may nevertheless benefit from having thus freed themselves from the victim position. They may additionally protect themselves by placing their protest on record.

- Similar considerations apply to requesting *appropriate supervisory training* from time to time (not just when newly appointed).

- Supervisors also need to argue for *realistic agency policies about supervision* and the powers and duties of supervisors.

- Any lack of *resources necessary for supervision* should be firmly pointed out. These can range from obvious practical matters like a room to the provision of a regular consultant to whom one or other supervisory function can be delegated (where the situation makes it impossible for one person to carry all of them). Making such demands may be the most important use to which a supervisor puts her professional authority.

- Finally, supervisors – who (like parents) spend so much of their time and energy on the development of others – need to decide on the areas in which they wish to *continue their own professional development*, and make sure they nurture these. Like previous suggestions, although this requires energy it may also free energy.

The last point is especially important since supervision is for much of the time a thankless task (Dearnley 1985); if it succeeds in helping supervisees, it does so by prompting the development of their own ideas and practice, which is not immediately attributable to the supervisor. Øvretveit (1993) observes that if a team leader is good the team will say 'the team decided, we did it ourselves' (p.135). Gratitude may sometimes be a later bonus, but cannot be a current expectation in supervision any more than in parenting. A supervisor needs her own sense of professional worth and development because, when all is said and done, she will probably have to rely on her own evaluation of whether she has been 'good enough'.

Conclusion

We ourselves have needed confidence in our own professional authority as we have attempted, in this book, to examine the realities and necessity of supervision amid contemporary turbulence. In stressing the essential inter-connectedness of process and task, our confidence in the continuing rele-vance of this way of thinking to an ever-changing world has been bolstered by our recent experiences of training supervisors from a wide range of disciplines and agencies.

Yet, throughout, we have been acutely aware that providing a thoughtful supervisory space in the organisational contexts where supervisors and first-line managers now work feels increasingly like an 'insurmountable' task (Waters 1992). The turbulence and contradictions of structure and ideology put enormous pressure on any capacity to provide containment. Any individual exercise of sane, mediating authority may be undermined by organisational and social failure to hold the inevitable tension – or bridge the chasm – between needs and resources, dependency and autonomy, care and control, feelings and actions. Moreover, whatever changes there may be in political fortunes and ideology in the coming years, turbulence is assuredly set to continue.

In such a context, our persistence in defining supervision as a place where tensions can be experienced and managed runs the risk of being seen as unbearably persecuting by staff who are struggling to survive. This can prompt a flight into either denigrating supervision as an out-of-date luxury or nostalgically idealising some 'golden age' when everything was possible (which makes the current tasks seem even more impossible). We remain convinced, however, that supervision is 'a life-saver not a luxury' (Dearnley 1985), and that active and connected attention to all three functions of supervision, linking process with task, is indispensable to the safe delivery of services.

As we said in Chapter 2, the history of supervision is notable for the gap between written exhortations and the actuality of supervisory practice. This book can be useful only if readers take their own authority to select whatever ideas help them to think realistically about what they do.

References

Addison, C. (1988) *Wandsworth's Study and Review of Supervisory Practice*. London Borough of Wandsworth Social Services Department.

Agass, D. (1992) 'On the wrong track: reflections on a failed encounter.' *Journal of Social Work Practice 6*, 1, 7–17.

Ainsworth, M., Bell, S. and Stayton, D. (1971) 'Individual differences in strange-situation behaviour of one-year-olds.' In H. Schaffer (ed) *The Origins of Human Relations*. New York: Academic Press.

Andersen, T. (1987) 'The reflecting team: dialogue and meta-dialogue in clinical work.' *Family Process 26*, 415–428.

Ash, E. (1988) *Acceptable Risk? Supervision in Child Abuse Cases Video and Training Guide*. London: Central Council for Education and Training in Social Work.

Ash, E. (1995) 'Taking account of feelings.' In J. Pritchard (ed) *Good Practice in Supervision*. London: Jessica Kingsley Publishers.

Atherton, J. (1986) *Professional Supervision in Group Care*. London: Tavistock Publications.

Bacon, R. (1988) 'Counter-transference in a case conference: resistance and rejection in work with abusing families and their children.' In G. Pearson, J. Treseder and M. Yelloly (eds) *Social Work and the Legacy of Freud*. London: Macmillan.

Baldwin, N., Johansen, P. and Seale, A. (on behalf of The Black and White Alliance) (1990) *Race in Child Protection: a Code of Practice*. London: Race Equality Unit, National Institute for Social Work.

Balint, M. (1957) *The Doctor, his Patient and the Illness*. Tunbridge Wells: Pitman Medical.

Biggs, S. (1994) 'New lamps for old: introducing the dynamics of community care' (Editorial). *Journal of Social Work Practice 8*, 2, 99–101.

Bion, W. (1959) 'Attacks on linking.' In W. Bion (1984) *Second Thoughts*. London: Karnac Books.

Bion, W. (1961) *Experiences in Groups*. London: Tavistock Publications.

Bion, W. (1962) 'A theory of thinking.' In W. Bion (1984) *Second Thoughts*. London: Karnac Books.

Blech, G. (1981) 'How to prevent "burn-out" of social workers.' In S. Martel (ed) *Supervision and Team Support*. London: Family Service Unit/Bedford Square Press.

Borland, P. (1995) 'Supervision in a statutory agency.' In J. Pritchard (ed) *Good Practice in Supervision*. London: Jessica Kingsley Publishers.

Bowlby, J. (1969) *Attachment and Loss, Volume I. Attachment*. London: The Hogarth Press.

Bowlby, J. (1973) *Attachment and Loss, Volume II. Separation: Anxiety and Anger*. London: The Hogarth Press.

Bowlby, J. (1980) *Attachment and Loss, Volume III. Loss: Sadness and Depression*. London: The Hogarth Press.

Bradley, G. and Manthorpe, J. (1995) 'The dilemmas of financial assessment: professional and ethical difficulties.' *Practice 7*, 4, 21–30.

Braye, S. and Preston-Shoot, M. (1993) 'Empowerment and partnership in mental health: towards a different relationship.' *Journal of Social Work Practice 7*, 2, 115–128.

Bridger, H. (1981) *Consultation Work with Communities and Organisations*. Aberdeen: Aberdeen University Press.

Britton, R. (1981) 'Re-enactment as an unwitting response to family dynamics.' In S. Box, B. Copley, J. Magagna and E. Moustaki (eds) *Psychotherapy with Families: an Analytic Approach*. London: Routledge and Kegan Paul.

Britton, R. (1989) 'The missing link: parental sexuality in the Oedipus complex.' In J. Steiner (ed) *The Oedipus Complex Today: Clinical Implications.* London: Karnac Books.

Britton, R. (1990) *Fundamentalism and Idolatry.* The Lincoln Clinic and Institute for Psychotherapy Annual Lecture.

Britton, R. (1992) 'Keeping things in mind.' In R. Anderson (ed) *Clinical Lectures on Klein and Bion.* London: Routledge.

Brown, A. (1984) *Consultation: an Aid to Successful Social Work.* London: Heinemann Educational Books.

Brown, A. and Bourne, I. (1996) *The Social Work Supervisor.* Buckingham: Open University Press.

Brown, G. and Harris, T. (1978) *Social Origins of Depression: a Study of Psychiatric Disorder in Women.* London: Tavistock Publications.

Brummer, N. and Simmonds, J. (1992) 'Race and culture: the management of "difference" in the learning group.' *Social Work Education 11,* 1, 54–64.

Burgess, R. (1994) '"You have an interesting way of seeing things": consulting within a social services department.' In C. Huffington and H. Brunning (eds) *Internal Consultancy in the Public Sector: Case Studies.* London: Karnac Books.

Butler-Sloss, E. (1988) *Report of the Inquiry into Child Abuse in Cleveland 1987* (Cmnd 412). London: HMSO.

Byng-Hall, J. (1980) 'Symptom bearer as marital distance regulator: clinical implications.' *Family Process 19,* 355–366.

Byng-Hall, J. (1988) 'Scripts and legends in families and family therapy.' *Family Process 27,* 167–179.

CCETSW (1992) *Paper 31. The Requirements for Post-Qualifying Education and Training in the Personal Social Services: a Framework for Continuing Professional Development (Revised Edition).* London: Central Council for Education and Training in Social Work.

Cardona, F. (1994) 'Facing an uncertain future.' In A. Obholzer and V. Zagier Roberts (eds) *The Unconscious at Work: Individual and Organizational Stress in the Human Services.* London: Routledge.

Carpenter, J. (1995) 'Doctors and nurses: stereotypes and stereotype change in interprofessional education.' *Journal of Interprofessional Care 9,* 2, 151–161.

Carpenter, J. and Wheeler, R. (1986) 'Supervising social workers using family therapy in social services departments.' *Social Work Education 6,* 1, 7–10.

Casement, P. (1985) *On Learning from the Patient.* London: Tavistock Publications.

City of Westminster, the Kensington and Chelsea and Westminster Health Authorities and the North West London Mental Health NHS Trust (1995) *Report of the Independent Panel of Inquiry into the Circumstances Surrounding the Deaths of Ellen and Alan Boland.* City of Westminster.

Clare, M. (1988) 'Supervision, role strain and social services departments.' *British Journal of Social Work 18,* 489–507.

Clarkson, P. and Gilbert, M. (1991) 'The training of counsellor trainers and supervisors.' In W. Dryden and B. Thorne (eds) *Training and Supervision for Counselling in Action.* London: Sage Publications.

Cleavely, E. (1993) 'Relationships: interaction, defences and transformation.' In S. Ruszczynski (ed) *Psychotherapy with Couples: Theory and Practice at the Tavistock Institute of Marital Studies.* London: Karnac Books.

Clulow, C. (1982) *To Have and to Hold: Marriage, the First Baby and Preparing Couples for Parenthood.* Aberdeen: Aberdeen University Press.

Clulow, C. (1994) 'Balancing care and control: the supervisory relationship as a focus for promoting organizational change.' In A. Obholzer and V. Zagier Roberts (eds) *The Unconscious at Work: Individual and Organizational Stress in the Human Services.* London: Routledge.

Clulow, C. and Vincent, C. (1987) *In the Child's Best Interests? Divorce Court Welfare and the Search for a Settlement.* London: Tavistock Publications in association with Sweet and Maxwell.

Cockburn, J. (1990) *Team Leaders and Team Managers in Social Services.* Norwich: University of East Anglia Social Work Monographs.

Cohen, A. (1995) 'A note protesting the betrayal of our social work heritage.' *Practice* 7, 4, 5–10.

Colman, W. (1989) *On Call: the Work of a Telephone Helpline for Child Abusers.* Aberdeen: Aberdeen University Press.

Conn, J.D. (1993) 'Delicate liaisons: the impact of gender differences on the supervisory relationship within social services departments.' *Journal of Social Work Practice* 7, 1, 41–53.

Daniell, D. (1985) 'Love and work: complementary aspects of personal identity.' *International Journal of Social Economics* 12, 48–55.

Davies, M. (1988) *Staff Supervision in the Probation Service.* Aldershot: Avebury.

De Board, R. (1978) 'Human behaviour and general systems theory.' In R. De Board *The Psychoanalysis of Organizations.* London: Tavistock Publications.

Dearnley, B. (1985) 'A plain man's guide to supervision – or new clothes for the emperor?' *Journal of Social Work Practice* 2, 1, 52–65.

Department of Health (1991a) *Child Abuse: a Study of Inquiry Reports 1980–1989.* London: HMSO.

Department of Health (1991b) *Working with Child Sexual Abuse: Guidelines for Trainers and Managers in Social Services Departments.* London: HMSO.

Department of Health (1991c) *The Children Act 1989: Guidance and Regulations. Volume 4: Residential Care.* London: HMSO.

Department of Health (1991d) *Care Management and Assessment: Managers' Guide.* London: HMSO.

Department of Health (1992a) *Choosing with Care: the Report of the Committee of Inquiry into the Selection, Development and Management of Staff in Children's Homes* (the Warner Report). London: HMSO.

Department of Health (1992b) Letter to Local Authority Social Services Authorities on *Community Care: Special Transitional Grant Conditions and Indicative Allocations* (Cmnd 27H).

Department of Health (1995) *Child Protection: Messages from Research.* London: HMSO.

Department of Health and Social Security (1968) *The Report of the Committee on Local Authority and Allied Personal Social Services* (the Seebohm Report). London: HMSO.

Department of Health and Social Security (1982) *Child Abuse: a Study of Inquiry Reports 1973–1981.* London: HMSO.

Devenney, M. (1993) 'User participation in quality assurance: fashionable dogma or professional necessity?' In D. Kelly and B. Warr (eds) *Quality Counts: Achieving Quality in Social Care Services.* London: Whiting and Birch Ltd and Social Care Association.

Devore, W. (1991) 'An ethnic-sensitive approach to supervision and staff development (parts I and II).' *Social Work Education* 10, 3, 33–43 and 44–50.

Dingwall, R., Eekelaar, J. and Murray, T. (1983) *The Protection of Children: State Intervention and Family Life.* Oxford: Blackwell.

Downes, C. (1988) 'A psychodynamic approach to the work of an area team.' In G. Pearson, J. Treseder and M. Yelloly (eds) *Social Work and the Legacy of Freud.* London: Macmillan.

Downes, C. and Smith, J. (1991) 'Description of a course model designed to develop advanced practice skills in supervision and consultation for qualified and experienced staff.' *Social Work Education* 10, 1, 30–47.

Downes, C., Ernst, S. and Smithers, M. (1996) 'Maintaining the capacity for concern during organisational restructuring for community care.' *Journal of Social Work Practice* 10, 1, 25–40.

Emery, F. and Trist, E. (1965) 'The causal texture of organizational environments.' In F. Emery (ed) (1981) *Systems Thinking 1: Selected Readings.* Harmondsworth: Penguin Books.

Faugier, J. and Butterworth, T. (1992) *Clinical Supervision: a Position Paper.* Manchester: University of Manchester School of Nursing Studies.

Festinger, L. (1963) 'The theory of cognitive dissonance.' In W. Schramm (ed) *The Science of Human Communication.* New York: Basic Books.

Fineman, S. (1985) *Social Work Stress and Intervention.* Aldershot: Gower Publishing Co.

Fonagy, P., Steele, M., Moran, G., Steele, H. and Higgitt, A. (1993) 'Measuring the ghost in the nursery: an empirical study of the relation between parents' mental representations of childhood experiences and their infants' security of attachment.' *Journal of the American Psychoanalytic Association 41*, 4, 957–989.

Foster, A. and Grespi, L. (1994) 'Managing care in the community: analysis of a training workshop.' *Journal of Social Work Practice 8*, 2, 169–183.

Furniss, T. (1983) 'Mutual influence and interlocking professional–family process in the treatment of child sexual abuse and incest.' *Child Abuse and Neglect 7*, 207–223.

Gardiner, D. (1989) *The Anatomy of Supervision: Developing Learning and Professional Competence for Social Work Students.* Milton Keynes: Society for Research into Higher Education and Open University Press.

Glaser, D. and Frosh, S. (1988) *Child Sexual Abuse.* London: Macmillan.

Grimwood, C. and Popplestone, R. (1993) *Women, Management and Care.* Basingstoke: Macmillan.

Grubb Institute (1991) *Professional Management.* London: Grubb Institute.

HMSO (1944) *A National Health Service* (Cmnd 6502). London: HMSO.

HMSO (1989) *Working for Patients* (Cmnd 555). London: HMSO.

Hallett, C. and Stevenson, O. (1980) *Child Abuse: Aspects of Inter-Professional Cooperation.* London: George Allen and Unwin.

Halton, W. (1995) 'Institutional stress on providers in health and education.' *Psychodynamic Counselling 1*, 2, 187–198.

Hanmer, J. and Statham, D. (1988) *Towards a Women Centred Social Work.* London: BASW/Macmillan.

Harding, T. (ed) (1992) *Who Owns Welfare? Questions on the Social Services Agenda.* Social Services Policy Forum Paper II. London: National Institute for Social Work.

Harkness, D. and Hensley, H. (1991) 'Changing the focus of social work supervision: effects on client satisfaction and generalized contentment.' *Social Work 36*, 6, 506–512.

Harrison, R. (1972) 'Understanding your organisation's character.' *Harvard Business Review 5*, 3, 119–128.

Hawkins, P. and Shohet, R. (1989) *Supervision in the Helping Professions.* Milton Keynes: Open University Press.

Heimann, P. (1950) 'On counter-transference.' *International Journal of Psycho-Analysis 31*, 81–84.

Herman, N. (1989) *Too Long a Child: the Mother–Daughter Dyad.* London: Free Association Books.

Hewitt, M. (1992) *Welfare Ideology and Need: Developing Perspectives on the Welfare State.* Hemel Hempstead: Harvester Wheatsheaf.

Hughes, L. and Pengelly, P. (1995) 'Who cares if the room is cold? Practicalities, projections and the trainer's authority.' In M. Yelloly and M. Henkel (eds) *Learning and Teaching in Social Work: Towards Reflective Practice.* London: Jessica Kingsley Publishers.

Inner London Probation Service (in collaboration with Greater London Probation Pre-Service Training Committee and Tuklo Associates) (1993) *Working with Difference: A Positive and Practical Guide to Anti-Discriminatory Practice Teaching.* London: Inner London Probation Service.

Jaques, E. (1955) 'Social systems as a defence against persecutory and depressive anxiety.' In M. Klein, P. Heimann and R. Money-Kyrle (eds) *New Directions in Psycho-Analysis.* London: Tavistock Publications.

Jones, S. and Joss, R. (1995) 'Models of professionalism.' In M. Yelloly and M. Henkel (eds) *Learning and Teaching in Social Work: Towards Reflective Practice.* London: Jessica Kingsley Publishers.

Jung, C. (1931) 'Problems of modern psychotherapy.' In C. Jung (1954) *Collected Works, Volume 16.* London: Routledge and Kegan Paul.

Kahan, B. (1994) *Growing up in Groups.* London: HMSO.

Kadushin, A. (1976) *Supervision in Social Work.* New York: Columbia University Press.

Kakabadse, A. (1982) *The Culture of the Social Services.* Aldershot: Gower Publishing Co.

Karpman, S. (1968) 'Fairy tales and script drama analysis.' *Transactional Analysis Bulletin* 7, 26, 39–44.

Kearney, P. (1994) 'Watching you.' *Community Care*, 8–14 December, 30–31.

Kemshall, H. (1995) 'Supervision and appraisal in the probation service.' In J. Pritchard (ed) *Good Practice in Supervision*. London: Jessica Kingsley Publishers.

Kirkwood, A. (1993) *The Report of an Inquiry into Aspects of the Management of Children's Homes in Leicestershire*. Leicestershire County Council.

Klein, M. (1940) 'Mourning and its relation to manic-depressive states.' In (1975) *Love, Guilt and Reparation and Other Works. The Writings of Melanie Klein, Volume I*. London: The Hogarth Press.

Klein, M. (1946) 'Notes on some schizoid mechanisms.' In (1975) *Envy and Gratitude and Other Works. The Writings of Melanie Klein, Volume III*. London: The Hogarth Press.

Knowles, M. (1973) *The Adult Learner: a Neglected Species*. Houston: Gulf Publishing Co.

Knowles, M. (1980) *The Modern Practice of Adult Education: from Pedagogy to Andragogy*. Englewood Cliffs, New Jersey: Prentice-Hall.

Kolb, D. (1984) *Experiential Learning*. Englewood Cliffs, New Jersey: Prentice-Hall.

Kraemer, S. (1983) 'Splitting and stupidity in child sexual abuse.' *Psychoanalytic Psychotherapy 3*, 3, 247–257.

Kraemer, S. (1990) *Creating a Space to Supervise – Opportunity or Persecution?* Paper given at a symposium on supervision at the Tavistock Clinic, July 1990 (unpublished).

Lane, S. and Mackey, S. (1995) 'Supervising staff in family court welfare teams.' In J. Pritchard (ed) *Good Practice in Supervision*. London: Jessica Kingsley Publishers.

Langs, R. (1994) *Doing Supervision and Being Supervised*. London: Karnac Books.

Lawler, J. (1994) 'A competence based approach to management education in social work: a discussion of the approach and its relevance.' *Social Work Education 13*, 1, 60–82.

Lawrence, W. (1977) 'Management development…some ideals, images and realities.' In A. Colman and M. Geller (eds) (1985) *Group Relations Reader 2*. Washington DC: The A.K. Rice Institute.

Leiper, R. (1994) 'Evaluation: organisations learning from experience.' In A. Obholzer and V. Zagier Roberts (eds) *The Unconscious at Work: Individual and Organizational Stress in the Human Services*. London: Routledge.

Levy, A. and Kahan, B. (1991) *The Pindown Experience and the Protection of Children*. Staffordshire County Council.

Lindsey, C. and Lloyd, J. (1982) 'The use of the family's relationship to the supervision group as a therapeutic tool.' In R. Whiffen and J. Byng-Hall (eds) *Family Therapy Supervision*. London: Academic Press.

London Borough of Brent (1985) *A Child in Trust: the Report of the Panel of Inquiry into the Circumstances Surrounding the Death of Jasmine Beckford*. London Borough of Brent.

London Borough of Greenwich and Greenwich Health Authority (1987) *A Child in Mind: Protection of Children in a Responsible Society*. London Borough of Greenwich.

London Borough of Wandsworth (1990) *The Report of the Stephanie Fox Practice Review*. London Borough of Wandsworth.

Loughlin, B. (1992) 'Supervision in the face of no cure – working on the boundary.' *Journal of Social Work Practice 6*, 2, 111–116.

Lousada, J. (1994) 'Some thoughts on the adoption of anti-racist practice.' *Journal of Social Work Practice 8*, 2, 151–159.

Main, M. (1993) 'Discourse, prediction and recent studies in attachment: implications for psychoanalysis.' *Journal of the American Psychoanalytic Association 41*, Supplement, 209–244.

Main, T. (1957) 'The ailment.' In T. Main (1989) *The Ailment and Other Psychoanalytic Essays*. London: Free Association Books.

Marris, P. (1974) *Loss and Change*. London: Routledge and Kegan Paul.

Marris, P. (1991) 'The social construction of uncertainty.' In C.M. Parkes, J. Stevenson-Hinde and P. Marris (eds) *Attachment Across the Life-Cycle*. London: Routledge.

Marsh, P. and Fisher, M. (1992) *Good Intentions: Developing Partnership in Social Services*. York: Joseph Rowntree Foundation in association with *Community Care*.

Marton, F. and Saljo, R. (1976a) 'On qualitative differences in learning: I. Outcome and process.' *British Journal of Educational Psychology 46*, 4–11.

Marton, F. and Saljo, R. (1976b) 'On qualitative differences in learning: II. Outcome as a function of the learner's conception of task.' *British Journal of Educational Psychology 46*, 115–127.

Mattinson, J. (1975; 2nd edition 1992) *The Reflection Process in Casework Supervision*. London: Tavistock Institute of Marital Studies.

Mattinson, J. (1981) 'The deadly equal triangle.' In *Change and Renewal in Psychodynamic Social Work: British and American Developments in Practice and Education for Services to Families and Children*. Massachusetts: Smith College School of Social Work; London: Group for the Advancement of Psychotherapy in Social Work.

Mattinson, J. (1988) *Work, Love and Marriage: the Impact of Unemployment*. London: Duckworth.

Mattinson, J. and Sinclair, I. (1979) *Mate and Stalemate: Working with Marital Problems in a Social Services Department*. (1981) London: Institute of Marital Studies.

Menzies, I. (1959) 'The functioning of social systems as a defence against anxiety.' In I. Menzies Lyth (1988) *Containing Anxiety in Institutions. Selected Essays, Volume 1*. London: Free Association Books.

Menzies, I. (1970) 'Pleasure foods.' In I. Menzies Lyth (1989) *The Dynamics of the Social. Selected Essays, Volume 2*. London: Free Association Books.

Menzies, I. (1979) 'Staff support systems: task and anti-task in adolescent institutions.' In I. Menzies Lyth (1988) *Containing Anxiety in Institutions. Selected Essays, Volume 1*. London: Free Association Books.

Middleman, R. and Rhodes, G. (1980) 'Teaching the practice of supervision.' *Journal of Education for Social Work 16*, 51–59.

Miller, E. (1986) 'Power, authority, dependency and cultural change.' In E. Miller (1993) *From Dependency to Autonomy: Studies in Organization and Change*. London: Free Association Books.

Miller, E. (1990) 'Missionaries or mercenaries? Dilemmas and conflicts in voluntary organizations.' *The Tavistock Institute of Human Relations 1990 Review*. London: Tavistock Institute of Human Relations.

Miller, E. and Rice, A. (1967) *Systems of Organization: the Control of Task and Sentient Boundaries*. London: Tavistock Publications.

Minty, B. and Pattinson, G. (1994) 'The nature of child neglect.' *British Journal of Social Work 24*, 6, 733–747.

Montaigne, M. de, translated by M. Screech (1991) *The Complete Essays*. Harmondsworth: Penguin Books.

Moore, J. (1995) 'Child protection: supervision in social services departments.' In J. Pritchard (ed) *Good Practice in Supervision*. London: Jessica Kingsley Publishers.

Morrison, T. (1991) 'The emotional effects of child protection work on the worker.' *Practice 4*, 4, 253–271.

Morrison, T. (1993) *Staff Supervision in Social Care: an Action Learning Approach*. Harlow: Longmans.

Mosse, J. and Zagier Roberts, V. (1994) 'Finding a voice: differentiation, representation and empowerment in organisations under threat.' In A. Obholzer and V. Zagier Roberts (eds) *The Unconscious at Work: Individual and Organizational Stress in the Human Services*. London: Routledge.

Moustaki, E. (1981) 'Glossary: a discussion and application of terms.' In S. Box, B. Copley, J. Magagna and E. Moustaki (eds) *Psychotherapy with Families: an Analytic Approach*. London: Routledge and Kegan Paul.

Nathan, J. (1993) 'The battered social worker: a psychodynamic contribution to practice, supervision and policy.' *Journal of Social Work Practice 7*, 1, 73–80.

Nathan, J. (1994) 'The psychic organisation of community care: a Kleinian perspective.' *Journal of Social Work Practice 8*, 2, 113–122.

Newburn, T. (1993) *Making a Difference? Social Work after Hillsborough*. London: National Institute for Social Work.

Nixon, S. (1982) 'The need for working agreements: social workers' expectations of their team leaders in supervision.' In J. Cypher (ed) *Team Leadership in the Social Services*. Birmingham: British Association of Social Workers.

Obholzer, A. (1994a) 'Authority, power and leadership: contributions from group relations training.' In A. Obholzer and V. Zagier Roberts (eds) *The Unconscious at Work: Individual and Organizational Stress in the Human Services*. London: Routledge.

Obholzer, A. (1994b) 'Managing social anxieties in public sector organizations.' In A. Obholzer and V. Zagier Roberts (eds) *The Unconscious at Work: Individual and Organizational Stress in the Human Services*. London: Routledge.

Obholzer, A. and Zagier Roberts, V. (1994) 'The troublesome individual and the troubled institution.' In A. Obholzer and V. Zagier Roberts (eds) *The Unconscious at Work: Individual and Organizational Stress in the Human Services*. London: Routledge.

Ogden, T. (1979) 'On projective identification.' *International Journal of Psycho-Analysis 60*, 357–373.

Oliver-Bellasis, E. and Vincent, C. (1990) *The Emotional Impact of Child Abuse: an Account of a Series of Case Discussion Seminars for Social Workers*. (Unpublished).

Orwell, G. (1949) *Nineteen Eighty-Four*. London: Martin Secker and Warburg.

Øvretveit, J. (1993) *Co-ordinating Community Care: Multi-Disciplinary Teams and Care Management*. Buckingham: Open University Press.

Parker, R. (1967) 'Social administration and scarcity: the problem of rationing.' *Social Work*, April, 9–14.

Parkes, C.M. (1971) 'Psycho-social transitions: a field of study.' *Social Sciences and Medicine 5*, 101–115.

Parkes, C.M. (1975a) *Bereavement: Studies of Grief in Adult Life*. Harmondsworth: Penguin Books.

Parkes, C.M. (1975b) 'What becomes of redundant world models? A contribution to the study of adaptation to change.' *British Journal of Medical Psychology 48*, 131–137.

Parsloe, P. and Stevenson, O. (1978) *Social Services Teams: the Practitioner's View*. London: HMSO.

Parton, N. (1994) '"Problematics of government", (post) modernity and social work.' *British Journal of Social Work 24*, 1, 9–32.

Pask, G. and Scott, B. (1972) 'Learning strategies and individual competence.' *International Journal of Man-Machine Studies 4*, 217–253.

Pask, G. and Scott, B. (1973) 'CASTE: a system for exhibiting learning strategies and regulating uncertainties.' *International Journal of Man-Machine Studies 5*, 17–52.

Payne, C. and Scott. T. (1982) *Developing Supervision of Teams in Field and Residential Work*. London: National Institute for Social Work.

Pengelly, P., Inglis, M. and Cudmore, L. (1995) 'Infertility: couples' experiences and the use of counselling in treatment teams.' *Psychodynamic Counselling 1*, 4, 507–524.

Peters, T. (1989) *Thriving on Chaos: a Handbook for a Management Revolution*. London: Pan Books in association with Macmillan.

Pettes, D. (1967) *Supervision in Social Work*. London: Allen and Unwin.

Pietroni, M. (1995) 'The nature and aims of professional education for social workers: a postmodern perspective.' In M. Yelloly and M. Henkel (eds) *Learning and Teaching in Social Work: Towards Reflective Practice*. London: Jessica Kingsley Publishers.

Pietroni, M., Poupard, S. and Wilford, G. (1991) 'Supervision and the career continuum.' In M. Pietroni (ed) *Right or Privilege? Post-Qualifying Training with Special Reference to Child Care*. London: Central Council for Education and Training in Social Work.

Pietroni, P. (1991) 'Stereotypes or archetypes? A study of perceptions amongst health-care students.' *Journal of Social Work Practice 5*, 1, 61–69.

Pottage, D. and Evans, M. (1992) *Work-Based Stress: Prescription is not the Cure*. Discussion Paper 1. London: National Institute for Social Work.

Pottage, D. and Evans, M. (1994) *The Competent Workplace: the View from Within*. Discussion Paper 2. London: National Institute for Social Work.

Reder, P. and Kraemer, S. (1980) 'Dynamic aspects of professional collaboration in child guidance referral.' *Journal of Adolescence 3*, 165–173.

Reder, P., Duncan, S. and Gray, M. (1993) *Beyond Blame: Child Abuse Tragedies Revisited.* London: Routledge.

Reynolds, J. (1994) 'Review of Grimwood and Popplestone (1993).' *British Journal of Social Work 24,* 2, 229–230.

Richards, M. and Payne, C. (1990) *Staff Supervision in Child Protection.* London: National Institute for Social Work.

Riley, P. (1995) 'Supervision of social services managers.' In J. Pritchard (ed) *Good Practice in Supervision.* London: Jessica Kingsley Publishers.

Ritchie, J. (1994) *The Report of the Inquiry into the Care and Treatment of Christopher Clunis.* London: HMSO.

Robertson, J. and Robertson, J. (1989) *Separation and the Very Young.* London: Free Association Books.

Robinson, V. (1936) *Supervision in Social Casework: a Problem in Professional Education.* Chapel Hill, N.C.: University of North Carolina Press.

Robinson, W. (1974) 'Conscious competency – the mark of a competent instructor.' *Personnel Journal 53,* 538–539.

Roscoe, M. (1995) 'Supervision in probation and bail hostels.' In J. Pritchard (ed) *Good Practice in Supervision.* London: Jessica Kingsley Publishers.

Rushton, A. and Martyn, H. (1993) *Learning for Advanced Practice: a Study of Away-Based Training.* London: Central Council for Education and Training in Social Work.

Rushton, A. and Nathan, J. (1996a) 'Internal consultation and child protection work.' *Journal of Social Work Practice 10,* 1, 41–50.

Rushton, A. and Nathan, J. (1996b) 'The supervision of child protection work.' *British Journal of Social Work 26,* 357–374.

Ruszczynski, S. (1991) 'Unemployment and marriage: the psychological meaning of work.' *Journal of Social Work Practice 5,* 1, 19–30.

Ruszczynski, S. (1992) 'Notes towards a psychoanalytic understanding of the couple relationship.' *Psychoanalytic Psychotherapy 6,* 1, 33–48.

Rutter, M. (1995) 'Clinical implications of attachment concepts: retrospect and prospect.' *Journal of Child Psychiatry 36,* 4, 549–557.

Saljo, R. (1975) 'Qualitative differences in learning as a function of the learner's conception of the task.' *Studies in Educational Sciences 14.* Göteborg: University of Göteborg.

Salzberger-Wittenberg, I., Henry, G. and Osborne, E. (1983) *The Emotional Experience of Learning and Teaching.* London: Routledge and Kegan Paul.

Sawdon, C. and Sawdon, D. (1995) 'The supervision partnership: a whole greater than the sum of its parts.' In J. Pritchard (ed) *Good Practice in Supervision.* London: Jessica Kingsley Publishers.

Sayers, J. (1992) 'Talking about child protection: stress and supervision.' *Practice 5,* 2, 121–137.

Schön, D. (1983) *The Reflective Practitioner: How Professionals Think in Action.* London: Temple Smith.

Schorr, A. (1992) *The Personal Social Services: an Outside View.* York: Joseph Rowntree Foundation.

Searles, H. (1955) 'The informational value of the supervisor's emotional experience.' In H. Searles (1965) *Collected Papers on Schizophrenia and Related Subjects.* London: Hogarth Press.

Senge, P. (1990) *The Fifth Discipline: the Art and Practice of the Learning Organisation.* New York: Doubleday.

Shapiro, E. and Carr, A. (1991) *Lost in Familiar Places: Creating New Connections between the Individual and Society.* New Haven and London: Yale University Press.

Simmonds, J. (1984) '"Crossing the boundary" – from student to qualified social worker.' *Journal of Social Work Practice 1,* 2, 3–12.

Skynner, R. (1964) 'Group analytic themes in training and case-discussion groups.' In R. Skynner (1989) *Institutes and How to Survive Them.* London: Methuen.

Sloboda, J., Hopkins, J., Turner, A., Rogers, D. and McLeod, J. (1993) 'An evaluated staff counselling programme in a public sector organisation.' *Employee Counselling Today 5*, 5, 10–16.

Smith, M. and Nursten, J. (1995) 'Murder, suicide and violence: impacts on the social worker.' *Journal of Social Work Practice 9*, 1, 15–22.

Social Services Inspectorate (1986) *Inspection of the Supervision of Social Workers in the Assessment and Monitoring of Child Care when Children, Subject to a Court Order, have been Returned Home.* London: Department of Health and Social Security.

Sproul-Bolton, R. (1995) 'Group supervision in an acute psychiatric unit.' In M. Sharpe (ed) *The Third Eye: Supervision of Analytic Groups.* London: Routledge.

Stanners, C. (1995) 'Supervision in the voluntary sector.' In J. Pritchard (ed) *Good Practice in Supervision.* London: Jessica Kingsley Publishers.

Steiner, J. (1976) 'Some aspects of interviewing technique and their relationship with the transference.' *British Journal of Medical Psychology 49*, 65–72.

Steiner, J. (1985) 'Turning a blind eye: the cover up for Oedipus.' *International Review of Psycho-Analysis 12*, 161–172.

Stevenson, O. and Parsloe, P. (1993) *Community Care and Empowerment.* York: Joseph Rowntree Foundation in association with *Community Care.*

Stokes, J. (1994) 'The unconscious at work in groups and teams: contributions from the work of Wilfred Bion.' In A. Obholzer and V. Zagier Roberts (eds) *The Unconscious at Work: Individual and Organizational Stress in the Human Services.* London: Routledge.

Stratton, P., Hanks, H., Campbell, H. and Hatcher, S. (1993) 'Countertransference in systems thinking and practice.' *Journal of Social Work Practice 7*, 2, 181–194.

Summit, R. (1983) 'The child sexual abuse accommodation syndrome.' *Child Abuse and Neglect 7*, 177–193.

Sutton, A. (1997) 'Authority, autonomy, responsibility and authorisation: with specific reference to adolescent mental health practice.' *Journal of Medical Ethics* (in press).

Symington, N. (1985) 'Phantasy effects that which it represents.' *International Journal of Psycho-Analysis 66*, 349–357.

Temperley, J. (1979) *The Implications for Social Work Practice of Recent Psychoanalytical Developments.* Lecture given for the Group for the Advancement of Psychotherapy in Social Work (unpublished).

Trist, E. and Murray, H. (eds) (1993) *The Social Engagement of Social Science: a Tavistock Anthology. Volume 2, The Socio-Technical Perspective.* Philadelphia: University of Pennsylvania Press.

Trowell, J. (1995) 'Working together in child protection: some issues for multidisciplinary training from a psychodynamic perspective.' In M. Yelloly and M. Henkel (eds) *Learning and Teaching in Social Work: Towards Reflective Practice.* London: Jessica Kingsley Publishers.

Trowell, J. and Miles, G. (1991) 'The contribution of observation training to professional development in social work.' *Journal of Social Work Practice 5*, 1, 51–60.

Tunnard, J. and Ryan, M. (1991) 'What does the Children Act mean for family members?' *Children and Society 5*, 67–75.

Twyman, M. (1984) *Oedipus – a Child at Risk: Some Reflections on Social Worker Experiences of Care Proceedings.* Lecture given at the British Psycho-Analytical Society (unpublished).

Valentine, M. (1994) 'The social worker as "bad object".' *British Journal of Social Work 24*, 1, 71–86.

Vincent, C. (1995) 'Love in the countertransference.' *Society of Psychoanalytical Marital Psychotherapists Bulletin 2*, 4–10.

Wandsworth Social Services Department and the Tavistock Institute of Marital Studies (1989) *Learning Supervision.* London Borough of Wandsworth Social Services Department.

Waters, J.G. (1992) *The Supervision of Child Protection Work.* Aldershot: Avebury.

Webb, D. (1992) 'Competencies, contracts and cadres: common themes in the social control of nurse and social work education.' *Journal of Interprofessional Care 6*, 3, 223–230.

Wells, P. (1995) 'Adolescent departments – wither on the vine? A Meeting with the Under-Secretary for State.' *Psychiatric Bulletin 19*, 4, 248–249.

Westheimer, I. (1977) *The Practice of Supervision in Social Work*. London: Ward Lock Educational.

Will, D. and Baird, D. (1984) 'An integrated approach to dysfunction in interprofessional systems.' *Journal of Family Therapy 6*, 275–290.

Wilmot, J. and Shohet, R. (1985) 'Paralleling in the supervision process.' *Self and Society 13*, Part 2, 86–91.

Wiltshire, K. (1995) 'Supervision of approved social work practice.' In J. Pritchard (ed) *Good Practice in Supervision*. London: Jessica Kingsley Publishers.

Winnicott, D. (1949a) 'Hate in the counter-transference.' In D. Winnicott (1958) *Collected Papers: through Paediatrics to Psycho-analysis*. London: Tavistock Publications.

Winnicott, D. (1949b) 'Mind and its relation to the psyche-soma.' In D. Winnicott (1958) *Collected Papers: through Paediatrics to Psycho-analysis*. London: Tavistock Publications.

Winnicott, D. (1953) 'Transitional objects and transitional phenomena.' In D. Winnicott (1958) *Collected Papers: through Paediatrics to Psycho-analysis*. London: Tavistock Publications.

Winnicott, D. (1960) 'The theory of the parent–infant relationship.' In D. Winnicott (1965) *The Maturational Processes and the Facilitating Environment*. London: The Hogarth Press.

Winship, G., Harniman, B., Burling, S. and Courtney, J. (1995) 'Understanding countertransference and object relations in the process of nursing drug-dependent patients.' *Psychoanalytic Psychotherapy 9*, 2, 195–207.

Woodhouse, D. (1977) 'Referral from general practice to specialised agencies.' *Proceedings of the Royal Society of Medicine 70*, 498–502.

Woodhouse, D. (1990) 'The Tavistock Institute of Marital Studies: evolution of a marital agency.' In C. Clulow (ed) *Marriage: Disillusion and Hope*. London: Karnac Books.

Woodhouse, D. and Pengelly, P. (1991) *Anxiety and the Dynamics of Collaboration*. Aberdeen: Aberdeen University Press.

Wright, K. (1994) 'The silent couple in the individual – which couple?' *Society of Psychoanalytical Marital Psychotherapists Bulletin 1*, 12–18.

Yelloly, M. (1995) 'Professional competence and higher education.' In M. Yelloly and M. Henkel (eds) *Learning and Teaching in Social Work: Towards Reflective Practice*. London: Jessica Kingsley Publishers.

Younghusband, E. (1978) *Social Work in Britain 1950–1975, Volume 1*. London: George Allen and Unwin.

Zagier Roberts, V. (1994a) 'The organization of work: contributions from open systems theory.' In A. Obholzer and V. Zagier Roberts (eds) *The Unconscious at Work: Individual and Organizational Stress in the Human Services*. London: Routledge.

Zagier Roberts, V. (1994b) 'The self-assigned impossible task.' In A. Obholzer and V. Zagier Roberts (eds) *The Unconscious at Work: Individual and Organizational Stress in the Human Services*. London: Routledge.

Zagier Roberts, V. (1994c) 'Conflict and collaboration: managing inter-group relations.' In A. Obholzer and V. Zagier Roberts (eds) *The Unconscious at Work: Individual and Organizational Stress in the Human Services*. London: Routledge.

Zagier Roberts, V. (1994d) 'Is authority a dirty word? Some dilemmas in idealistic organisations.' *Journal of Social Work Practice 8*, 2, 185–192.

Index

Page numbers in italic refer to Examples